INSIDE
OUTER CANADA

To Mom,
who began
it all (with
Dad), with thanks
and
much love,

D—

7 Dec 90

INSIDE
OUTER CANADA

DAVID KILGOUR

LONE
PINE

The Publisher:
Lone Pine Publishing
206, 10426-81st Avenue
Edmonton, Alberta
T6E 1X5

Canadian Cataloguing in Publication Data
Kilgour, David, 1941-
  Inside Outer Canada

Includes bibliographical references and index.
ISBN 0-919433-86-3

  1. Regionalism--Canada. 2. Nationalism--Canada. 3. Political
alienation--Canada. 4. Canada--Politics and government--1984-
I. Title
FC98.K54 1990   321.02'0971   C90-091725-3
F1026.K54 1990

Cover design: Beata Kurpinski
Cover illustration: John Driedger
Cover portrait: Con Boland
Editorial: Gary Whyte
Layout: Gary Whyte
Printing: Gagné Printing, Louiseville, Québec, Canada

Publisher's Acknowledgement
The publisher gratefully acknowledges the assistance of the Federal
Department of Communications, Alberta Culture, the Canada Council, and
the Alberta Foundation for the Literary Arts in the production of this book.

To the memory of my brother,

Donald,

who left the West as a young man
and chose to live the remainder of his life,

mostly in French, in east Montréal.

CONTENTS

ACKNOWLEDGEMENTS

The idea for this book came from the fertile mind of Grant Kennedy, founder and president of Lone Pine Publishing, Ltd. in Edmonton. Mary Walters Riskin, his former editor-in-chief, provided invaluable advice and major editing assistance from the beginning. Gary Whyte completed the final edit.

The cover illustrations are the results of hard work by two Edmonton professionals: thanks to John Driedger for the excellent illustration and to Con Boland for the fine portrait.

Danuta Tardif did most of the research, even though as a Polish national, Canada was but a geographical expression to her a few years ago. She estimates that the research for this work involved approximately five times as much effort as that done for our first book, *Uneasy Patriots*. I thank Nancy Beauchesne, who typed and retyped much of the manuscript. Cynthia Guibord, who did a good deal of the typing, managed the enterprise with one hand, pulled out her hair with the other, and with Daniel Fine, Corinne Kucey, Jane Swinton and Lesia Stangret, kept up on the rest of the office work. Adam Barratt, Elizabeth Kwasniewski, Jef Bodwich and Dan Mathis helped with research as well. Romas Garbaliauskas prepared the graphs in the chapter "Dealer's Choice."

Much of this book was written on flights between Ottawa and Edmonton, or at home. My wife, Laura, provided good judgement and advice on all of the chapters. I thank our children, Eileen, Margot, David and Hilary, for putting up with their father's preoccupation over the past months.

ACKNOWLEDGEMENTS

A number of experts are also to be thanked by name. For review of the chapter on Atlantic Canada, I thank Professor John Reid, Professor Cyril Byrne, Harry Bruce, Eugene Forsey and the Hon. George Stanley. I am grateful for assistance with the chapter on the North to Professor Michael S. Whittington, Ann Ray, and Dr. Louis-Edmond Hamelin. For his major contribution to the chapter on regional development, I thank Dirk de Vos. For the one on federalism ("Reconcilable Differences"), the contributions of Gordon Robertson, Professor John Courtney and Professor Théodore F. Geraets must be acknowledged. I also thank Professor Maurice Yeates for his comments on the chapter entitled "Main Street," the term he coined himself. For his knowledge of the Australian Senate and flaws in Canadian Parliamentary democracy, I thank Graham Eglington. Thank you to the staff of the Library of Parliament for their endless patience and unwavering assistance during long months of research.

All translations from French are my own unless otherwise indicated.

As is true of *Uneasy Patriots*, all author's royalties from *Inside Outer Canada* will be remitted, by the publisher, to the Receiver General of Canada.

This book belongs mainly to those listed above. None is responsible for the views expressed in it — except where they are directly quoted — or for the errors it undoubtedly contains.

A NOTE TO THE READER

We Canadians are known virtually the world over for our cherished national values of generosity, moderation, fairness, civility, and reasonable compromise. This book is a call for elected and appointed policy makers in our national capital to begin living up at home to our reputation abroad.

The focus is on our peripheral regions, which I call Outer Canada, including in the term virtually the entire country outside of Toronto-Montréal-Ottawa. Inner Canadians, more precisely, are a few thousand residents of Toronto's Old Forest Hill Village, the Bridle Path and upper Rosedale; Montréal's upper Westmount and sections of Outremont; and Ottawa's Rockcliffe Park and New Edinburgh. In short, they are those who by means of private wealth, position, and political clout have called most of the shots on national policy since Confederation.

In each of these three favoured cities, homeless people, food banks, functional illiteracy and soup kitchens today co-exist alongside obscene affluence and luxury. Many hard-working individuals in all three centres get by each month only with great difficulty. Others, with what appear to be huge family incomes, spend up to half of it paying for mortgages with fourteen to fifteen per cent interest rates. Such people in the context of this book are really no more Inner Canadians than is a resident of Canso, Rankin Inlet, or Nanaimo. One important difference, however, is that the present federal cabinet, like others before it, is much more concerned about the well-being of one group than the other. In consequence, someone losing a job in Inner Canada usually has much better prospects of replacing it than does someone across Outer Canada.

Outer Canadians are the approximately eighteen million of us who live outside Toronto-Montréal-Ottawa. I include all of us, admittedly somewhat arbitrarily, because the evidence is overwhelming that many of the policies of successive national governments have cost us dearly in terms of population, opportunity, economic stability and self-respect. The cost of official Ottawa's short-sightedness is greater in some provinces than in

11

others, but the differences are mostly in degree.

The experience of my friend, Wilf Aucoin, formerly of Cheticamp on northern Cape Breton Island, Nova Scotia, illustrates the point. He and nineteen male classmates graduated there from Notre Dame Assumption High School in June of 1962. No jobs were available locally. Nor were there opportunities for further training, so ten of the male graduates immediately enlisted in the armed forces. The remaining ten, along with some of their female classmates, caught the same train for Toronto. A similar exodus of young men and women probably repeated itself in hundreds of Outer Canadian communities that year and in most years since. Today, there are more economic reasons than ever for Atlantic Canadians to "go down the road to Upper Canada."

Some in both Outer and Inner Canada will reply, "Thank goodness for the strength of Toronto's economy then and now." Others will salute the recruitment policies of our armed forces. Yet both reactions miss the deeper point that these continuing migrations weaken local communities and our national unity. Outer Canadian parents want their children to have a reasonable opportunity to settle near them.

I am not suggesting that young or older Canadians should not be able to start again in some other region of this unique country. New starts in new locations form a necessary feature of life in any open society. The basic argument here is that any national government worthy of the name must bring in a new National Policy which pays far more attention to equality of opportunity for Outer Canadians. For example, Cape Bretoners are capable of growing good hay, which is badly needed by dairy and sheep farmers in Newfoundland, but federal and provincial policy does not encourage the formation of farm enterprises that could produce the needed product efficiently. Ottawa farm policy in Cape Breton promotes only micro-farms, which are unable to export anything.

In these perilous times, it is tempting to wait until the dust from the Meech Lake process settles, in Québec and elsewhere, before beating the regional drum. But continuing to sweep major national problems under the carpet will only compound them. A large number of Québeckers in the periphery, as indicated in the chapter, "Life on the Shield," are charter members of the Outer Canadian Club. Addressing their legitimate concerns more effectively than at present, with due regard to the limits of federal jurisdiction, is more likely to aid the all-important issue of national unity than continuing what, in essence, amounts to ignoring peripheral Québeckers. To demonstrate that the concept of Outer Canada is no mere state of mind, the first chapter, "Main Street," shows how flagrantly Ottawa has long played regional favourites.

The present plight of many Atlantic Canadians has been caused to a considerable extent by a fairly continuous indifference from our national governments since the 1880s. The Atlantic story in Confederation to date is particularly vexing because decades ago the region enjoyed a genuine

A NOTE TO THE READER

and stable prosperity. Nothing in history is irreversible, as events in Eastern Europe are showing, and in a nation like our own, a number of economic and political reforms can today achieve much for 2.2 million Atlantic Canadians. They must no longer confront indifference in Ottawa's political and mandarin circles.

Northern Ontario's ongoing problems with national policy makers are combined with those of residents of the Québec sub-regions because they share similar circumstances. The long and deeply-rooted discontent of Westerners with Ottawa policy-making constitutes a separate chapter. The chapter "Up North" focuses on the predicament of the Yukon and Northwest Territories. In many ways, regional alienation is exemplified most dramatically by conditions north of sixty degrees latitude because the lives of Northerners are probably still more dominated by Ottawa than are those of Canadians anywhere else. Concluding the first part of the book is an essay entitled "Canadians Speak Out" which presents opinions on problems dividing the country and on ways of building unity held by some reasonably representative voices among 26 million Canadians.

Part two of the book begins with a piece, "Dealer's Choice," which is mostly an indictment of the insensitivity of the Mulroney government to Outer Canada. The attitudinal problem in Ottawa certainly did not begin in 1984. Some major current national issues, including culture and communications, the failed Meech Lake process, and the goods and services tax are discussed in a second chapter here.

The final section of the book looks at some possible solutions. The chapters "Kickstarting Development" and "Reconcilable Differences" attempt to reach to the heart of two distinctive Canadian twins, "executive democracy" and :executive federalism." Each of them as practised now, encourages the continued existence of Inner and Outer Canada. In the final chapter I have offered some remedies likely to help us all to live together more amicably.

My overriding purpose is to explore ideas that might strengthen national unity, to seek a political catharsis that might produce a unifying vision for Canadians generally, and to serve as a catalyst for those everywhere making a genuine effort to reconcile regional differences in future national policy making.

This book, then, is a modest attempt to contribute to the necessary national effort to keep Canadians together. It is my firm belief that by staying together as one country, Canadians in all regions of it can better serve their interests, reach their goals and achieve their aspirations.

David Kilgour
Ottawa and Edmonton
September 1, 1990

13

PART I

TWO CANADAS

ONE

MAIN STREET

Since 1867, Ottawa policies have helped to create two Canadas. One is economically diverse, stable, populous and prosperous and exists within Inner Canada. The other is characterized by small populations (often shrinking further through out-migration), resource-dependent economies, low political clout and various degrees of regional discontent. This is Outer Canada. Large portions of both Ontario and Québec lie within Outer Canada; each of the two provinces accordingly have partial membership among the officially disfavoured regions of our country. Although the focus of this volume is Outer Canada, a brief overview of Inner Canada as the heartland of the country seems necessary as a point of reference. It should provide evidence that the division between "Outer" and "Inner" Canada is not a mere state of mind.

Various contrasting terms are used to describe the economic, political, societal and cultural structures which characterize Canada: core vs. periphery, inner vs. outer, metropolis vs. hinterland, centre vs. margin, heartland vs. hinterland. The two-tier model is both more enduring and more deeply entrenched in Canada than in most nations. In the United States, for example, the Boston-Washington corridor has, over a long period, lost its former national dominance in many spheres. More than half of the American population today lives west of the Mississippi River. Taking Winnipeg to be the approximate mid-point of Canada, there is little likelihood of ever duplicating this phenomenon in our own country.

In Canada, the communities which lie within the trading and transportation systems of the "Commercial Empire" of the St. Lawrence River have become more dominant in every sphere almost continuously over the decades. The late Toronto historian Donald Creighton and many of his followers have made it almost a heresy to approach our national experience in other than Laurentian terms. To the Creighton school, whatever enhances the quality of life along the axis is good; whatever does not is essentially "un-Canadian." Central to it all is the notion of Toronto and Montréal as the main creators, directors and beneficiaries of peripheral development. As Maurice Careless, another essentially heartland historian, puts it, Paris and London reached across the Atlantic to create Montréal and Toronto as "bases, garrisons, or entrepots on the frontiers of commerce and resources." By the close of the eighteenth century, he goes on, the hegemony of Montréal through the fur trade reached as far as the Pacific Ocean. Its rival Toronto would rise to dominance in the national order only later in the cycle.

Central domination has gradually weakened the sense of partnership and provincial equality that allowed Confederation to occur and to flourish in the hearts and minds of Canadians everywhere. One manifestation of the hinterland anguish was a comment made by Newfoundland premier Clyde Wells in the early spring of 1990 that the earnings of Newfoundlanders (then only fifty-six per cent of the national average) had risen only three

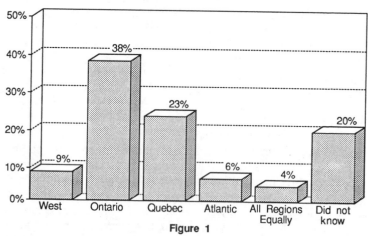

Who Benefited Most From Confederation
Opinions in a Gallup Poll 1989

Figure 1

percentage points in twenty-six years. "At that rate," he complained, "it would take us six hundred years to reach the national average." A Gallup poll released in November, 1989 indicated that only four per cent of Canadians felt all regions of our country had benefited equally from Confederation whereas 38 per cent thought Ontario had done best; 23 per cent said Québec; six per cent, Atlantic Canada; and nine per cent, Western Canada (Fig. 1).

As the twentieth century draws to a close, most residents of Outer Canada continue to be denied equal opportunities and first-class memberships in our national family. By indicators such as personal income, types of economic activity, settlement patterns and political clout, our country can now readily be divided into two distinct regions. The centre, the industrial heartland of southern Ontario and southern Québec, has remained the privileged core of Confederation for most of twelve decades. Except for the rapid economic growth of Alberta's energy boom in the 1970s and to a lesser degree by British Columbia's impressive population growth to about three million residents since 1945, the hegemony of the centre has, if anything, increased during the second half of the twentieth century. Inner Canada's initial advantage of location along our Great Lakes-St. Lawrence River drainage systems was complemented by a good natural resource base and the best access to foreign markets for both staples and manufactured products. Other strengths were added as time went by: a large and growing regional population, control of Western Canadian development, strong financial institutions, and unchallenged political dominance in Ottawa.

Inner Canada has been at different times, identified with Ontario, Québec or both. It is only a narrow southern band of each province, three hundred kilometres wide and one thousand long, extending from Windsor to Québec City. This core is larger than England and Wales combined and is about two-thirds the size of France. It was termed "Main Street" by Maurice Yeates, an authority on Canadian urban and regional geography. Its centre today is clearly Metropolitan Toronto and to a lesser extent Greater Montréal. Standing astride these two dominant centres are the neighbourhoods of Toronto's Bridle Path, Old Forest Hill Village and upper Rosedale and Montréal's Upper Westmount and parts of Outremont. According to 1987 figures released by Revenue Canada on the average income of individuals filing income tax returns, seventeen of Canada's twenty wealthiest communities are found in this Inner Canadian core.

The concentration of so much of Canada's population, political clout, manufacturing industry, service sector, and research and development has created growing problems for both Outer and Inner Canada. Outer Canadians are increasingly alienated by what they see as major and ongoing national injustices and inequalities, justified by what has been seen until now as "the Canadian way." Inner Canadians, on the other hand, face the social, housing, transportation, pollution and other problems associated with overpopulation everywhere.

Maurice Careless's view of Canada's metropolis-frontier experience is that our metropolitan areas have been essential to the development of all our frontiers through history and down to the present day. "As a prime focus of trade, wealth, leadership, and enterprise," he contends, "the metropolis could effectively dominate wide economic hinterlands, whether in territories adjacent or lying far remote." What he doesn't stress is that a long series of policy initiatives in Ottawa have provided our two core cities with an additional "leg up," something rarely offered by the national government to the rest of the country.

A Western Canadian historian, the late William Morton, effectively attacked this metropolitan view. He charged Careless with presenting a Central Canadian imperial perspective, neglecting most regional history, and attempting to impose a centralist mind-set on Outer Canadians. Like Outer Canadians generally, Morton felt strongly that Ottawa — having pursued policies which strengthened Inner Canada at the expense of Outer Canadians for decades — should adopt a strategy designed to strengthen the peripheries as well.

Domineering Heartland

Often erroneously perceived as a single political entity, Inner Canada in fact remains sharply differentiated along linguistic and cultural lines. Two communities, predominantly French-speaking in Lower Canada and English-speaking in Upper Canada, worked together over several generations for political and economic reasons, while maintaining what Hugh MacLennan called "two solitudes," socially and culturally. This partnership of convenience began with the export of furs, and later timber and wheat, to Western Europe. All three products left Canada primarily through the Great Lakes-St. Lawrence waterways. Shrewd and aggressive merchants in Montréal took charge of the movement of commerce in and out of the St. Lawrence basin, first by exchanging our staples for foreign manufactured products. During their golden age in the eighteenth and nineteenth centuries, Montréalers also perfected transportation systems, business contacts, and linking mechanisms for both Lower and Upper Canada.

Because of their dependence on the St. Lawrence and Great Lakes transportation systems, ports were the most dynamic early urban centres in both Ontario and Québec. The development of canals, railways, roads, telegraph and telephone lines later improved domestic and foreign trade significantly. It also prompted a host of new manufacturing centres to appear away from the St. Lawrence River and Great Lakes. By the 1850s, the southern portions of Upper and Lower Canada had both achieved national importance. The development of manufacturing and financial institutions was accompanied by the building of numerous Inner Canadian railways, which further strengthened the regional economy. After Confederation, many businesses in the heartland expanded into Outer Canada, both east and west. Using their greater financial clout and their better access to credit, they absorbed or otherwise eliminated numerous manufacturing rivals in Atlantic Canada.

Because of John A. Macdonald's 1879 National Policy, with its high protective tariffs on most agricultural machinery, farm producers in Prairie Canada eventually found themselves able to buy tractors and other machinery only from the Canadian core. Ottawa's Bank Act of 1871, which opted for branch banking rather than following the American model of state-regulated and usually locally-owned banks, resulted in the rapid rise of large banks controlled from their head offices in Montréal and Toronto. Low postal rates, another Ottawa policy, assisted Inner Canadian retailers with catalogues, such as Eaton's, to effectively challenge local retailers and regional wholesalers throughout Outer Canada. Limp-wristed anti-trust laws enacted by our national Parliament also encouraged heartland companies in various sectors to absorb their competition, initially in Atlantic Canada, later throughout Western Canada as well. In short, Inner Canada, with the help of the "national" government, eventually came to control most wholesale and retail prices, interest and insurance rates, electronic communications, trading and investment policies, from St. John's to Nanaimo to Yellowknife. This essentially colonial economic pattern persists to the present day.

A few sectors in Outer Canada matured quite independently of Central Canada, including the British Columbia and New Brunswick forest industries, the Alberta and Saskatchewan oil and natural gas industries, and fisheries on both coasts. The disproportionate concentration of economic clout at the centre remains, however, a distinct feature of Canada. It is all the more conspicuous among industrial democracies, given the diversity of the country and its mammoth size.

In general terms, with good incomes derived from a rich agricultural economy and foreign trade in staples, early Inner Canadians made use of the tariff, railway-building and other features of the National Policy to establish their regional dominance everywhere in manufacturing, transportation and financial spheres. Their successors, entering the twentieth century, had the additional advantages of large local markets, ready access to prosperous and huge American markets, proximity to transportation routes, and above all the political and administrative muscle in Ottawa necessary to enhance the heartland role of Central Canada. Managers in fast-growing cities located within southern Ontario and southern Québec, themselves products of an industry-led civilization process, became in many areas the effective managers of Atlantic, Northern and Western Canadians.

Numerous indicators of Inner Canada's economic and political dominance underscore the continuing pivotal role of the Windsor-Québec City corridor in modern Canada. In 1986, it was estimated that 13.9 million people — over fifty-five per cent of the population of the country — lived within the core, an area which constitutes about fourteen per cent of the populated area of the country. More than half of the population of this axis lives in the metropolitan areas of Montréal, Ottawa and Toronto.

Using data from 1982, the geographer Maurice Yeates demonstrates that the core/periphery division is readily apparent in the character of Canada's international trade. The figures for 1989 confirm the continuation of this pattern. Staples and food products constitute a large share of exports; Outer Canada is the source of most of them. Inner Canada dominates both the export and import of manufactured products. The periphery dominates national trade in crude oil, forest products, and natural gas, most of which go to the United States. Other materials are partially fabricated in our heartland, and then exported primarily to the United States. Manufactured end products, such as auto parts, are produced virtually only in the core and are usually exported to the United States.

An ongoing feature of the axis is its dominance in the industrial field. Seven out of every ten manufacturing jobs in Canada are located within the core (Fig. 2), with the bulk of employment in manufacturing being in a few major central cities: Toronto, Montréal, Hamilton, Kitchener. Among our twenty-two metropolitan areas, fifty-seven per cent of the national employment in manufacturing is located in Toronto and Montréal. This manufacturing region contains all types of industry, particularly those which involve a high level of processing, such as machinery and transportation equipment, metal fabricating and chemical products.

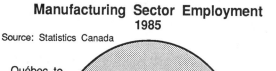

Manufacturing Sector Employment
1985

Source: Statistics Canada

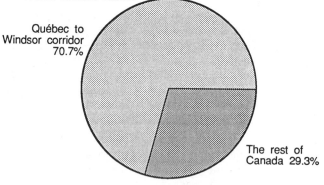

Québec to Windsor corridor 70.7%

The rest of Canada 29.3%

Figure 2

There are various types of manufacturing: industries are often divided into so-called "low and high value-added industries." The former entail relatively low wages; the latter just the opposite. In Inner Canada they tend to be concentrated in different locations. Our high value industries (machinery, petroleum and coal products, chemicals, transport, metal fabricating) are prone to cluster in our largest metropolitan centres — Toronto and Montréal — and in particular within the "golden horseshoe" around western Lake Ontario from Oshawa-Whitby to Hamilton. Low value-added sectors (clothing, furniture and textiles), on the contrary, tend to be dispersed in smaller Ontario towns and in Qubec's part of the axis.

The geographic concentration of high and low value-added industries is, of course, explained by the availability of capital and labour. Southern Ontario initially offered more abundant capital than labour and therefore has attracted capital-intensive, high value-added industries. In Québec, labour has traditionally been more abundant than capital; more labour-intensive and low value-added industries have tended to locate there.

Yet, service industries within the axis today provide three times as many jobs as manufacturing. Three major groups prevail: wholesale trade, finance, and business management services. Not surprisingly, a high percentage of labour forces in Ottawa-Hull and Québec City are in services and government activities. Metropolitan Toronto and Montréal specialize in finance, services to business management, and wholesale trade. Kingston and London are dependent on health and education-related services.

The predominant role, then, of Canada's heartland can be found in past and in present patterns of manufacturing, trade and service industries, not to mention cultural activities and political clout.

The Major Cities

The direction and intensity of the movement of people, goods and information as a result of these economic activities point to the high volume in the core; they show a clear pattern of interaction between the core and periphery. As Yeates demonstrated in 1985, and as my own more recent research confirms, Montréal and Toronto continue to be the major generators and destinations of this movement. The pattern of road traffic, for example, indicates that the major flows occur on highways that are at least four lanes and follow the corridor from Windsor to Québec City, with Toronto and Montréal as the major nodes and Ottawa-Hull and Québec City as lesser ones. The pattern of interaction as measured by airline passengers points to a direction of flows involving both business and politics. The figures for 1987 and 1988 (the most recent available from Statistics Canada) on air passenger origin and destination demonstrate that the largest volume of traffic is between Montréal and Toronto. Ottawa-Toronto ranks third, after Toronto-Vancouver.

Montréal and Québec City

Careless sees both Québec City and Montréal as leaving deep imprints on all Québeckers for more than three centuries. During the 1760s, the British conquest of New France transferred effective metropolitan supremacy over the St. Lawrence from Paris to London, thereby displacing French-speaking merchants in both Canadian cities and rendering Québeckers more rural in outlook than they had been before. Careless argues that even under the British rule Québeckers continued to focus on Montréal and Québec. From Confederation onwards, Québec City remained the political champion and cultural centre of the province. Montréal's commercial network spread into the West and Atlantic Canada after Confederation, and dominated both regions well into the twentieth century. Today Montréal is unquestionably the economic capital of Québec. When comparing the two cities, Montréal is usually referred to as the metropolis and Québec City as "the old capital."

During the summer of 1964, as a university student working in the largest Québec lower town branch of the Bank of Montreal, I experienced Montréal's economic domination over Québec City in various ways. One day, a fellow employee asked my assistance in composing a letter to the bank's head office in Montréal. Why, I wondered, did he need my help with a letter I presumed would be in French? He responded that the bank's head office required all communications from employees, even ones living in Québec City, to be in English only.

Today, Québec City is more than ever the political capital of the province. The Quiet Revolution of the 1960s, the Parti Québécois victory in 1976, various measures aimed at unilingualism, and a host of other political factors have given it pre-eminence in terms of government over the much larger city of Montréal. In addition, Québec City, as the seat of the National Assembly, intervenes directly in decisions by Hydro Québec, the giant provincial Crown corporation.

Metropolitan Montréal, with almost half the provincial population, is Qubec's business, theatre and communications heart. The city dominates the southern and western regions of Laurentian Québec, and it is a major national business centre with a large quantity and variety of manufacturing. However, it is a distant second today to Toronto in banking, investment and insurance activities. Until 1977, Montréal was the country's premiere city. Today, it has 2.9 million residents compared to Toronto's 3.4 million. During 1989, nine to ten per cent of Montréal residents were unemployed, compared to less than four per cent in Toronto.

Nonetheless, Montréal is the motor of the province's economy, accounting for fifty-two per cent of Qubec's gross domestic product and almost half of the work force. The region of Montréal, according to the 1988 Statistics report by the Government of Québec, contains sixty-seven per cent of the industrial establishments of Québec and accounts for almost seventy per cent of the province's manufacturing employment. Nearby Dorval airport is a hub of activity; Mirabel has yet to catch on as an international gateway. Montréal's maritime shipping remains important in Canada.

The dominance of metropolitan Montréal over other regions of Québec is impressive. An analysis of all Québec provincial cabinet ministers between 1867 and 1960 by geographic origin shows that on average half of them came from the Montréal region. A 1977 paper by the provincial government's office of planning and development documents that the city contains fifty-seven per cent of the population of the province, sixty-nine per cent of the industrial employment, sixty-nine per cent of the volume of the province's manufacturing and sixty-one per cent of textile employment. It concludes, "Québec is divided into two: Montréal and the rest."

Personal income in 1987 for the Montréal economic region was the highest in the province at $18,459 per capita, with some communities in Greater Montréal at $19,784. The average per capita income for the province was $17,256, while some communities in the Gaspé and the North of Québec had average personal incomes as low as $11,405 and $12,151 respectively. In his 1981 article, "Regional disparities: the more it changes the more it's the same," Michel Gailloux refers to Montréal as "Québec's breast," traditionally feeding its hinterland regions but increasingly unable to do so. Jean-Claude Thibodeau and Mario Polse, the authors of a study "The effects of the domination of Montréal on the other regions of Québec" bluntly state that economic development in Québec must pass through the region of Montréal, which by the weight of its influence is the fundamental factor in bringing growth and economic development to the province. It is necessary to revitalize Montréal first, they contend, and the whole of Québec will benefit as a result. This is, of course, only another application of the trickle-down economics of the Reagan, Thatcher and Mulroney governments.

Montréal is no typical North American city, despite its plentiful downtown skyscrapers: it is far more a European one. It now covers virtually the entire length of Montréal Island. According to the Québec government's figures, in 1982 Montréal attracted 1.3 million Canadian tourists from other provinces, 52.2 per cent of the total number for the province. (Québec City, the third most popular destination after the Outaouais region, was visited by 233,000 Canadians.) Manufacturing plants are found almost everywhere in Montréal, especially along the river banks, in Laval and along the freeways to Dorval.

French-speaking Québeckers, who comprise four-fifths of the province's population of 6.6 million, claim only fifty-six per cent of the residents on the island of Montréal. People of countless origins and languages work downtown at the foot of Mount Royal, but upper Westmount remains an almost exclusive preserve of its still mostly English-speaking captains of industry. Stone and mahogany-filled mansions with splendid gardens are abundant there, a mute testimony to the ongoing clout of at least this part of Montréal as a key piece in the Inner Canadian puzzle. Most other districts of the city, especially the walk-up apartments in east Montréal, are really far more a part of the Québec Branch of Outer Canada.

Metropolitan Toronto

Within Ontario, Toronto, designated a city in 1834, outpaced its early rivals — Hamilton and Kingston — through the natural advantage of location on rich farm land, and by becoming a regional railway link and attracting immigrants. Following Confederation, the city added financial and manufacturing muscle to the transport dominance it had already acquired over Outer Ontario. But only well into the twentieth century did it finally successfully challenge Montréal in a number of sectors, notably mining and lumbering, for dominance of peripheral regions such as the Prairies. The whole of Outer Canada outside Québec became its oyster after World War II. Entering the 1990s, Toronto is our dominant metropolis. Frederick Fletcher, a Toronto political science professor, has said Ontario is "the spider at the centre of the web of Confederation." If this is the case, then its provincial capital is the directing head of the creature.

Toronto is our largest national metropolis, occupying 632 square kilometres and extending forty kilometres along the north shore of Lake Ontario and inland about sixteen kilometres. It is home to 3.4 million people, thirteen per cent of Canada's entire population and thirty-five per cent of Ontario's. The Greater Toronto area, which includes adjacent communities in Halton, Durham, Peel and York, contains almost four million people. It is the national business capital, accounting for a quarter of our country's gross national product and half of our national exports. Forty-four per cent of the sales of Canada's top one hundred industrial companies take place in Toronto — a yearly financial flow of $19 billion. Equally significant, the Greater Toronto area today provides half of all income taxes paid by Ontarians to the federal and provincial governments.

"Metro has real manufacturing muscle and has the highest income, output and invested productive capacity of any municipality in Canada," boasts the 1987 annual report of the Municipality of Metropolitan Toronto. More than five thousand separate manufacturing firms are located within its communities and about one third of Canada's retail market is located within 200 kilometres of Toronto's CN Tower. The Toronto Stock Exchange now accounts for about three-fourths of the activity on all Canadian stock exchanges. Per capita income within the city in 1987, the most recent year for which statistics are available, was $21,905. During the same year, it was $12,541 in one district in northeastern Ontario; $12,400 in Newfoundland; $13,138 in PEI; $14,685 in Nova Scotia; $13,752 in New Brunswick; $17,256 in Québec; $16,709 in Manitoba; $15,862 in Saskatchewan; $18,176 in Alberta and $17,731 in British Columbia.

In the film business, more than thirty-five feature films were produced in the city in 1987 alone. Toronto is also Canada's construction leader. Office space is abundant and prestigious, with the city having almost thirty per cent of Canada's total urban office space, twice the proportion of New York City which has only fifteen per cent of the available American office accommodation. 1989 was the eighth consecutive year of economic growth and development for Metro Toronto. With its diversified economic base, Toronto led the country in new business activity, retail sales, manufacturing and small business growth, ending 1989 with a 3.7 per cent unemployment rate and new building permits in excess of $3 billion.

Toronto is home to half of Canada's largest five hundred companies (Manhattan includes only about one tenth of the U.S. Fortune 500 companies). Sixty per cent of our computer firms and four out of five foreign banks operating in Canada are located in Toronto.

Toronto housing prices in early 1990 averaged $289,000 — having approximately doubled since 1986 alone — when average prices were $95,000 in Halifax and $76,000 in Regina. Despite John Crow's interest rates, which have in recent months caused a major fall in housing prices nation-wide, Toronto's home prices have made it the most expensive city in North America for a home-owning family to live in.

A survey of eighty-three of the world's most expensive cities published by a Geneva-based organization released in May, 1990 showed that Toronto ranks as the most expensive on this continent, ahead of New York, Chicago and Washington. The study was based on a basket of 151 products, including food consumed at home, alcohol, tobacco, clothing, transport, sports and leisure, but not including housing. Toronto was the most expensive city in the Western hemisphere.

During the 1970s, almost half of the new immigrants to Canada were understandably attracted to Metro by its strong industrial base and employment opportunities. It continues to be a magnet for at least a quarter of all immigrants to Canada and in 1988, 35 per cent of newcomers located in Toronto. The unemployment rate, at 4.1 per cent in mid-1990, was among the lowest in the country. In the 1988 Annual Report of the Municipality of Metropolitan Toronto, the chairman of its Council wrote: "It is no secret that the very many who flock to Metro see us today as a safe and vibrant community; the hub of Ontario's economy; the industrial heartland of Canada, a cultural and tourist mecca . . . ."

There are drawbacks. An article in the January/February 1990 issue of *Saturday Night* magazine, "Welcome to Toronto" by David Eddie, reflects the inevitable result of too much development. "Welcome to Toronto means," he wrote, "welcome to a typical metropolis of the late twentieth century; grid-locked, crime saturated, thoroughly compromised . . . ." The lack of affordable housing and the choking traffic top the list of big city woes which afflict the greater Metro Toronto area. A survey by Goldfarb Consultants commissioned by the *Toronto Star* in the spring of 1989 found that a huge majority of those surveyed — 85.9 per cent — were dissatisfied with the lack of affordable housing in Metro. More than half of the residents surveyed didn't expect to ever own a home within a commuting distance of the city, and nearly one in four families is thinking of moving away — a quarter of them because housing costs in the Metro area are too high. Some residents say housing prices and mortgage costs have been the most important topic of conversation for many months.

Peter Ustinov has praised Metropolitan Toronto as "New York City, run by the Swiss" and Canadians everywhere have reason to relish the thought. Many might even share the boosterism of a *Globe and Mail* editorial published in the final days of the 1980s: "While most Canadian cities generally improved their situations (especially Montréal), Toronto seemed to grow into another order of urban being. Narcissistic as the city became, it is simply descriptive to say that Toronto bloomed as a national city on a wider stage, with all the virtues and frustrations that implies. We dare to say it here first: Canadians everywhere have a right to be proud of Toronto, Canada."

Seldom grateful that unemployed neighbours, friends and family have found new opportunities in Toronto, Outer Canadians generally might fail to notice that the biggest contributor to Toronto's housing, rent, traffic and other congestion problems is our national government itself. For example, the single federal constituency of Etobicoke-North in suburban Toronto alone received $1.3 billion in federal procurement contracts during 1987, whereas all four western provinces together with their 7.2 million residents, received only $933 million in federal contracts the same year.

I am not arguing that the Greater Toronto area should be penalized for its many successes. It is the mega-locomotive of the national economy and therefore what hurts the metropolis probably affects Outer Canada in an even more severe way as a result of the ripple effect. On the other hand, a nationalized federal government should do what it can to avoid the patterns of France and Great Britain where little of consequence is encouraged to locate outside the two national capitals.

Ottawa-Hull

Boarding a plane in Ottawa for Edmonton last year, I overheard two Western businessmen discuss their just-concluded visit to the national capital. One nodded in full agreement when the other shook his head and muttered, "It's the most subsidized city in the country." My mind went back to 1969 when the $6 million cost of a special acoustics system in Ottawa's recently-completed National Arts Centre alone approximated the entire cost of Winnipeg's Manitoba Theatre Centre, which was built at about the same time. The capital seemed to me like a modern Babylon then; it still does. What, however, are the current facts about Ottawa of special interest to Outer Canadian tax payers?

"Sorry, Ottawa, but Statistics Canada has the evidence in black and white. Almost any way you measure it, we look like Fat City," wrote the *Ottawa Citizen*'s Daniel Drolet earlier this year. The statistics are persuasive:

- Ottawa families have the highest average income compared with other cities in the country — $48,600. Nearly one-third of all Ottawa households report an annual income of more than $50,000.
- Ottawa-Carleton has fewer people at low-income levels, proportionately, than the Canadian average. Only 13.2 per cent of all households in Ottawa-Carleton reported incomes of less than $20,000. The Canadian average is 19 per cent.
- The region has the highest proportion of university graduates — twenty per cent more than anywhere else in the country.

— Despite announced cuts, mostly cosmetic, by the Mulroney government in spending in the area, the National Capital Region was named by a Toronto consulting firm as the top economic performer among some twenty-seven Canadian cities during the last half of the decade. Approximately three and a half million visitors came to Ottawa during 1988. High tech and development sectors accounted for a big part of the region's performance. The local economy seems to be growing less dependent on the federal government. In 1980, for example, the federal government employed 30.2 per cent of Ottawa-Carleton's work force. By the end of the decade, the figure was 21.8 per cent.

In 1893, Canada's future prime minister, Wilfrid Laurier, expressed his wish to see Ottawa become "the centre of the intellectual development of this country . . . the Washington of the North." The Ottawa Improvement Commission founded in 1899 was the first planning agency for the area. With a yearly budget of $60,000, it tried to change the image of Ottawa's "sub-arctic lumber village" past. Following a number of name changes and enormous increases in power and budget the National Capital Commission came into being in 1959. Its primary purpose is to develop and improve the federal capital, "in order that the nature and character of the seat of the government of Canada may be in accordance with its national significance." In other words, it is to make the city look really elegant at the expense of Canadian taxpayers.

Contrasted to the period when the Ottawa Improvement Commission made do with an annual grant of $60,000, the National Capital Commission's resources are breathtaking. Total expenditures by the Commission for 1988-89 were $113 million, with the parliamentary portion amounting to $61.5 million. During 1988-89, the NCC spent $8.7 million for the development of its Confederation Boulevard, which it wants to make "as distinctive to Canada's capital as the Mall is to Washington or the Champs-Élysées is to Paris." It further spent $3.3 million on landscaping the grounds of the National Gallery and the Canadian Museum of Civilization.

Other prominent features of the federal presence in the Ottawa area are the many government institutions established simply because it is the capital. These buildings, particularly the Parliament Buildings, are clearly of major importance to regional tourism. It is, however, Ottawa's cultural institutions, ostensibly established in the interests of Canadians generally, which benefit most directly and continuously the residents of the capital region. The National Arts Centre, the National Library, the National Gallery, the Canadian Museum of Natural Sciences, the Museum of Science and Technology, the National War Museum, the National Postal Museum and the National Aviation Museum — all are located in Ottawa, which demonstrates the national government's efforts over the years to enrich primarily the cultural lives of residents of the National Capital region.

It is ironic that with all the public money spent to bring Ottawa closer to Canadians, almost half of us are unable to locate Ottawa on a map of the country according to a July 1989 Gallup poll. It appears that our national capital fails to evoke pride and a sense of nationhood and is far from a unifying symbol for citizens everywhere. In many countries, the capital is a cherished national symbol, a place around which the population can rally in times of uncertainty and trouble. London and Paris have been the seat of government throughout centuries of history. Ottawa, a relatively new capital, has largely failed to develop this symbolic status, despite the federal government's direct efforts to provide the city with enhanced significance through increased spending.

Douglas Fullerton, a former NCC chairman, noted one of the side effects of the government's efforts to make Ottawa an important national symbol. "A capital of growing physical appeal may have had a favourable impact on visiting Canadians, helping them accept special federal spending in the region, but the consequences are sometimes two-edged. 'Fat City' is a phrase that comes easily to Canadian visitors from areas in economic trouble."

Right across the Ottawa River and close to all this government-created pomp and luxury lie the three western Québec communities of Pontiac, Gatineau Valley and Papineau. In mid-1990, a report by the Québec Social Affairs Council identified all three as among the poorest in the province, with the average family income being about $25,000. Equally distressing, the unemployment levels in the three were dreadful. Those who know the by-ways of the National Capital region should be troubled by this public affluence and private poverty co-existing so close to one another. It would be far better to direct part of the huge sums spent in recent years on buildings like the Museum of Civilization ($257 million) and National Art Gallery ($162 million) on improving the skills and the lot of Western Québeckers and other similarly depressed Canadians across the country.

The millions of dollars spent on beautifying the capital region and on such grandiose projects as the ceremonial route will win neither the affection nor the pride of Outer Canadians. A more caring and just federal government associated with the city would certainly put "the capital into the heart and mind of every Canadian" — the elusive dream of one chairman of the NCC — more effectively than will all the attempts to concentrate value, interest and beauty in Ottawa.

TWO

DOWN HOME

A century of Atlantic de-industrialization, de-population, growing dependence on Ottawa and lost opportunities is a major national tragedy, shrieking to be righted now. A chain of events has led to the decline in the economic potential and in the political clout of the three Maritime provinces, a phenomenon the rest of Canada, and politicians of all three major political parties in Ottawa, observed mutely for the most part and failed to stop.

"Haggard," "poor cousins," "economic basket case" — each is among the terms thrown at the region by Canadians from other parts of the country who should know better. The leader of one national political party, the late David Lewis, told his party's national council in 1971 as he left a meeting for a short interval, "Talk about something unimportant while I'm gone — talk about the Maritimes." Too many leaders of all three parties have been perfectly capable of saying the same thing in unguarded moments. Almost a decade earlier, a prominent Ontario historian, the late Frank H. Underhill, proclaimed to a CBC radio audience: "As for the Maritime provinces, nothing of course ever happens down there." Many others have committed the same intended or accidental slight before and since.

Atlantic academics continue to assert that most Canadian textbooks and historians display a deep ignorance and profound indifference to their region. John G. Reid, a historian, in an assessment of some recent books about Canadian history, concluded many gave short shrift to his region and some contained errors about even basic facts pertaining to it. He scolded Toronto historian J.L. Granatstein's *Canada, 1957-1967: The Years of Uncertainty and Innovation*, noting: "Outside of the introductory chapter, the three Maritime provinces are barely mentioned and Newfoundland comes off marginally better only because of Premier Smallwood's clashes with Prime Minister Diefenbaker in 1958-59." Another work, *Twentieth Century Canada*, by five prominent non-Atlantic historians, was also

31

criticized by Reid for stating boldly, but incorrectly, that the Maritimes "experienced an almost continuous depression since Confederation."

A related perspective was provided by Prince Edward Island Premier Joe Ghiz. In a letter to the *Globe and Mail* in June 1989 on the budget-proposed closure of the Canadian Forces Base at Summerside, PEI and the paper's editorial supporting the proposal, he noted that the closing of the base would in proportional terms be of similar impact in Ontario to closing down its auto industry or eliminating 35,000 military jobs in Québec. Ghiz concluded: "We (Islanders) are not your poor cousins — we are equal as Canadians, deserving of hospital and health care, of education and of transportation facilities equal to those provided to you. And, incidentally, we also believe that the defence spending should not be primarily spent in Central Canada, thereby giving you the ability to earn a good income while dumping on the 'have-not' regions of the country."

A stirring definition of the regional identity was provided by the educator William B. Hamilton at Mount Allison University during 1984. Calling on Atlantic Canadians to recognize that respect abroad begins with dignity at home, he asked them to reflect positively on their "common historical and demographic background, the far-reaching legacy of the sea, tell-tale traces of our architectural history; the deep relationship with the land and its people that runs through so much of Maritime literature. All of these are qualities that illustrate and illuminate the commonality that sets the Maritime region apart and have helped make it what it is today."

In short, the picturesque but generally negative perception held of the region by the rest of our country is a major obstacle to a better Atlantic future.

The West and the Maritimes

Ironically, Atlantic and Western Canada, each dubbed a "Cinderella of Confederation," have found themselves in conflict on several fronts over the years. As the population grew in the West, the regional redistribution of seats in the House of Commons resulted in a growing number of MPs for that region at the expense of the Maritimes. Political power in the West, at least theoretically, was growing while, as their number of seats dropped, Maritime Canada's voice and role in the national political community were declining. As Alberta and Saskatchewan benefited from becoming provinces in 1905, and during 1912 Québec, Ontario and Manitoba each saw their surface areas grow considerably, the Maritime provinces were left not only without new land — there was none available on the east coast — but with a diminished percentage of the national land surface. This weakened their position in Confederation even further. Moreover, Maritimers felt the new provinces in the West had received unreasonably generous financial subsidies from the federal government. For example, Saskatchewan's annual federal subsidy was, for a period, approximately three times that of Nova Scotia's subsidy even though at the time Nova Scotia had twice

Saskatchewan's population. Maritimers felt that the settlement of the West was occurring at their expense.

The frustration of the Maritimes with the ascendancy of the West and their own decline, combined with other sources of political discontent, culminated in the Maritime Rights Movement that swept the entire region between 1919 and 1927. The movement helped foster a regional consciousness and sense of identity. It did not secure any significantly different approach in federal government policies.

At the beginning of the 1990s, the four Atlantic provinces have less than half as many MPs as the West. Many Atlantic Canadians concluded that government policy in respect of VIA Rail cut backs (sixty per cent of the VIA job losses announced in October, 1989 were to be in Atlantic Canada), and the Wilson budget during the spring of 1989 (fifty per cent of the jobs affected by the various spending cut backs were in Atlantic Canada) were punishment for having voted mostly Liberal in the 1988 national election.

In the fall of 1989, premier Ghiz told a Toronto audience that Atlantic Canada feels the same sense of frustration and alienation as Western Canada. We have the "deep-seated feeling we're not cared about, that policies made in Ottawa are insensitive to the region," he stressed. He called for an elected Senate with an equal number of senators from each province to act as a counterweight to the House of Commons. The three other Atlantic premiers appear to be united with Ghiz on the need for a Triple-E Senate (Elected, Equal, Effective). In an open letter to Robert Stanfield and Jack Pickersgill about flaws in the Meech Lake accord, Newfoundland's Clyde Wells noted in early 1990 the resounding silence of premiers Bourassa and Peterson on that score. "It is abundantly clear," he stated, "that if ever the Meech Lake accord were approved as it is, Senate reform involving a true Triple-E Senate would be virtually impossible." His continuing opposition to the unanimity requirement of the Meech Lake accord for any constitutional amendment to pass became one of the rocks upon which the agreement smashed on June 23, 1990. With the collapse of Meech Lake, the 1982 amendment formula — approval by the legislatures of seven provinces together having half the population of Canada — is still in effect.

Atlantic Confederation Experience

Atlantic Canada's experience in Confederation is a story of hesitation and triumph followed by successive disasters. By the mid-nineteenth century, Nova Scotia, New Brunswick and Prince Edward Island were thriving within a trade network involving themselves, Great Britain and the West Indies. The shipyard industry, at its peak in the 1860s, had built much of the fleet that made the world's fourth largest shipping power of what soon was to become Canada. The financial network included a dozen banks, — the Bank of Nova Scotia and antecedents of the Royal Bank of Canada, as well as other important institutions. Halifax — the centre for

Nova Scotia by mid-century — Toronto historian J.M.S. Careless called "the wealthiest most advanced metropolitan city in the British North American provinces." Culture flourished in the region. There emerged a strong regional outlook which gave rise to the romantic notion of a golden age of "Wooden Ships and Iron Men."

The crisis of Confederation soon hit each of the three Maritime provinces. Wooden ships began giving way to an economy based on railways and coal. Charles Tupper, premier of Nova Scotia, pitted this emerging industrial model against a departing era of "wind, wood and sail" in favour of his province's joining Confederation. Public support for union was so low that he passed the necessary motion to bring Nova Scotia into Confederation in the provincial assembly without calling an election on the question. In the federal and provincial votes called shortly after Confederation, anti-Confederationists won thirty-six of thirty-eight provincial and eighteen of nineteen federal seats in Nova Scotia. In New Brunswick, Premier Samuel Leonard Tilley, who more courageously called a provincial election in 1865 on the Confederation issue, was defeated overwhelmingly by opponents who mistrusted Canadians generally and worried about a loss of autonomy. On Prince Edward Island, opinion initially was virtually unanimous against union from fear of losing both independence and island-identity.

Eventually, the tide of Maritime public opinion turned in favour of union due to other factors, including what the historian George Rawlyk saw as the "loyalty" of many Maritimers to the Queen: it was plainly the wish of Queen Victoria and also of Westminster politicians that the entire region enter Confederation. Nevertheless, resentment would long smoulder actively below the surface.

There was also, in the thought of David Alexander, a Newfoundland economic historian, "fear that the provinces would be reduced to colonies of Upper Canada, and optimism that they would develop into the workshop of the new dominion."

John A. Macdonald's National Policy and its high tariffs introduced in 1879 to stimulate national manufacturing prompted a Maritime industrial boom. The completion of the Intercolonial Railway from the Maritimes to Central Canada that same year, with its freight rates favourable to moving products westward, was also a powerful tonic to regional manufacturing. By the mid-1880s, Maritimers controlled three of Canada's five sugar refineries, one of three national glass works, two of seven ropeworks and eight of twenty-three cotton mills. Nova Scotia's iron and steel industry and related sectors were also thriving. In the decade of the 1880s, Nova Scotia increased its industrial output by two-thirds, substantially greater than the growth in Québec and Ontario. Nova Scotia's per capita growth in manufacturing led the nation and Saint John's exceeded that of Hamilton. The rapid industrialization, for a time, abundantly fulfilled the hopes of Maritimers to become a prosperous and cultural model for Canada and to play a role similar to the one New England has long played in the United States.

The second golden era was not to survive for long. In an attempt to reduce competition, Montréal and Toronto businessmen, with more cash reserves or better access to bank credit, bought out a large number of Maritime firms. During the 1890s, Montréal replaced Halifax and Saint John as the dominating metropolitan influence. The process was largely completed early in the new century and at the outbreak of World War I the region had become a branch-plant economy. By the 1930s, Torontonians, who didn't operate a single branch in the region in 1881, owned 228 regional business operations.

A number of Ottawa policies played a significant role in the economic subjugation of Maritime Canada. One was the branch banking system established by Parliament's Bank Act of 1871. Quite predictably, it quickly shifted all real banking clout to a small number of banks in Montréal and Toronto. As the historian T.W. Acheson notes: "Between 1900 and 1920 every component in the century-old Maritime banking system was swept away and replaced by branches of great national banking consortia." Central Canadian shareholders took control of the Bank of Nova Scotia, for one, and moved its effective ownership and directors to Toronto.

Earlier promises by national politicians to the Maritimes soon weakened in favour of concentrating manufacturing in the St. Lawrence valley. The Maritime industrial sector went into rapid decline. The Intercolonial Railway, based in Moncton, had at first itself operated as an effective regional transportation device through rates which encouraged long haul traffic out of the region but mildly discouraged finished goods from coming into Maritime Canada. This made Maritime manufacturers competitive with Central Canadian factories; under it, freight tonnage quadrupled between the years 1899 and 1917. The Intercolonial also made a modest profit.

While it lasted, the regionally-oriented freight rate system permitted the Maritimes both to industrialize and to share in the general economic prosperity accompanying the settlement of Western Canada. It was probably the only way Maritimers could benefit over a longer term from Macdonald's National Policy. In 1912, Central Canadian manufacturers astonishingly persuaded the newly-elected government of Robert Borden, himself from Halifax, to completely abolish the east-west differential of the Intercolonial. A final Ottawa nail in the region's manufacturing coffin was added in 1919 when the Intercolonial was absorbed in the nationalized Canadian National Railway and its management abruptly moved from Moncton to Toronto. The special freight rates for sugar and coal were quickly eliminated and its freight charges generally levelled with those in Central Canada. By 1920, cumulative freight rate increases had the effect of raising rates on the Intercolonial by 140 to 216 per cent. The new rate was a terrible blow, further maiming a regional economy already in shock from attempting to adjust to a host of technological changes.

Ironically, the strong Maritime case for special freight rate treatment was advanced in the Arthur Meighen cabinet by A.E. Kemp, a Toronto manufacturer. The general increases went ahead and all Maritimers were affected adversely. Robb Engineering of Nova Scotia, for example, had planned to produce farm tractors for the Prairies; it soon abandoned production when it was hit with a 40 per cent freight increase. By 1926, a majority of its 350 highly-trained employees were laid off; they found work and brighter futures in the United States.

Rapidly growing out-migration itself became the major cause of Maritime economic grief. At least 100,000 people, including my great grandparents, left the Maritimes in each of the decades between 1881 and 1931, mostly the young, skilled and ambitious. At least three-quarters of these talented Canadians appeared to follow the traditional Maritime route to the United States. Prince Edward Island was the worst affected and it would not regain its 1881 population level until a full century later in 1986. The loss of so many vigorous people from those provinces, which as a whole in 1881 held only 871,000 persons, was clearly the main cause (or some say the major symptom) of the region's economic and political decline.

The decline of the regional population had a highly negative impact on the local industry which survived. The common pattern was for machine shops, cotton mills, rail car factories and steel mills either to be transferred to Ontario or Québec, closed by head offices, or forced into bankruptcy.

World War II

Economic stagnation in Maritime Canada has never been inevitable or beyond a 'turn-around.' World War II provided an excellent opportunity for a fresh start because of the massive wartime role of the federal government. Adam Smith and his laws of the market were suspended by the Mackenzie King government between 1939 and 1945 when controllers were appointed over each major industry to develop and implement an industrial program. The man who dominated Ottawa's wartime thinking on most economic issues was C.D. Howe. Direct grants were made by Ottawa to many private businesses and tax incentives were also available to designated ones. For Maritime and Western coal, however, senior Ottawa officials, who seem forever unable to see Canada as a whole, during mid-1940 recommended against continuing transportation subsidies, arguing it was better to purchase coal in the U.S. and to absorb Maritime and Western Canadian miners thrown out of work into other sectors of our war effort. The King cabinet accepted this to the extent of reducing the subsidies by more than a third.

It is now well documented how Maritime coal, steel, shipbuilding, ship repair and manufacturing companies were, for more than a year into the war, denied federal funds for modernization and expansion. The historian Ernest Forbes states that C.D. Howe and his controllers "with the realization of impending commodity shortages and the great strategic importance of the region, finally turned to Maritime industries only to encounter manpower shortages and a limited infrastructure." The C.D. Howe vision, Forbes concludes, "of a centralized manufacturing complex closely integrated with the United States apparently did not include the Maritimes in any significant role."

The case of the Dominion Steel and Coal Company (DOSCO), the largest manufacturing employer in the Maritimes and one of Canada's "Big Three" steel producers, is illustrative. Howe provided $4 million in tax money to assist each of its two Ontario competitors, the Steel Company of Canada in Hamilton and Algoma Steel in Sault Ste. Marie, to modernize and increase capacity. Arthur Cross, DOSCO's president, was reduced to pleading that his was the only primary steel producer in the country receiving no government assistance whatsoever. A continued failure to provide a level playing field for all, Cross wrote to Howe, would make inevitable the conclusion that Ottawa was intending "to discriminate against the post-war future of this corporation and in favour of its Central Canadian competitors."

Howe's unexplained hostility towards DOSCO and his campaign to concentrate steel manufacturing on the Great Lakes alone had devastating repercussions for the Maritime steel industry. In 1944, Ottawa's steel controllers were even advised by Howe to use DOSCO "to the minimum extent possible even if we have to buy the steel from the United States" as reported by Duncan MacDowall in his book on the Algoma Steel company. Nor was DOSCO included in the federal government's invitation, extended to other companies as part of the postwar economy adjustment plans, to develop proposals for a sheet steel mill.

Wartime Ottawa also financed two new shipbuilding facilities on the Great Lakes and reserved for major naval contracts ten of fifteen existing shipyards across Canada which were capable of building freighter class vessels. Conspicuously absent from this list, however, were the Halifax and Saint John yards. Angus Macdonald, Nova Scotia's representative in the wartime cabinet, later defended the exclusions on the basis that they were needed for repairs and service. In fact they were used for neither of these purposes. The reality was that steelmaking, shipbuilding and even ship repairs were, by Ottawa order, first to be done in Québec and Ontario. More skilled Maritimers were thus forced by Ottawa to move inland.

The failure to develop a good naval repair service on our east coast resulted in some Canadian navy vessels becoming frozen in St. Lawrence ports and the dispatching of others to British Columbia and American ports. The Canadian navy, notes Forbes, "was forced to watch 'from the sidelines' while the better-equipped British escorts brought victory to the allies in the Battle of the North Atlantic." Maritimers and knowledgeable Canadians elsewhere could only mutter about the egregious stupidity of Ottawa's defence planners.

As early as 1940, British naval authorities opposed Ottawa's plan to ignore the potential of Atlantic Canada. Later, the British Admiralty mission in Ottawa would object, on the grounds of effectiveness, to building ships in Central Canada yards which were cut off by ice from the Atlantic for five months yearly and to forcing vessels to travel up the St. Lawrence River for servicing. They specifically wanted Ottawa to build an adequate repair facility at Halifax. Since the capital's czars were unmoveable, the British turned to the United States for the North American refit of their larger vessels. The Americans, too, were surprised by the Canadian nonchalance at the state of their repair facilities. In the spring of 1942, they completed their own survey of the port of Halifax and were strongly critical of the scarcity of repair berths. The investigators recommended that the American government send tug boats to Halifax to 'rescue vessels of all nationalities . . . detained for an unreasonable length of time in Canadian waters awaiting repairs.'"

As the war escalated, the federal government eventually made an investment in Maritime plants and equipment. It was modest and involved industries with poor prospects for post-war continuation. None of the 28 federal Crown corporations that existed at the time had its head office in the region. Of $823 million of Ottawa wartime spending on industrial expansion which could be identified on a provincial basis, the Maritime share was a pitiful 3.7 per cent. PEI didn't receive a dime; Nova Scotia — $20.8 million; New Brunswick — $6.5 million.

After the war, Ottawa started allocating money to enable industries to make the transition to peacetime production. By mid-1945, 48 per cent of the funds went to Ontario, 32 per cent to Québec, 15 per cent to British Columbia and the remaining 5 per cent was divided among the remaining six provinces under the assistance formula used. Ministry of Reconstruction officials justified this grossly discriminatory approach with gibberish and doubletalk. The problem of transition, gushed one, will be "most acute in the Maritimes . . . where wartime dislocations have been superimposed on the special problems of a depressed area." The post-war reconstruction policy reinforced the dreadful economic status quo for Maritime Canada.

Federal wartime policy was destructive to the Maritimes mainly because it created virtually no industries of a lasting nature. Compared to its two major competitors who received some of Howe's millions, DOSCO came out of the war weakened. Canadian National's repair shops in Moncton were undermined by the presence of a modern new shop in Montréal, converted by the railway — at C.D. Howe's suggestion — from a munitions factory at the end of the war.

Why this perverse wartime ministerial hostility toward Maritime industry? One can only speculate as to motives as Howe's biographers shed little light on that aspect of his many decisions. Presumably, he felt Maritime industry must inevitably decline and this became a self-fulfilling prophecy. He used enormous amounts of public money to ensure that it would occur.

Newfoundland: The Rock

Probably no province anywhere in Canada has a longer, more vexatious and contradictory history than Newfoundland and Labrador, the most recent partner in Confederation. That history deserves attention: its understanding may generate an improved national partnership between Newfoundland and the rest of Canada.

From the standpoint of national unity, it is no accident that in one recent poll done before the demise of the Meech Lake accord, 47 per cent of Newfoundlanders identified themselves with their province first, the highest showing in the country. Newfoundlanders maintain a strong sense of independence which could in some circumstances threaten Canada's continuation as one nation. Post-Meech Lake comments as the one by an Inner Canadian MP, Don Blenkarn, that consideration might be given to towing the province out to sea are adding fuel to Newfoundland fires instead of building much-needed national unity.

The province is physically divided into two major units: the mainland territory of Labrador to the north and the much smaller island of Newfoundland to the south. Part of the Canadian Shield, Labrador contains picturesque, rugged and isolated scenery, characterized by bare rock and barren tundra, forest, rivers, innumerable fjords, bays and inlets. Labrador is a vast storehouse of natural resources, mostly undeveloped. Approximately 27,000 Labradorians in eleven communities cling to a way of life which reflects the harsh realities of geography and politics.

For four centuries, Newfoundlanders fought for economic prosperity and political independence. It is ironic that their endless efforts achieved the opposite effect: greater dependence and economic decline. Almost a century after first being wooed by Canadian Confederationists, they were finally drawn into the North American orbit. Still, only a razor-thin majority of Newfoundlanders opted for provincehood, seeing it as a means of achieving economic development. Instead of being a "ward" of Britain's Royal Navy, as George Rawlyk puts it, by 1970 Newfoundland was transformed into a reluctant "ward" of Canada.

Until 1949, a series of territorial conflicts with France, the United States and Canada helped Newfoundlanders mould and strengthen their well-founded sense of national identity. This sense of national identity still endures as the twentieth century comes to a close. Today, Newfoundlanders weigh the benefits and disadvantages of the union, pondering upon the balance between humiliating dependency and proud but poor independence. The words "Having lost nothing they have surely gained a great deal ...," expressed by an enthusiastic Toronto newspaper 40 years ago, must be ironic not only to hundreds of thousands of Newfoundlanders who left the island in search of opportunity but also to those who stayed. As of January, 1989 there were some 568,000 residents on the Rock, most of whom owned their own homes. Compared to the national average a higher percentage of its residents are self-employed. The island also supports a proportionately larger service sector than does Ontario.

As the Economic Council of Canada has pointed out, in Newfoundland and Labrador the "incidence of suicide, murder, divorce, mental illness, cirrhosis of the liver and cancer is low compared with that in more privileged provinces like Alberta, British Columbia and Ontario. The human condition in short is a good deal better than is indicated by economic statistics alone." Indeed, one Council study is hopeful that Newfoundland and Labrador can break out of a circle of poverty and dependence if intelligent investments are made in its ideas and its people.

A Proud Past

Newfoundland's earliest role in the New World was as a dry mothership for English fishermen in the Grand Banks and as a possession of the Royal Navy. Despite British attempts to limit all permanent settlement on the island, approximately 15,000 permanent residents lived on the island by 1770, mostly on its eastern tip. They were joined each year for the fishing season by 10,000 Irish and English fishermen. Despite official British support for Confederation, the strong pro-British sympathy on the island made the going easy for those opposing it in the 1860s. A popular folk song went in part:

"For a few thousand dollars Canadian gold,
Don't let it be said that our birthright was sold.
Newfoundland's face turns to Britain.
Her back to the Gulf.
Come near at your peril,
Canadian wolf."

Most Newfoundlanders resisted the financial and other blandishments offered by the Fathers of Confederation even though the colony probably had more to gain in terms of cash inducements than any other part of the nation. Less than a fifth of Newfoundland's two-way trade was with London's North American Colonies and the merchants of St. John's feared they would lose their hammerlock on the island's economic power if exposed to mainland business competition. Many Newfoundland Roman Catholics, who by the 1800s had lobbied successfully for responsible government and government-supported denominational schools, were also reluctant to put such hard-won achievements in jeopardy through union with Canada. They saw an obvious parallel between the Irish economic and political decline following the 1801 Act of Union of England and Ireland and what would happen following Newfoundland's union with Canada. Many independent Newfoundlanders also deeply resented being pressured by Westminster to become Canadians. In consequence, anti-Confederationists swamped the supporters of Confederation in the 1869 election.

Hopes of Newfoundland joining Canada had been dashed for a generation. The next serious look at the issue came in the late 1880s. After a period of high employment in the cod and seal industries, the industry was severely battered by an export price collapse. Instead of restructuring the industry that employed virtually all of its labour force, the Newfoundland government chose to provide no assistance. Employment in the sector dropped from 60,000 in 1884 (87% of the work force) to 35,000 by 1935 (half of the labour force). Other sectors failed to take up the slack. Chronic unemployment and out-migration inevitably followed.

In 1890, Newfoundland negotiated a reciprocity agreement with the United States which might have improved things. Ottawa, concerned that the result might be harmful to Maritime fishermen, mischievously persuaded the British government to veto the agreement. This did serious harm to Canada-Newfoundland relations and contributed to a further postponement of Newfoundland entering Confederation.

The financial crisis of 1894 in Newfoundland reopened the issue of Confederation, viewed as a possible solution to the island's problems. The failure of talks with Canada in 1895 on the financial terms of entering Confederation had enduring consequences for public opinion on the island. There was little sympathy for a deeper involvement with Canada for a very long while.

During the first third of the twentieth century, St. John's merchants, 'the Water Street set', dominating a proudly independent island population, kept most heads turned firmly away from Canada. The Great Depression, however, all but wiped out foreign markets for Newfoundland's resource-based economy and shook the population to its foundations. Bankruptcy loomed for its government with a massive public debt. After unsuccessful attempts to raise money, including an effort to sell Labrador to Canada, it voluntarily suspended its self-government and dominion status within the Commonwealth in favour of a Commission of Government composed of British and Newfoundland appointees.

The Commission of Government did have some important achievements, in social services, tax reform, agriculture and fishing development programs. Yet, by the end of the 1930s, popular disenchantment had set in. There were still as many unemployed as in 1933; nor had the Commission achieved anything positive to restore self-government to the island. In the words of one of the Commissioners, Thomas Lodge, "To have abandoned the principle of democracy without accomplishing economic rehabilitation is surely the unforgiveable sin." By 1940, most Newfoundlanders seemed to agree.

Because of its strategic importance during World War II, the United States and Britain built bases at various locations across Newfoundland. Prosperity reached most corners of the island as thousands of jobs were created. Many British residents moved toward the greater prosperity on North America. World demand for primary goods exploded—fish exports alone quadrupled during the war years; newsprint sales climbed about 60 per cent and mineral production increased by almost fifty per cent. The best indicator of the massive change was that there was full employment on the island by 1942 compared to approximately 30 per cent of the population on relief just before the war began.

After the war, a referendum was held in mid-1948 on three options for the future: retention of the Commission of Government; reversion to responsible government; or confederation with Canada. The winner was responsible government by a small margin over joining Canada. Seven weeks later in a second referendum containing two choices only — responsible government or confederation — union with Canada narrowly won with only 52 per cent of the vote. Interestingly, Joey Smallwood, leader of the pro-Canada side, won most of his support in rural areas where incomes were lowest. An immediate result of joining confederation was higher personal incomes because of the new family allowance and unemployment insurance benefits from Canada. Other Confederation advantages were harbour facilities, the Trans-Canada Highway, and considerable equalizing of incomes within the new province.

On the negative side, the effective price of Canadian consumer goods fell sharply on the island since custom duties were removed and generous transport subsidies granted. "Within months," the Economic Council of Canada noted, "most of Newfoundland's substantive agriculture had succumbed to competition from imports of meat, vegetables, and canned milk, paid for with the baby bonus." Island manufacturing suffered similarly and within a year a paper bag producer, a mattress manufacturer and an underwear plant closed. The warning by Newfoundland's Responsible Government League, that Confederation would ruin local industry, seemed to be correct.

By entering Confederation, Newfoundland also lost control of its most important industry, the fishery. The result has been devastating. It need not have happened in the judgement of at least one expert, Michael Staveley, if Ottawa had drawn on lessons taught by the Commission of Government and dealt sensitively with the island fishery.

During the 1950s, neglect by the federal government and internal structural problems arising from a divided jurisdiction over the industry caused the fishery to slip even further into decay. Ottawa's slow response to the problems of off-shore fishing by huge foreign fleets led to quickly diminishing stocks. The island's entry into Confederation had legally given the federal government its fishery and oil resources. The 1985 Atlantic Accord ceded a substantial share of resource control and revenue to Newfoundland and entitled its residents to a major say in how and when they are to be developed. The post-Meech Lake "postponement" of the huge Hibernia oil project by the Mulroney government was understandably seen by many Newfoundlanders as a revenge because its assembly ultimately did not vote on the Meech Lake accord.

Whither Self-Reliance

Throughout history, Newfoundlanders have attempted grand projects and initiatives devised to raise incomes and increase employment. Some of them worked to a degree, but the island experienced more than its share of misfortune and adversity. Confederation brought transfers and subsidies that improved family incomes and social services. As a result, the province is dependent on money flowing from Ottawa: half of every dollar spent in the province now comes from the federal government. At the same time, the province forgoes a lot of money in revenue from natural resource development. Moreover, the disparity in income and unemployment between Newfoundland and the rest of the country is real and persistent.

In its 1980 study *Newfoundland: From Dependency to Self-Reliance*, the Economic Council of Canada studied development problems and opportunities in Newfoundland. It determined that it was possible to reduce the unemployment rate in the province and to lower its dependence on transfer payments. It also stressed that improvements could and should be made within existing subsidies and programs, without increase in aggregate government expenditures: "We are convinced that ways can be found to reduce Newfoundland's disparities in income and unemployment by reallocating the hundreds of millions of dollars already going to the province through subsidies on transportation, shipbuilding, and fishing; the program budgets of the Department of Regional Economic Expansion, the Department of Fisheries and Oceans, and the Department of Industry, Trade and Commerce; and the transfers under Established Program Financing and the Unemployment Insurance Act."

One very straightforward Council argument was that Canadians generally should recommend changes in national policies if those policies are perceived as having undesirable effects in places like Newfoundland. Optimistic that Newfoundland's situation can be improved, the authors pointed out many changes that would help the Newfoundland economy; some of them imply removing some undesirable aspects of provincial and federal government policies.

Suggesting that Ottawa give Newfoundland a new deal in order to overcome entrenched economic problems, the study concluded that to lower its unemployment and raise its productivity the province must foster the efficiency and self-reliance of its economy and its people. The authors do not see the main hope for Newfoundland in the resource industry but they rather stress the human talent in the province. We must, says the Council, go "with the ways in which they organize themselves and their activities into cities, towns, and outposts, and with how they develop their transportation and distribution systems and their businesses."

A partial update of the 1980 study was published in 1986 under the title *Newfoundland Revisited*. Noting the devastating impact of the 1980s recession on the economy — Newfoundland's unemployment rate reached

26.1 per cent in January 1985, the highest level recorded since the province joined Confederation — the Council pointed out again that there are very large transfers of income from Newfoundland to the rest of Canada, most notably the annual transfer of hundreds of millions of dollars from the Churchill Falls hydro-electric power project in Labrador to Hydro-Québec under the terms of the notorious 65-year Churchill Falls Power contract. With the benefit of hindsight, the Council concluded that most of the economic analysis proved to be correct. Most of the recommendations of its 1980 study remain to be fully implemented.

The overall conclusion of the study was that with an expanded fishery, oil developments, improved productivity, and better income maintenance systems, Newfoundland will move from dependency to self-reliance. Its century-long quest for a measure of prosperity and independence could be finally realized for its proud people.

The promises and hopes of Confederation might be fulfilled even before the Newfoundlanders celebrate the 50th Anniversary of the union.

Recent Days

Since the 1950s, Ottawa has taken a wide assortment of federal initiatives in an attempt to undo the damage done to Atlantic Canada. Regional Economic disparities have persisted nonetheless. The Maritimes and Newfoundland and Labrador are constantly positioned last among Canadian provinces in all the economic indicators. Productivity and capital formation are lowest. Despite the presence of many universities and colleges, educational levels tend to be lower, partly because so many Atlantic Canadians continue to seek opportunities outside the region. In out-migration, the four easterly provinces continue to win hands-down. In terms of personal income per resident, Atlantic Canadians have been lowest almost continuously since 1926. In both 1931 and 1933, farm-devastated Prairie incomes fell below Atlantic ones, but the pattern has since been unbroken. During World War II there was an improvement, but a deep Maritime slump followed between 1946 and 1951.

The gains Atlantic Canada has made since the early 1950s are pensions, unemployment payments, industrial incentives and other social payments from Ottawa. Despite the improvements to personal incomes from these transfers, the average income of Atlantic Canadians continues to vary between 65 and 80 per cent of the national average. In Nova Scotia, the highest income province in the region, personal incomes were only 81 per cent of our national average during 1984. For New Brunswickers and Prince Edward Islanders in the same year, the comparable figures were 74 and 72 per cent respectively, whereas Newfoundlanders stood at a mere 67 per cent.

Excluding transfer and incentive payments of various kinds, the so-called "earned" incomes of Atlantic Canadians as a whole during 1984 were only two-thirds of the national average compared to 65.2 per cent in

1926. Combining "earned" and "unearned," total personal income per person in the mid-1980s for Atlantic Canadians was still only about three-quarters of the national average. This gap is simply unacceptable today to any thoughtful Canadian.

Unemployment rates are a good indicator of disparity. In mid-1989, the regional unemployment rates were: Newfoundland — 15.5 per cent, PEI — 13 per cent; Nova Scotia — 9.4 per cent and New Brunswick — 12.2 per cent. Unemployment soars disproportionately faster in Atlantic Canada during national recessions and falls much more slowly than elsewhere across Canada during recoveries. For example, following the 1982 recession, it took two more years for the Atlantic unemployment rate to show any improvement whatsoever. Atlantic participation rates in the work force are, moreover, lower than elsewhere. Transfer payments from governments to individuals are much higher. Economic output per person is also lower and a larger part of it is accounted for by public administrators and defence spending.

Equalization payments are made on the basis of a formula that awards the most to provinces with the lowest revenue-raising capacities. They average about $800 per capita for Nova Scotians; more than $1,000 per person for all other Atlantic Canadians. These large amounts of overall government spending in the region when added to the public sector and all other government spending equalled two-thirds of the Atlantic economy in 1987.

Atlantic Canada vs. New England

The impressive economic turnabout of New England in the mid 1970s and 1980s is often contrasted with the opposite experience in Atlantic Canada during the same period.

The six New England states and Atlantic Canada are similar in geography and population roots but not in patterns of population growth and economic development. Major differences were already clear in 1640, and have persisted ever since. The political and social fabric of New England differs significantly from that of Atlantic Canada. There is also a marked difference in the relative size of the business community and industrial base in these two regions.

The Atlantic Provinces Economic Council undertook a study of the two regions on behalf of the Department of Regional Industrial Expansion and published its findings in 1985. It perceived the two regions as quite dissimilar due to significant differences in the political systems and due to the existing economic base, the availability of capital and the willingness to take risks in New England.

The key economic indicators for New England and Atlantic Canada show a dramatic contrast in the economic growth of the two regions. In 1975, the unemployment rate in New England was 10.4 per cent, higher than that of Atlantic Canada at 9.8 per cent. Nine years later, the rate in New

England had dropped to 4.5 per cent while that in Atlantic Canada had increased to 15.4 per cent.

The Council identified four major factors that were instrumental in prompting New England's recent impressive economic growth. First, the historical presence of a strong economic base which provided the foundation of a vibrant economy. The region has been in the forefront of "high-tech" industries in the U.S. for almost 200 years. Second, defence spending has had a major effect on the New England economy. Over 13 per cent of the supply contracts for U.S. defence awarded in 1982 went to Vermont, Massachusetts and Connecticut alone. The statistics provided by our Department of National Defence for 1985/86 indicate that 77 per cent of the contracts in Canada were awarded in Montréal-Ottawa-Toronto and only 23 per cent in the remaining eight provinces and two territories. Before 1985/86, DND did not keep records of financial activities in specific geographic areas.

New England also enjoys an abundance of venture capital. Twenty of the top 100 venture capital firms in the U.S. are located in New England. Conversely, there were no Canadian venture capital investment companies in Atlantic Canada in 1987 and 1988. It was not until 1989 that venture capital investors held their national convention in the region during their 10-year history.

Finally, world class educational centres have been a large New England source of R & D, highly skilled personnel, spin-off technologies and entrepreneurs.

Other factors contributing to overall growth within the New England states include research and development; a good business environment (e.g., tax levels, wage rates); transportation infrastructures; entrepreneurship; government programs; and rationalization and adjustment within the manufacturing sector.

Building on its analysis of New England's economic success, the Atlantic Economic Council identified a number of conclusions and recommendations for Atlantic Canada. It stressed the need to expand the region's limited economic base through the encouragement of local entrepreneurs and the creation of inter-industry linkages. Noting that Atlantic Canada holds a significant representation of armed forces personnel — as was the case before the 1989 Wilson budget — it called for a higher level of spending on military production, contracts and research. It suggested that special investment policies be considered. It called for improvement in the education levels and stressed the need for regional universities to develop better links with the local business community and to become centres of innovation.

Other recommendations included encouraging an increase in applied research and development; reducing high tax levels; attracting more business investment through better government attitudes and policies; modernizing, rationalizing and diversifying traditional Atlantic Canadian industries; improving transportation links and stabilizing transportation costs to businesses. The service sector is of great importance in the region, and should receive more attention in economic planning. Finally, a special effort should be made to relocate head offices to Atlantic Canada. At present not a single one of the forty biggest or best known federal crown corporations has its head office in Atlantic Canada.

New initiatives in Atlantic Canada must recognize the nature of the region: this is the only way to overcome barriers to growth and the creation of an environment which will promote sustained economic growth. Atlantic Canada's future is still in our hands.

Prospects for the 1990s

Following the spectacular pre-release of the Wilson budget by the television journalist Doug Small in April, 1989, a wave of disappointment and anger swept across Atlantic Canada as its consequences for the region became fully understood. Timothy O'Neill, chairman of the Atlantic Provinces Economic Council, complained that about half of the federal government cuts as measured by employment were in Atlantic Canada. No one across the region disagreed except for some local federal cabinet ministers.

Two years of relative prosperity across the region had just ended; now an estimated 10,000 Atlantic Canadians were expected to lose their jobs either permanently or temporarily because of the proposed closing or reduction in six Canadian Forces Bases in the region, the postponement of the Hibernia oil mega-project and a deeply depressed fishery. Many of the residents of Atlantic Canada are faced with an all-too-familiar regional dilemma: to remain unemployed in their home province or to go job hunting in Central or Western Canada.

The Armed Forces base closings were fresh Ottawa kicks in the face for Atlantic Canadians. The closing of the Summerside base would result in the disappearance of 1,300 direct jobs over two years. The Atlantic Provinces Economic Council estimated that as many as 5,000 individuals might in consequence be obliged to leave Prince Edward Island with the loss of $40.8 million in salaries and $20 million in local contracts. The local impact of additional base closings at Barrington and Sydney, Nova Scotia, and Moncton, New Brunswick and the scaledowns at Gander, Newfoundland, and Chatham, New Brunswick would also be disproportionately heavy. The establishment of a data processing centre for his proposed goods and services tax in Summerside, announced in May, 1990, promised 400 full and part-time jobs by the time it is to open in 1992. This was far fewer than the 1,300 direct and 1,700 indirect jobs that would be lost by the time the base closes in mid-1992.

Why, Atlantic Canadians ask, must military operations be further concentrated in high-cost regions such as Ontario? Must PEI's unemployment rate be raised by two or three points when it was already 14.3% in

April, 1989? The Mulroney government replied woodenly that military spending is not regional development. Bases must, however, go somewhere: don't they provide an opportunity to distribute some federal spending in a way that entails regional benefits? Doesn't the location of a penitentiary within the Prime Minister's constituency fulfil a similar goal? In short, why should Atlantic Canadians carry the heaviest share of Ottawa's thus far largely futile effort at cutting its deficit?

"There is no crisis in Atlantic Canada," protested Prime Minister Mulroney in the Commons during an exchange with opposition members in January, 1990. At that time it became apparent the region would bear most of the pain from deficit cutting measures and present economic slowdown. Also, the consequences of the latest crisis in fisheries had become obvious. The fall in cod stocks forced Ottawa to cut the 1990 fishing quotas by a ratio that would throw 3,000 Newfoundlanders and Nova Scotians out of work.

A report by a special panel to investigate the state of cod stock, headed by Leslie Harris of Memorial University in St. John's, concluded that the 1991 quota of 190,000 tonnes might well contribute to a further decline in stocks, and that it will be necessary to further decrease the 1991 quota. In short, more Atlantic jobs are doomed. As to the region's share of federal industrial assistance it has fallen steadily since 1980 as indicated in a 1989 study by the Atlantic Economic Council. That year, Ottawa aid to Atlantic Canada amounted to $1,045 per person, compared with $229 per person in the rest of Canada and $302 per person for all of Canada. By 1987, the per person federal spending in the region was $200 (in 1980 dollars), while for the rest of Canada it was $258. The national average that year was $253 per resident.

The underlying message of these numbers — dismissed by some federal cabinet ministers as nonsense — was evident: though the region is getting some band-aid assistance in the form of various "show-case" programs, such as the Atlantic Canada Opportunities Agency, and a recent half-billion dollar aid package spread over five years, meaningful aid in the form of a coherent overall development plan for the region, backed up by a substantial dollar value, is not on Ottawa's current agenda. There is no plan that would mobilize existing resources and industrial potential, build on the human talent and develop technologies for tomorrow. Ottawa development dollars are mostly by-passing Atlantic Canada because of policy-makers who are incapable of envisaging a future for the people there other than a hand-to-mouth existence.

Atlantic Canadians appear to have been among the major victims of recent federal government changes in the tax system. In preparing to replace a 13.5 per cent tax at the manufacturing level, which applied to a limited number of products, with a seven per cent tax on virtually every good and service at the retail level, the impact will clearly be greater on middle- and low-income Canadians generally. The proposed tax credit for low-income families will arguably reduce the blow for a while for some Atlantic families. However, without full indexing for cost of living increases, Canadians who earn the least will soon be hit the hardest.

The Atlantic Provinces Economic Council pointed to the probable impacts of the GST on the region, noting that because Atlantic Canadians have lower average income levels than people elsewhere, "it would seem critical to ensure the tax credit be of sufficient size and be indexed to inflation." It also said that removing the manufacturing tax would initially benefit a number of industries (motor vehicle, furniture, household appliances, alcohol, tobacco, construction materials) concentrated in southern Ontario. Extending the federal sales tax to sectors such as services and food-processing, moreover, would strike regions like Atlantic Canada, which lack a strong manufacturing sector, disproportionately hard. It warned that Atlantic Canadian consumers will be forced to pay more of the new sales tax than Canadians in denser population centres where greater market competition will encourage producers to absorb some of the increased costs created by the new tax. The effects of a multi-stage tax on transportation services is particularly worrisome to the region because both producers and consumers remote from Central Canada face higher transportation costs than persons close to population centres in Ontario and Québec. Overall, the regional Council doubted the new tax would prove neutral in its geographic implications. It disputed proceeding with such a major initiative in the absence of a detailed study of its regional consequences.

Regional Hope

New directions, new development techniques and new technologies can bring sustainable development for Atlantic Canada during the 1990s and beyond. The catch-up instruments of the past have clearly failed. These include the development policies of federal departments and many provincial development policies. At the current rate, it will take a full century to raise per person incomes across the region to our national average. Only some new directions can produce changes to achieve major improvements in the living conditions of Atlantic Canadians.

A late summer of 1989 edition of the *Globe and Mail* carried an article "Farewell to Toronto" by writer Alexander Bruce, son of Harry Bruce and grandson of Charles Bruce — both Maritime authors. Three generations of Bruces drew strength and inspiration from the region, its people and their century-old homestead Down Home: "The Place." In his father's account of a 1986 Christmas spent in "The Place," Alexander, visiting from Toronto, remarked, "Boy, if I could get a decent job down here, I'd be back in a flash." It took him longer than that and there is no indication that "a decent job" was located, but eventually he left Toronto as a successful writer "for the second and probably last time."

The Toronto-born Alexander Bruce's decision to move his family to

Halifax epitomizes the plight of many other Atlantic Canadians by birth, by choice or by family heritage. Today or a century ago, wherever they live outside "Down Home," and no matter how successful they are, they never fully detach themselves from the spot on the map where they feel they really belong. They will always come back even if it is only in thought, memory or spirit.

THREE
LIFE ON THE SHIELD

The Canadian Shield is, to most Canadians and foreigners alike, the quintessential Canada. I share this view having lived in the Gatineau Park spur of it for more than a decade and having often vacationed at Lake of the Woods for many more years. In countless ways, the Shield is idyllic. I think, for example, of the hundreds of motor boats which gather each July 1st in Kenora Bay at the north end of Lake of the Woods to watch Canada Day fireworks. Mingled with townspeople at these annual events under the stars are summer residents from all over the country. Many would move to the area to live year round if they could somehow earn a living; some do.

Approximately two million Québeckers and Ontarians combined live on the Canadian Shield. Since its borders are physical rather than political, residents on both sides of the provincial boundary lack effective structures through which they can pursue common regional concerns. The north of both provinces contains relatively thinly-populated frontier hinterlands; for many years, each of them has had only a limited influence on its respective provincial parliament and upon Ottawa policy makers.

The Shield in fact occupies more than forty per cent of our national territory across five provinces, but contains only eight per cent of our national population. In recent years, vigorous natural resource competition from developing countries, a declining resource-orientation of the world economy, and the weakened political position of the American economy have reduced mineral exploration and development across the region. Decades ago, it also contributed to the development of our national self-identity through the art of the Group of Seven and considerable writing about Northern self-reliance.

John Diefenbaker's view that our national future lay in harnessing the distant North was popular in its day. Economic historians also accorded the Shield a large role, one competing even with the Laurentian school of thought. Some of them concluded that our national resource export patterns have entrenched metropolitan hegemony over various hinterlands such as the Shield.

The Shield is Canada's largest and best-known physiographic feature: 4.6 million square kilometres of a lake-dotted plateau ranging from Labrador in the East to the Arctic in the Northwest. Distinguished by a mosaic of rock, deep lakes and forests, it offered the challenge of minerals of vast value hidden in a hostile wilderness. For most of the nineteenth century, its mineral potential was largely ignored and it was seen as a useless barrier blocking the northern and western expansion of farm settlement. In 1864, *The Toronto Globe* dismissed the Shield as "gaps of rough and . . . barren country which lie between us and the fertile prairies of North-Western British America."

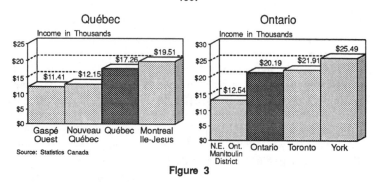

Personal Income Per Capita
Provincial and Sub-Provincial Regions
1987

Figure 3

The regional variations of the Shield have determined a discontinuous and thinly scattered pattern of settlement. The first to arrive were farm communities established on land opened during the westward lumber boom of the nineteenth century, including the Ottawa Valley and Lac Saint Jean lowlands. Between 1880 and 1915, the second group of settlements sprang up along the CN-CP rail routes; some of these, notably Thunder Bay and Sudbury, achieved national significance during these years. Finally, more recent centres such as Lynn Lake in Ontario and Schefferville in Québec were created to mine resources. The Shield's aboriginal residents today often live near single-industry mining or forest towns with narrow job opportunities, but continue travelling over large areas to seek fish and game.

As a result of these three types of settlement and the boom and bust cycles of natural resources, the urban structure of the Shield today consists of small and medium-sized communities with no large metropolis. Single-enterprise resource communities, vulnerable to the loss or depletion of their resources or a necessary international market, is a classic urban Shield feature.

The tendency of Southern cities to diversify their economies through import replacement seems not to apply to smaller communities on the Shield. Dozens of them in both Ontario and Québec depend on single employers and their service sectors. The isolation of most such centres, with limited employment opportunities and few social and cultural outlets, has encouraged considerable out-migration. Most communities on the Shield run from a few hundred to more than a thousand residents. According to the 1986 census, there are only three sub-regional cities even within our two largest provinces with populations of more than 100,000: Chicoutimi-Jonquiere (158,500), Sudbury (150,000) and Thunder Bay (122,200).

These three cities are connected much more closely to Montréal, Toronto and Winnipeg respectively than to each other. Their local industries are invariably controlled from one of the larger Canadian cities or from the United States. In addition, successive Ontario and Québec governments have for the most part shown an inadequate understanding of their own provincial north. A common regional identity has unfortunately failed to emerge that might have provided an effective voice in setting both public and private policies for a relatively large group of Canadians.

The construction of the CPR line across Canada solidified Montréal's position as the dominant Shield metropolis during the late nineteenth century. It connected such major centres as Sudbury, Sault Ste. Marie, Thunder Bay and Winnipeg to Montréal before later rail links to Toronto provided any real competition. Torontonians caught up and passed Montréalers in Shield dominance well into the twentieth century by becoming the financiers of most Shield mines. Through forest company mergers during the 1970s, the Ontario capital also reduced Montréal's earlier dominance over Shield wood product industries. Together, however, the two cities, home to large natural resource companies such as Alcan, Noranda, Inco, Abitibi-Price and Hydro-Québec, effectively control the Shield's economy today to an astonishing degree. Consequently, Sudbury, Chicoutimi, Thunder Bay and other towns are in essence merely regional centres of services. The smaller communities are even less protected than these larger ones from the common boom-bust cycles of ore industry resource towns.

The Shield forest industry in both provinces is illustrative of a common sub-regional problem. From the early 1800s until World War I, a breath-takingly wasteful cutting of Shield trees lunged westward across both provinces. There was very little forest regeneration and it became necessary to move northward after 1918 for fresh pulp and paper stocks. Earlier mills were founded in the St. Lawrence and Ottawa Valleys, but later ones extended from Chicoutimi to Kenora, providing pulpwood logs mainly to northern American newsprint markets. Various attempts by provincial Ontario governments to bar the export of raw pulpwood logs — "the manufacturing condition" — ultimately failed when governments in Québec City declined to enact similar legislation.

Only when American publishers, foreseeing a shortage in wood, succeeded in persuading legislators in Washington to allow the tariff-free admission of Canadian newsprint did large new investments create a number of new pulp and paper mills across the Shield. The resulting excess capacity, combined with the arrival of the Great Depression, brought severe drops in newsprint prices and major havoc for a host of newsprint-dependent communities. Québec and Ontario politicians and Canadian banks made various attempts to create an industry cartel that would end price competition and reduce production — a mechanism comparable to OPEC's attempts to control oil. This failed for various reasons, but the banks' and provincial governments' motivation probably had little to do with keeping hinterland mill employees out of the ranks of the unemployed.

During the 1960s and early 1970s, another wave of pulp and paper mills was built, often financed with the help of Ottawa and provincial regional development grants. Unfortunately, long-term negligence by the two provincial governments acting as forest landlords has created severe problems, especially in northwestern Ontario where three out of four manufacturing jobs today still depend on trees. In recent years, both governments have improved their forestry practices a good deal.

Given that almost ninety per cent of the Shield's pulp and paper and about sixty per cent of our newsprint goes to the United States, the current high exchange rate of the Canadian dollar — a ten year high — is causing real marketing problems. The Bank of Canada Governor appears to have kept Canadian interest rates at high levels mostly to keep the Canadian dollar at levels which will persuade Japanese and American institutions to buy Canadian government bonds. As a result, residents in the Shield believe they and the condition of the forest industries in which they earn their living have scant influence on the policies of the Bank of Canada.

Mining on the Shield began during the 1890s in response to demands from various international markets. At Sudbury, where the CPR discovered ample nickel deposits during construction of its line westward to the Prairies, the mines enjoyed almost a world monopoly on the product for a long period. It was not, however, until after 1945 that the mining age on the Shield flourished, following some very large investments in railway construction. Minerals from new sources, such as the Québec-Labrador iron fields, then came into production.

Since the 1982 economic recession across Canada, the Shield mining industry has faced an uncertain future. Severe competition from a number of developing countries and from Australia has hit the Canadian Shield. This, combined with uncertain ore prices, threatens the economic future of numerous Shield communities.

Shield minerals constitute an essential part of the Ontario and Québec economy; mines in Québec brought in $2.2 billion during 1986 and employed more than 20,000 people. They are a mixed blessing, though, since they are developed for outsiders and usually by firms from the south — thus perpetuating a hinterland status for the North.

The case of Elliot Lake illustrates the fortunes of communities affected by decisions taken thousands of miles away. Located 140 kilometres west of Sudbury, Elliot Lake, a community of 16,000 people, came into being in 1955, two years after the discovery of uranium in the area. The American military's demand for uranium during the height of the Cold War was so great that a boom developed lasting from 1956 until 1963. By 1959, a dozen mining companies were in operation in the district. Almost 25,000 people were living in the carefully-laid out community when Washington announced in 1959 that it would not renew its contracts. As a consequence of this devastating news, Elliot Lake's population collapsed six years later to only 6,600. By 1970, only Denison Mines and Rio Algom were still in operation. A better period emerged in the 1970s with the advent of nuclear-generated power in Canada. The fortunes of the "Uranium Capital of the World" improved slowly until the early 1980s when sales to Ontario Hydro stimulated a second surge in growth.

The prospects of uranium are much less bright for the last decade of the century. In 1990, with the announced closures of the Rio Algom and Denison uranium mines as a result of plummeting uranium prices and rising production costs, 2,500 miners are expected to lose their jobs; an additional 2,000 service and support sector jobs will disappear as well. The impact on the local population and business community could be compared to job losses in Metro Toronto of one million. The expected exodus of the laid-off miners and their families again threatens to reduce Elliot Lake to the ghost town it resembled in the mid-1960s. The community is bracing itself in anticipation of tough times. Its enterprising mayor has attempted to find salvation for his thirty-five-year-old mining town by persuading Canada's seniors to move in. During the last two years, more than a thousand of them have been persuaded to move to Elliot Lake under the retirement program sponsored by the town and the mines. Doubts persist that even the 3,000 more seniors whose arrival is anticipated will be able to sustain the town once designed for ten times that number. Still, local citizens are determined not to let their community die. "Many of us have a lot of faith in the town and this community that it just can't become a ghost town. We'll adjust," a miner's wife said defiantly.

Since 1950, the major demand for the Shield's cheap electricity has come from the urban-industrial heartlands within Canada and the American Northeast. The Churchill Falls project, started in 1953 in Labrador by a consortium of Europeans, set a standard for others to follow. Unfortunately for residents of Newfoundland and Labrador, in 1965 the Smallwood government entered into a sixty-five-year contract with Hydro-Québec to provide ninety per cent of the power generated at a price which during the 1980s was approximately one-tenth of its value in American markets. In 1984, the Supreme Court of Canada, displaying an unusual respect for the sanctity of contracts, saw no legal reason to rescind the agreement. The Québec government goes on selling Labrador's power for huge profits in the U.S. and uses the product domestically to attract industry into Québec. Meanwhile, the two provincial governments continue to disagree hotly over where the Labrador-Québec boundary should be drawn.

Northern Ontario Disaffection

Life in the Shield has been far too little examined but one of its features is well known: the grossly unequal struggle between the heartland of southern Ontario and metropolitan Québec and the northern hinterlands. Manufacturing firms have no incentive to locate on the Shield because metals refined there are by direction of head offices rarely sold at prices set at the mine gate. Gasoline sold in Red Lake, Ontario, goes at the Sarnia price plus a two thousand and fifty kilometre freight charge to Red Lake even though Red Lake is only about five hundred kilometres from oil refineries in Winnipeg. Another case is Matagami in northern Québec, whose residents complained in 1976 that their community was relocated more than a half century ago to make room for a hydroelectric dam, while they themselves did not obtain electricity until 1971.

For generations, federal policies have been designed to suit southern Ontario's needs. "New Ontario," as northern Ontario was known a century ago, has today approximately three-fourths of the province's land area but only ten per cent of its population. In terms of Canada as a whole, however, northern Ontario lies not in northern Canada but close to its centre. Draw a straight line from Edmonton eastward and it runs into James Bay. Residents of North Bay, Sault Ste. Marie and Sudbury might occasionally call themselves "Northerners", but they live south of some parts of the United States. A few northern Ontarians have sought provincial status for their sub-region at various intervals since Confederation as a solution to their isolation from Queen's Park but with very little success or popular support.

In many ways, northern Ontario is a microcosm of Canada as a whole: eighty-five million hectares within the Shield's rugged, lake-dotted geology; a scattered population; a colonial economic system; a sizeable French-speaking community in the northeast; a neglected native population who have finally begun to lobby for their rights at many isolated points everywhere. While it is true that Ontario, in the words of the late Ontario Premier John Robarts, is the "golden hinge" of Confederation, it is equally true that northern Ontario is "the rusty linchpin." As Don Scott notes, "If Canada is to work, then Northern Ontario, where all the alienations meet, must be made to work for it. It is here that Eastern Canada meets the alienated West. It is here that English Canada meets alienated French

Canada. It is here that the Indian suffers a silent alienation within sight of a standard of living far above his own. It is here that a colonial industrial system functions with an alienated work force."

When Ontario's Ministry of Northern Affairs sponsored a history of the region during the province's bicentennial in 1984, the author of one chapter concluded cheerfully: "No longer is Northern Ontario simply a place in which to work or survive; rather it is a place in which three-quarters of a million Ontarians choose to live satisfying and productive lives. Ontario's north has finally come of age." The realities of everyday life in northern Ontario scarcely warrant such optimism. Discontent is a sentiment which surfaces readily in discussions held north and west of any line drawn down the Mattawa River, Lake Nipissing and the French River. It reflects the feeling common among many residents of the sub-region that they are being short-changed; that their natural resources, local residents and money are constantly removed from them in order to serve southerners; that southerners in return have little or no concern for balanced economic and cultural development, environmental protection or local government structures and services. This sense of grievance and feeling of powerlessness tends to be reinforced by the perceived impotence of elected representatives at both the federal and provincial levels throughout northern Ontario.

Many northern Ontarians share with Outer Canadians generally the view that while they do much of the really hard work in often inhospitable places, rewards "go south." Northern Ontarians also share the hinterland conviction that both federal and provincial government services are only grudgingly provided in their communities and that they are victimized by a host of transport and trade policies which leave them with undiversified resource economies vulnerable to every drop in world commodity prices. "Northern Ontario is for the rest of the province what the Prairie West is for Canada," notes Tom Miller, with the difference that "the Prairie West has provinces and a political voice; northern Ontario is a part, and electorally a very small part, of the province that exploits it. Political frustration gives northern resentment a very special bitterness." During the summers I spent in the Kenora district of northwestern Ontario I was able to fully verify this feeling.

In Northern Ontario today, the sense of belonging to an exploited hinterland is both widespread and reinforced by geographic and other natural factors. Timmins has only ninety-two frost-free days, Sudbury and the Soo — 112, compared with Toronto's 160. Thunder Bay is a two-long-days' drive from Toronto, and residents west of the lakehead are for all practical purposes really Manitobans who happen to live in Ontario. Lakehead residents often read Manitoba newspapers and watch Manitoba television. Many go to university in Winnipeg and find it closer for serious medical problems. The thought that things would have been better if everything west of Thunder Bay had been joined formally to Manitoba keeps few northerners awake at night today, but a persuasive case can still be made for it.

Kenora, one of the most idyllic settings anywhere in Canada, is northern Ontario in its most perfect state. On most summer weekends across northern Ontario there are about 300,000 vacationers among 800,000 local residents. Visitors generally drive better cars and own the better lakeside locations. When a high-powered motor boat full of carefree holidayers speeds down the lake, almost swamping a family of Indians in a canoe, many of us are horrified. Tourism is the region's third-largest industry, yet it is badly paid, seasonal, often harmed by pollution, and to a degree pre-empted by better incomes in the forest industries. Looking deeper, one discovers that freight practices and rates maximize the movement of raw materials out of the north; decent roads are usually built reluctantly by the Ontario government and late in the day; most communities lack dentists; and doctors are scarce. The tourists probably do not notice the brisk out-migration of young Northerners seeking better job opportunities to the South.

North of the Fiftieth Parallel

In addition to its northeast and northwest, Ontario also has another north, the one beyond the fiftieth parallel where boreal forests become tundra. Sioux Lookout, Moosonee and Red Lake/Balmertown are its major cities; places like Pickle Lake and Ear Falls are its "towns." Most of its approximately 30,000 residents live in isolated communities, accessible mostly by bush planes.

Culturally, the various Ontario Norths differ both from each other and from the southern part of the province. Many non-British newcomers reached parts of northern Ontario and Prairie Canada in roughly equal numbers and at about the same time. Today, despite the passage of three generations, multiculturalism has triumphed in numerous northern communities. Francophones are found everywhere in northern Ontario, although most numerous in the northeast, and today command reasonable access to francophone education, radio and health services in a number of census districts. A second major group is the aboriginal peoples who predominate "north of fifty" either as status Indians, with treaty rights, as non-status Indians, or as Métis. Ojibway is spoken in the south; Ojibway and Cree in the centre; Cree only in the north. Band councils and Band chiefs are the municipal governments of these peoples. It troubles small native communities who live from fishing and hunting that their band chairmen are not yet recognized by Queen's Park and Ottawa as they are by other Indians.

The living conditions of Ontario aboriginals tend to vary with the situation of the neighbouring white centres. The Fort William band members near Thunder Bay live quite well; conditions for people living near less prosperous centres are often outrageous. Native communities in some remote reserves compare unfavourably with settlements in developing world nations. Virtually nowhere today do hunting, fishing, trapping, and wild rice harvesting provide decent livings. High school and junior education is generally inadequate for young persons choosing either to remain in the north or to seek future-oriented jobs in the south. An Indian brief to a recent Ontario Royal Commission noted: "Our traditions, stifled within this foreign system, could no longer guide or support us, and we gradually sank into a pool of despair: a despair that led to alcoholism, violence and the numbing apathy that characterizes a colonized and dependent people."

Many northern Ontarians were deeply concerned that areas around Sudbury were chosen by American astronauts as a practice moonscape. Most know that industrial pollutants released both in Canada and in the United States have killed thousands of lakes within the Shield. Most also know that the Shield ecosystem, fragile enough because of thin soil, poor drainage systems and lakes vulnerable to acid rain, grows ever weaker as one goes north.

The most tragic occurrence of Ontario Shield water pollution was the Reed Paper Company mill at Dryden on the English/Wabigoon River system. For years, the Dryden Chemicals mill at Dryden in northwestern Ontario had, in full compliance with Ontario government permits, dumped large amounts of mercury into the local river. Until the Japanese discovered the fact at Minimata, few in North America knew that mercury does not diffuse, but instead becomes highly toxic and, being absorbed in plants, is then eaten by fish.

Ultimately, much of the fish was consumed within the Indian communities of Grassy Narrows and Whitedog north of Kenora. The health, food and tourism consequences lingered for many years. At one point in the late sixties, the Schreyer government in Manitoba passed legislation aimed at holding liable anyone who polluted rivers flowing into Manitoba. An action was initiated by the province against Dryden Chemicals for what it had done with its mercury; it ultimately failed when the courts held the statute was unconstitutional for attempting to legislate against acts occurring beyond Manitoba territory. The vulnerable residents of the district had been victimized by official ignorance, but the many more years until the mid-1980s it took to arrive at a settlement of damages with Ottawa was also very troubling.

In northern Ontario, the radicalism created by alienation and economic and political domination from outside the area has been mostly immobilized because of small populations, ethno-cultural fragmentation, and ideological rivalries. Trade unions were slower to make headway in company towns such as the Nickel Belt than in communities such as Timmins where employees did not live on company premises. In addition, internal disputes weakened union activity in Sudbury between 1940 and the 1960s. Only in recent years have significant improvements been achieved in working conditions and work safety issues generally.

Politically, northern Ontarians persist in dividing their votes among three political parties at both the federal and provincial levels, a practice that results in a lack of any serious political impact both at Queen's Park and on Parliament Hill. C.D. Howe, when minister of virtually everything in Ottawa, had great difficulty in keeping the Port Arthur shipyards (now Thunder Bay) at work: they were located within his own constituency. Lester Pearson was prime minister when Elliot Lake, within his own Algoma East riding, suffered its greatest economic difficulties.

It bothers many northerners that some one-industry northern towns are so vulnerable as to be receptive to the most blatant bullying. Atikokan, for one, was reduced to accepting an offer of a nuclear waste disposal site and a thermal power station even without scrubbers for the chimneys. On the brighter side, other northern communities have diversified. Sault Ste. Marie won an Algoma Steel plant. Thunder Bay's Canadian Car company has made aircraft, buses, tree harvesters, prefabricated houses, rail and subway cars for international markets since as long ago as World War II. Its high-tech products appear to have overcome high transportation costs. Contrary to conventional wisdom about it being essential for manufacturers to be close to their markets, Canadian Car is a beacon for all who seek economic diversification across both northern Ontario and Outer Canada as a whole.

Northern Ontario's economic structure often reinforces the psychological basis for disaffection. When nickel ore from Falconbridge goes to Norway, iron ore from Atikokan to Cleveland, uranium from Elliot Lake to Japan, this troubles some local residents. There are enough northern ghost towns that Northerners worry about working themselves out of both jobs and town sites as mines become exhausted. Too many rivers and streams are polluted and there are too many pollutants in the sky. Federal and provincial officials, rather than taking action, prefer making self-serving speeches about doing regional justice. Discriminatory freight rates compound economic problems within the sub-region. The area from Levis, Québec, to Armstrong in northern Ontario has the highest freight rates in Canada. In addition, because favourable rates apply for the export of raw resources out of the north, those for moving many manufactured products into the north are higher.

Northern Québec

Québec's North is a moving frontier, as full of the same social and psychological importance for the rest of the province as the American West holds for the United States. As early as the middle of the nineteenth century, Northern Québec had assumed far more significance than its geography implied. For many Québeckers, it became both a symbolic region and a myth: they needed reassurance about their dwindling population relative to other regions of Canada. The rapid industrialization of the

United States in that period, the threat to Québeckers' culture, language and religion caused by surging anglophone immigration, the dangerous overcrowding of provincial land already settled, and the uncooperative reception given French-speaking families who sought to settle in the English-speaking Eastern townships — all these factors encouraged the development of the province's north as Québec's region of hopes and myths.

Québec's North acquired a legendary status from well-known geographer Arthur Buies. During the years 1850-1860, "the North" for many Montréalers meant a vast region with no precise boundaries but one where the southern edge was almost at Montréal's city limits. As Buies put it, "It was believed that the limits of cultivable lands had been reached and that the name 'North' meant there was nothing beyond Saint-Jérome but a fleeting spring, an illusory summer. The railway to Saint-Jérome opened up, just a few leagues behind Montréal, an almost unknown, sparsely-cleared region. At the time, the North was the forbidden region, closed to any attempt at colonization or even habitation, doomed to the immutable stillness of sterility and even the imagination did not dare probe its remote and sinister depths."

The Laurentian mountains near Montréal and Québec City were the closest ramparts of the North. Only a few Montréalers were conscious of the potential of the North; many others believed the province was worthless beyond the St. Lawrence Valley. In the developing "Open Country North" myth, the sub-region gradually became the province's promised land. At first, it was seen as a desert, only becoming a Garden of Eden later. Providence would use the area to help Québeckers survive: though hostile, the northern land would be settled and cultivated.

Like the Canadian and American frontiers, Québec's north also held within it the crucial element of regeneration: new people for a new country. Frederick Jackson Turner, the American historian, proclaimed in the American western frontier the birth of a new spirit, a long-lost purity in the bosom of virgin territory. Similarly, Québeckers would be regenerated in their North, a promised land in which courageous spirits might figuratively cross a Red Sea. The North was also widely seen across Québec as the symbol of a new and classless society. The significance of Québec's North during the second half of the nineteenth century has been seriously underestimated by recent historians. In fact, the parallels, despite obvious differences, between Québec's North and the American West were substantial. Each carried the aspirations of the nation and each became first symbols and later myths for their respective peoples. In Québec's case, however, the myth of the North now seems largely forgotten, victim mostly of the lure of the two large provincial cities and the draw of the much closer Appalachian region.

A 1983 publication by the government of Québec, *The Québec North, regional profile*, identifies the southern boundaries of Northern Québec with the limits of the administrative regions: Abitibi-Témiscamingue, Sauguenay-Lac-Saint-Jean and North Shore. According to this publication, the total area of Northern Québec covers one million square kilometres or two thirds of the total territory of the province, the equivalent of the combined land area of Spain, the two Germanies and Portugal but with a population of approximately 100,000 people.

The geological exploration of Northern Québec dates back to 1684 when the Hudson's Bay Company sent ten men from Fort Charles to the mouth of the Eastmain to exploit a mica mine. Two names stand out in the history of geological explorations of the area: an Oblate missionary, Father Louis Babel, the first to discover iron ore in Northern Québec between 1866 and 1870; and a geologist, Albert Low, who with his partner covered 5,675 miles at the end of the nineteenth century, carrying out his scientific studies. Low identified millions of tons of iron ore along the shores of Lake Cambrian. The mineral resources of the North of Québec are abundant, particularly in its southern parts and the Labrador trough. However, factors like access to the resources and current economic conditions severely minimize their exploitation.

The names of many places in Northern Québec reflect the presence of the Northern peoples in the area for thousands of years. The Amerindians of the Algonquin tribe arrived almost 8,000 years ago. The Inuit crossed over from Baffin Island almost 4,000 years ago to the northern shores of Québec's Far North and settled along the coast of Hudson Bay. They played important roles as guides, helpers and interpreters during the days of the fur trade and its explorations. They still pursue traditional activities like hunting, trapping, and fishing, but are gradually becoming more dependent on social assistance for survival. Recent decades have witnessed the native peoples' fighting more successfully for self-determination and becoming more aware of their rights. The agreements between James Bay Crees, the Inuit and Québec are examples of the more effective participation nowadays by Québec aboriginal peoples in controlling their own lives.

The Case of Schefferville

The case of Schefferville in the heart of the Québec-Labrador peninsula, 1,400 kilometres northeast of Montréal in one of the most peripheral regions of the province, illustrates the uncertainties of life in northern Québec. In 1981, its population was 1,997; by 1986 it had collapsed to three hundred and twenty-two residents. In November, 1982 the Iron Ore Company of Canada, based in Montréal, announced it would close its Schefferville mine by mid-1983. The company had built the community in 1953 with initial reserves of ore estimated at 420 million tons. At the peak, there were 4,500 community residents. When I visited it as a student during the summer of 1964, the future seemed bright to everyone.

A fall in the world price of iron in the early 1980s dashed many hopes. The company's president of the day, Brian Mulroney, announced a $10 million severance package for employees losing their jobs, amounting to $9,200 per family, with three-quarters to be paid by the federal and provincial governments and one-fourth by the company. Thirteen months later, only 274 of the 2,000 non-aboriginals who had lived in the town a year earlier still remained. Approximately 900 Naskapis and Montagnais Indians who live on two local reserves remained, thereby preventing it from becoming a ghost town, but of 500 modern home 375 were unoccupied. The school and hospital continued as public services. A proposal to establish a federal correctional institution in the area was rejected by Ottawa, because it would have resembled ones in Siberia and a proposal by Mulroney to create a national park in the area also met with little enthusiasm at Parks Canada.

Schefferville and many other communities are victims of boom and bust cycles and the inability of governments to develop a comprehensive policy for northern resource towns. "The end of the great collective dream," declared the headline of a 1984 issue of Québec City's *Le Soleil*. The dream of many Québeckers to provide their province with an integrated steel industry had also collapsed with it.

Life in the Québec north continues to be harsh and is often made more so by insensitive measures devised by southern policy-makers. Guy St-Julien, MP for the Abitibi riding in Northern Québec, located mostly beyond 50 degrees and extending northward beyond the 60th parallel, attempted in vain to bring his Ottawa colleagues attention to the plight of his constituents during late 1989 and early 1990. The devastating impact on northern communities of the combined effects of Canada Post rate increases and proposed elimination of the tax benefits provided to northern and isolated areas had become fully apparent. The mayor of Umiujag community was alarmed at the increase in the cost of living as a direct result of the Canada Post Corporation decision to eliminate cheap rates for food shipments. In February 1990, the mayor wrote that a bag of apples that had earlier sold for $2.86 now cost $4.44, bread had gone up from $1.70 to $3.88, a can of evaporated milk from $1.60 to $2.60. Native communities are going to suffer the most as they struggle to make a living off the land and from the scarce number of jobs available. The residents of Chapais, who stand to lose their status as an isolated post, must travel long distances by car to obtain special services or specialized care mostly available in Chicoutimi (378 kilometres away) or Québec City (524 kilometres away)." The loss of these tax benefits will inevitably and tragically contribute to the exodus of workers to the south," said St-Julien, " . . . life in the north is harsh, isolated and expensive. We have very little compared to the south and we are producers rather than consumers."

Québec's Peripheral Sub-regions

Québec's five peripheral sub-regions are Eastern Québec, the Saguenay-Lac-Saint-Jean, Abitibi-Témiscamingue, the North Shore, and

James Bay (New Québec). Together they contain slightly more than half of the province's land mass, but only thirteen per cent of its population. Services in each of them are significantly inferior to those available to other Québeckers in part because the managers usually live outside them and have an inadequate knowledge about them. The per person income of residents of the peripheries was also well below the Québec average in 1987 of $17,256: Eastern Québec — $13,558; Saguenay-Lac-Saint-Jean — $14,581; Abitibi-Témiscamingue — $15,833; North Shore — $15,185; James Bay (New Québec) — $12,151. Living costs are often greater in the peripheries than in Montréal and Québec City.

Statistics Canada reported the following unemployment levels for the province's different economic regions in September, 1989: North Shore — 12.1%; Gaspé — 23.1%; Saguenay-Lac-Saint-Jean — 14.3%; Abitibi-Témiscamingue — 13.3%. These compared to 9.9% in Québec City and Montréal Centre. The common complaint in Gaspé that provincial taxes go mostly to Montréal was only sharpened by such figures.

Ranging in size from 42,000 kilometres (East Québec) to 350,000 square kilometres (James Bay), the five peripheries are at different economic stages as well. East Québec and the Abitibi region are attempting to urbanize and industrialize while reducing their out-migration. Hydro-electricity development around James Bay is having a heavy impact on the 10,452 mostly Crees who live there. Overall, the residents of all five sub-regions face some common problems: a peripheral location, a marginal local economy, and a heartland core in the province rushing to urbanize and industrialize. The transformation toward a post-industrial information economy is also creating serious growth and social disparity problems for all five regions.

Tourism continues to be a source of major hope for Québec's periphery regions because visitors from all parts of North America and beyond find their scenery and natural environment, their human qualities and culture, their socio-economic diversity, fresh air, and wildlife to be fascinating even if only during two or three brief summer months. In Gaspé there are so many summer visitors that the local tourist services remain inadequate.

For more than twenty-five years, residents of Québec's outer regions have fought fiercely in many ways to overcome difficulties. A number of committees and structures have been put in place; all kinds of experiments have been tried to pull the regions out of their difficulties and to create development opportunities. It would appear, however, that the chief beneficiaries of these efforts were businessmen, politicians, researchers, technocrats, planners, experts and consultants from outside the areas who discovered in under-development greater income and fresh soil for their theories. If so, the Québec peripheries have lots of company here with other parts of Outer Canada.

Both isolation and economic disparities aggravate the perceived inferior status of peripheral Québeckers. A major cause of peripheral alienation is the fact that so many decisions affecting the five sub-regions are made in Québec City, Montréal, Toronto and the United States. Decisions made in far-away centres are often based on inaccurate data, further distorted by distance, misconceptions and urban prejudices. As a consequence, they are often inappropriate for the region concerned and do not result in sustainable development. The policy-makers are simply unaware of relevant facts.

Residents of Québec City, Montréal, Ottawa and Toronto usually follow developments in peripheral Québec only when the provincial or national media focus attention on some picturesque story. This is vexing to residents of the five regions who are largely dependent on Québec City, Montréal, Ottawa and Toronto. Most of the administrative and economic decisions concerning them are made in these cities and it is to Québec City and Montréal that they must go for specialized services. Important news is filtered and broadcast from Québec City or Montréal. These two cities are also the cultural and scientific centres exercising an influence on the entirety of the province. Fellow Outer Canadians in St. John's, Yellowknife, Sudbury and Nanaimo face, of course, the same problems.

Major strikes, demonstrations (including the riveting one at Oka), large-scale relocations of people, violent storms, school closings, poor health conditions, communications problems — such items are the usual news fare about the peripheries broadcast or published in Montréal and Québec City. Given the metropolitan bias to electronic and print media, periphery residents accordingly know a great deal more about metropolitan Québec than about residents of other peripheral or neighbouring regions. They also tend to know about other hinterland regions through the metropolitan media filter and through public officials. No single medium, written or electronic, private or public, covers all of Québec's sub-regions. The coverage of events in the peripheries by the Montréal and Québec City media at times is almost comical. During 1979, Montréalers were more informed by their media about the socio-economic problems of Port-Cartier than were the residents of North Shore generally. A regional consciousness and pride is in consequence very difficult to develop and sustain. There is little regional solidarity among the Québec peripheries, as elsewhere in Outer Canada, mostly due to distance, disparity and poor communications. Attitudes in the regions are also characterized by parochialism preventing regional consciousness to develop. This is an observation also made about Northern Ontario as typical for alienated regions.

A related factor is economic fragility with its consequent high unemployment and low incomes, which themselves promote considerable migration from all five sub-regions. This phenomenon exists despite large forests, fertile soil for farming and plentiful mineral resources. Moreover, each sub-region has its own special economic strengths: mining in Abitibi-Témiscamingue, hydro-electricity and aluminum in Saguenay-Lac-Saint-Jean, fishing and fleet maintenance in Eastern Québec, hydro-electricity and iron ore on the North Shore, and electricity around James Bay. For each region, however, part of the price of having such natural resources is that the output is mostly consumed beyond the district and its price and development are determined by factors beyond the periphery.

Limited economic diversification appears to be a further part of the employment problem in each of the five. One in four residents of Eastern Québec and five in ten in Abitibi-Témiscamingue live from work with wood. Almost four in ten employees in Saguenay-Lac-Saint-Jean and three in ten on the North Shore work in mines. Paper-making employs almost a third of the North Shore work force, twenty-three per cent of Saguenay-Lac-Saint-Jean's, seventeen per cent of Abitibi-Témiscamingue's, and fifteen per cent of Eastern Québec's. In other words, with so many of northwest Québeckers working in the wood and paper sectors, the rise and fall of international demand for their products is a daily and dominant concern. The three in ten residents of East Québec who earn their living from fish are similarly vulnerable to the ups and downs of foreign markets and a very short working season.

In this context, few Québeckers were surprised when the new government of Robert Bourassa opted in 1971 to develop the immense hydroelectric potential of James Bay with its promise of 125,000 jobs, many to be in the farthest periphery of the province. Five important northern rivers were to be dammed and a huge amount of land, including that of approximately five thousand natives, was to be flooded. Soon after the announcement, it became clear that the government had consulted no native residents, had done no environmental study, and had not even determined on which rivers the work would be done.

Following the 1970 October crisis and Prime Minister Pierre Trudeau's invoking of the War Measures Act, Premier Bourassa found himself with an uproar in parts of rural Québec as well. Operation Dignity, led by Catholic priests, was soon in full flower across Eastern Québec. The lack of proper consultation with local people about the Baie James project produced a hinterland backlash over other major projects as well. The proposed pipeline to Eastern Québec, a cablevision war in the lower St. Lawrence, and the establishment of Forillon park in the Gaspé all reinforced the widespread view that regional interests were of secondary importance in the plans of both Québec City and Ottawa.

Montréal and Québec continue to have a large influence on Shield Québeckers, providing, for example, supplies for most of their businesses and almost all public and semi-public services. This reality compels rural managers to travel to these two cities to meet public officials, business people and investors and to attend exhibitions and information sessions. Such frequent inconveniences, time consuming and expensive as they are, are part of the price of dependence.

In summary, northern Ontario and peripheral Québec are not only Canadian hinterlands but also provincial ones of their respective southern industrial metropolitan centres. The degree of progress and relative prosperity reaching the people living there proves elusive; depending on southern economic interests or needs of the day rather than policy designed for the long-term interests of the area. Residents already disadvantaged by an often hostile and harsh natural environment, continue to fight for a degree of dignity against the indifference of both senior levels of government and global and Canadian market forces. They fight often hopeless battles to hang on to a way of life they favour. To give up would mean moving south to be absorbed by a faceless megalopolis and becoming just another statistic in the success story of Inner Canada.

FOUR

OUT WEST

In 1929, Herman Wiebensohn, a young immigrant from Germany, began work on a wheat farm in southern Saskatchewan. During his next six years in the dust bowl, virtually nothing grew. His only pay for the entire period, aside from room and board, was a team of horses, harness and wagon. He drove them north in the mid-1930s looking for work and finally, after eleven years as a hired man, was able to rent and later buy his own farm. He married, raised an equally hard-working family, and today in his eighties retains his unquenchable optimism and curiosity about life. The Wiebensohns are representative of many Westerners.

What has grated on the Western consciousness for generations, however, is deep-seated indifference and condescension from successive national governments. Shouldn't Ottawa represent all Canadians equally and play no regional favourites? Canadians living outside the West may feel mystified by the intense and rising disaffection across the four Western provinces towards the federal government and Inner Canada in general. Why, they ask, are so many Westerners angry when ten of their MPs have held portfolios in the Mulroney cabinet during the past six years? The region is fed up with watching jobs, opportunities and people being removed from their natural location across the West and relocated in Inner Canada. Examples are legion.

A crown corporation at the time, Air Canada first moved its head office and later its maintenance base from Winnipeg to Montréal. Many Westerners were enraged with the fact that a government in which they had placed their confidence in 1984, barely two years later rejected the better and cheaper CF-18 aircraft maintenance contract offer by a Winnipeg company and handed it to Canadair of Montréal instead.

In Vancouver, a promised project to build a Polar-8 ice breaker was recently cancelled in the name of restraint by a cabinet which had failed to reduce the deficit significantly since taking office in 1984. A promised natural gas pipeline to Victoria was abandoned on the same basis. The same for the OSLO synthetic crude oil plant in northern Alberta, which will inevitably make Canada even more dependent on imported oil from OPEC member countries. As well, Ottawa's high interest-high dollar policy is contributing to an increase in the number of bankruptcies among Prairie farmers.

Indications of growing Western alienation can be observed in many opinion surveys. One of the first formal samplings of the Western mood, done during 1969, indicated that 55-60% of Albertans felt the Trudeau government was neglecting the West. By late 1981, following the introduction of the National Energy Program, an Environics sounding showed that 82% of Westerners agreed with the statement that "the West usually gets ignored in national politics because the political parties depend upon Québec and Ontario for most of their votes."

Another poll, conducted by the same firm shortly after the CF-18 contract was awarded, found that more than four in five Westerners thought the Mulroney government played regional favourites. Shortly before the November 1988 national election, the Winnipeg pollster Angus Reid reported that two-thirds of the residents of the four Western provinces thought the Conservative government favours Québec. With the Meech Lake process behind us, I think virtually all Westerners would now agree that some provinces are more equal than others in today's Ottawa. An Angus Reid poll taken in mid-summer of 1990 indicated that 87% of Prairie Canadians were dissatisfied with their national government. A few months after the 1988 election, a poll by Environics found that the percentage of Westerners who then agreed with its statement about the West usually being ignored had risen to 85%. In other words, alienation across the West was higher after four years of Brian Mulroney than it was in 1981 after the introduction of the National Energy Program by the detested Trudeau government.

Most Westerners who have supported the PC party since John Diefenbaker's rise to leadership in the mid-1950s felt we had won a government by 1986 but had lost a meaningful voice in the government party. These dashed hopes created deeply felt bitterness. The recent cancellation of VIA Rail's "Canadian," which has in one form or another provided passenger rail service across the southern part of Western Canada for more than a century, is only one of many illustrations of this reality. One consequence of this is the rise of a new party and its subsequent success in Alberta. The Reform party's Deborah Grey won a by-election in northeastern Alberta, and the party's Stan Waters, a province-wide Senate election.

In short, the West is weary of being dealt with as if it were Inner Canada's vast domestic colony. From John A. Macdonald to Brian Mulroney, Westerners have been treated mostly with polite indifference and subdued contempt by national governments. The exceptions seemed to occur only when it was in the interests of Inner Canadians to do something such as peopling the region in order to provide captive markets. Justice for the outer regions of Canada is as distant today as it has ever been. An important difference is that Westerners are now much better informed about the nature of official discrimination against us than was the case before. With a Prime Minister in office who, to many Westerners, is more an auxiliary premier of Québec than a prime minister of all Canadians, our demands for equal economic and political status are mounting.

An Anguished Past

Western discontent with Ottawa is the cumulative effect of a long series of grievances and frustrations. Let me recall a few of them.

Most Canadian students, including Westerners until more recently, were taught through the published works of Toronto historians Donald Creighton, Harold Innis and others that the National Policy proclaimed by John A. Macdonald in 1879 was beneficial to all parts of Canada. These apologists for what I call the core-periphery view of Canada gave no serious attention to the effect of the policy on, for example, generations of hard-working and dollar-poor producers in Saskatchewan.

Farmers were long the dominant occupational group in Prairie Canada. Under the National Policy, they either had to pay a 35 per cent tariff on imported machinery from the United States or Britain or were forced to purchase more expensive substitutes from Inner Canadian manufacturers like the Masseys. Somehow the latter could never locate any of their production facilities near their important Prairie customers. Since, on the other hand, Western farmers were compelled to sell grain into fiercely competitive international markets, they began as early as the mid-1880s to lobby for the removal of the tariff on farm machinery and building materials.

Their hopes for fair play were dashed at the end of the 1911 national election campaign when manufacturers, retailers, bankers and railroaders in Inner Canada united to defeat a proposal by Prime Minister Wilfrid Laurier's Liberals to enter into a limited reciprocity agreement with the United States. In the Conservative rhetoric of the campaign, a Prairie grain farmer who wanted to sell his grain in Minneapolis was a traitor whereas a Toronto banker who did as much business as possible in Manhattan was a patriot. Incredible as it may sound, the disloyalty charge proved effective even in two Western provinces: virtually all the seats in Saskatchewan and Alberta went Liberal. In British Columbia, the Conservative leader Robert Borden's moronic demand for voters to choose between the Union Jack and the Stars and Stripes won him all the seats. In Manitoba, the Conservatives elected eight of ten MPs, largely, it appears, due to the strong organization of Conservative Premier Rodmond Roblin. The reciprocity question does not seem to have been the dominant issue in the province. Considerable Western bitterness lingered on afterwards, partly because the reciprocity agreement, dealing mainly with natural commodities and unfinished products, would barely have affected the privileged in Inner Canada.

Another farm issue was freight rates. Why, Western grain farmers asked, did the CPR charge twice as much to move wheat in parts of the Prairies as it did in Ontario and Québec? Myopic Ottawa rail officials, moreover, later approved as "fair discrimination" railway rates by which Manitobans were to be charged more for moving the same items the same distance as Central Canadians, residents of what are now Alberta and Saskatchewan were to pay more than Manitobans, and British Columbians were to pay even higher rates. It would require decades for a united Western lobby to correct this federal government-sanctioned abuse.

There were plenty of other abuses during the era of railways. In Manitoba, for example, the first threat of secession arose during 1882 over the issue of why the CPR had been given by Ottawa a virtual monopoly over all goods moving to and from the province. When Manitoba's premier, John Norquay, attempted to build a provincial railway to the American border, Prime Minister Macdonald used his influence to prevent a bond sale in London and New York. He later forced Norquay's ouster as premier by spreading rumours about financial irregularities he probably didn't commit.

A decade later, the CPR obtained a cash grant from the Laurier government to build a new line from Lethbridge to Nelson, B.C. through the Crowsnest Pass. In return, the railway agreed to cut its rates by approximately a fifth on grain moving from Winnipeg to what is now Thunder Bay. In fact, however, this first Crow rate was an illusory concession because, during the 1903-1918 period, the railway accepted an even further cut. The "Holy Crow" was later shown to be rather hollow when it came to light that shortly before 1914 the charges for other freight moved on the Prairies were 30 to 50% higher than in Ontario. The additional surcharge for B.C. freight was not removed by Ottawa until 1949.

Three years earlier, as World War II ended, both the CPR and the CNR had applied for a thirty per cent general increase in rates across Canada. Seven of the nine provincial governments -- Ontario and Québec excepted -- opposed it vehemently. The government of Mackenzie King allowed a twenty-one per cent increase. Today, as inflation is eroding the real worth of the remaining Crow benefit, it is still for many Westerners a potent symbol of regional grievance primarily because it was seen as the West's one real offsetting factor to a century of industrial benefits going to Inner Canadians as a consequence of the tariff and other protections created by Ottawa.

Wheat was a major preoccupation of Prairie Canadians for decades, but national governments rarely did much to help in its marketing. When Prime Minister Pierre Trudeau once asked "Why should I sell your wheat?" he was touching a very sensitive Western nerve. Following World War I, for example, Prime Minister Arthur Meighen, a Conservative originally with a Manitoba constituency but always with Inner Canadian ideas, stopped government control of grain marketing despite the opposition of most grain farmers. In 1920, the Canadian Wheat Board, created to cope temporarily with chaotic world grain export conditions, ceased to operate. The three Prairie wheat pools were thus forced to market grain themselves and did so with considerable success. Only with the virtual collapse of world grain prices could Prime Minister R.B. Bennett, himself a Prairie MP, be persuaded during the dying days of his doomed mandate to re-create the Wheat Board in 1935. The newly elected Liberals offered more hope to financially-desperate farmers. Yet, Mackenzie King also intended to eliminate the Board four years later. The united protest of angry Prairie producers dissuaded him from doing so.

Political Subordination

For a long time, the political inequality of Western Canadians has been the most potent cause of regional alienation. In British Columbia, many resent that Ontarians and Québeckers dictate the policies of every national government. Yet, because of the province's dependence on forestry, mining and fishing, the first two of which have until recently only rarely interested Ottawa policy-makers, the national government is not constantly obtrusive on the West coast. More Prairie Canadians than British Columbians are affected on a daily basis by Ottawa policies on transportation, agriculture, energy exports and resource taxation.

Some Prairie residents recall the shameful way their own provinces came into being. Manitoba became a province in 1870 due to the earlier successful uprising by Louis Riel and his provisional government at Red River. Yet the province was so tiny that it was simply not viable. Moreover, unlike the founding provinces, it lacked ownership of its limited land and resources. Its boundaries were later extended, but it was not able to obtain ownership of its natural resources from Ottawa until it was sixty years old, almost a pensioner as a province.

Alberta and Saskatchewan became provinces only in 1905 following long years of advocacy by Frederick Haultain, chairman of the North-West Territories Assembly, and many territorial residents. There is persuasive evidence that two provinces rather than a more viable single one were created by Prime Minister Laurier mostly because he did not want Haultain, a political opponent, to become premier of one large Prairie province. Neither province, moreover, even in 1905 received ownership of its land or resources. To compound the insult and leave a lasting bitterness about Ottawa politicians generally in the minds of many residents of the new provinces, Laurier appointed well-known Liberal supporters as first lieutenant-governors of the new provinces. They in turn appointed Liberals as interim premiers, and a small army of fellow partisan workers established as homestead inspectors and the like helped ensure that Liberal governments were elected in each of the two new provinces.

Progressives and Reformers

The Progressive Movement emerged on the Prairies during the 1920s.in response to such tactics by Ottawa politicians. Essentially, it was a delayed Western revolt at the ballot box against the major features of Macdonald's National Policy and the two old parties which were seen by many Westerners as equally committed to that policy. By 1918, many Prairie farmers who had broken virgin land with oxen or horses felt themselves engulfed by interest rates and railway and grain elevator charges. When Wilfrid Laurier's government, in office from 1896 to 1911, repudiated the Liberals' traditionally low tariff policy, it was the last straw for many Prairie wheat growers.

During the 1911 reciprocity election, Laurier resorted to his party's longstanding free-trade position, but this sharply divided his own party which had become as welded to the National Policy as had the Conservatives. Clifford Sifton, the second most influential Liberal in the country until his resignation as minister during 1905, even defected noisily to Borden's Tories. The high tariff policy of the Ottawa Conservatives helped wreck its provincial wings in both Saskatchewan and Alberta after 1911; its Manitoba affiliate all but disappeared for several decades as well.

The arrival on the Prairies of thousands of settlers from the American Midwest after 1896 weakened regional ties to both national parties because many of the new arrivals had supported American third parties. Settlers from England were frequently supporters of the Labour Party, at that time a third party as well. In short, the Progressive Movement was a unique combination of Jacksonian democracy and British radicalism.

By the time of the 1917 election, Laurier's Liberals had collapsed across the West. Borden's Union government, a coalition formed to maximize the war effort mainly through conscription, gave itself several legs-up in the election: disenfranchising citizens of foreign birth, and so on. It won fifty-five of fifty-seven seats in the four Western provinces as the result of its win-at-any-cost measures.

In essence, as William Morton, the most knowledgeable authority on the movement concluded, the 1917 election purged many Westerners of their previous political loyalties. Another major factor was the Union government's withdrawal in 1918 of its promise that farmers' sons would be exempt from the draft. This caused widespread revulsion among Western farmers. When Arthur Meighen, the successor to Borden, attempted to make trade protection the main issue of the campaign and attacked the Progressives for wanting to destroy the National Policy, he was doomed in the region. The Conservatives won only fifty seats, coming third after the Progressive Party, in the new Parliament.

The Progressives were also determined to destroy the Liberals and Conservatives in the provinces. Their allies on the Prairies, the United Farmers, were largely successful in both Alberta and Manitoba for a period.

In Saskatchewan, the Liberal government of William Martin avoided the 1920-21 tide only by temporarily ending his ties with the federal Liberal party.

Whether the Reform Party is a 1990s successor to the Progressives is a very lively subject today across Western Canada. High interest and bankruptcy rates, major debt problems for many Prairie farmers, the proposed GST, the Meech Lake process and the widespread conviction that the Prime Minister sees the West primarily as a place for reliable votes and docile MPs, have helped recruit about 45,000 members for the new party, mostly among Albertans and British Columbians. A party meeting in Victoria in the summer of 1990 attracted 1,500 persons and, even more surprising, an opinion survey done at the time indicated that 59 per cent of Calgarians, the most loyal PC voters in the nation for a generation, would vote Reform today compared to 11 per cent who would vote PC.

Preston Manning, the Reform Party leader, is widely seen in the West as an articulate individual whose personal qualities contrast favourably with the Prime Minister's. Jean Chrétien, the new Liberal leader, is also well-regarded in the West and is also an excellent foil to Brian Mulroney. He is deemed to be less right-wing than the Reformers, an advantage to some and a disadvantage to others. He favours cultural pluralism whereas the Reformers are seen as both unsympathetic to minorities and distinctly cool to immigration. The federal New Democrats are strong in much of British Columbia, across Saskatchewan, in urban Manitoba and in Edmonton. As of the late summer of 1990, the next general election is likely to be a Gotterdammerung in Western Canada. Only one party, the Conservatives (the perennial favourite), is likely as of now to emerge from the campaign as an also-ran.

Recent Years

A dreary past in terms of the impact of national policies on the West was compounded by a series of events occurring during the 1970s and 1980s. Each of them reinforced for Westerners the idea that a national government controlled by Inner Canadians for the benefit of Ontarians or Québeckers, or both, was imposing policies deeply harmful to the legitimate interests of Western Canadians.

Oil was probably the most important of these major friction points even though it affected mostly Alberta and Saskatchewan as the producing provinces. During 1974, as OPEC member governments began to raise world oil prices from about $4 (U.S.) a barrel to $11 and later much higher, the product became the focus of fierce differences between the Trudeau government and the West.

In response to the rising prices, Ottawa first imposed an export tax on oil the West was exporting to the U.S. and froze the domestic price. Alberta premier Peter Lougheed protested strongly at the time. The only reason for exporting to the south at all, he argued, was the persistent refusal by every

Ottawa government since the 1960s to have the Western oil pipeline lengthened to Montréal. An extension was rejected on the premise that it was cheaper for Canadians east of the Ottawa river to buy oil from the Middle East or Venezuela. One result of this official myopia, said Lougheed, was that a good number of Canadian-owned oil firms which could not afford to operate at other than full capacity had been forced to sell out, usually to Americans.

The Alberta premier also noted that as recently as early 1973, the federal Energy Minister, Donald Macdonald, later appointed by the Mulroney government to be Canada's High Commissioner in Britain, had again refused a Western request to extend the pipeline with the usual rationale that offshore oil was cheaper. Once again, rejoined Lougheed, the national government "had weighed Alberta's needs for markets against the economic advantages to Eastern Canada, and decided against us."

Many across the West wondered why the non-renewable oil of Alberta and Saskatchewan was the only Canadian export to be subject to a federal export tax when renewable exports, such as Québec's growing electricity sales to the United States, were not similarly taxed. The Trudeau government replied that oil was unique. Having been discriminated against so often in the past by national governments, Westerners were mostly unconvinced. The continuing support of the Western constitutional position by the Québec governments of both Robert Bourassa and Ren Levesque became a feature of a West-Québec alliance which too many Westerners later forgot during the Meech Lake process.

Eight months after Pierre Trudeau and his Liberals defeated Joe Clark's Conservatives in February, 1980, Marc Lalonde introduced the West's most hated of all Ottawa policies: the National Energy Program (NEP). Suffice it here to say that despite attractive features, such as promoting energy conservation, the policy was quickly seen across the West as deeply harmful to the region. For example, oil exploration and development were redirected by costly tax incentives away from the Western provinces toward the North and off our three coasts, all of which were controlled by Ottawa. The incentives being unavailable to foreign-owned companies, a number of them soon moved about 200 oil drilling rigs (each employing approximately 200 people) to the United States. This convinced many Westerners that petroleum self-sufficiency was not a goal of the NEP at all. The real objective, it appeared, was for an anti-Western regime in Ottawa to continue buying off-shore oil at $37 (U.S.) a barrel (the price as of 1980), from sources such as Libya while at the same time refusing to buy it from numerous capped wells in Alberta and Saskatchewan for $18 a barrel.

One of the unstated objectives of the NEP was to relocate the leadership of the energy industry to Ottawa. Rather clearly, the plan was to create a new community of energy leaders with a primary loyalty to the federal government. It would join the industrial-financial elites within Inner Canada who have historically identified closely with Ottawa because of various federal measures such as the Bank Act. The NEP was thus profoundly anti-Outer Canada because until 1980 the oil and gas industry was one of the very few sectors based in Western Canada.

Reorganizing the ownership for the industry was a major goal of the NEP. The federal government took advantage of the rapid rise in international oil prices to buy out some foreign-owned parts of our domestic industry. To persuade targeted firms unwilling to sell to do so, the NEP created a series of tax incentives and other measures which discriminated blatantly in favour of Canadian-owned companies. The best known of these was the twenty-five per cent back-in provision through which Ottawa was to take an automatic one quarter of the revenue from any oil or gas discovered on lands it controlled. The government of Canada soon found itself accused internationally of legislated theft. The avalanche of protests following the initial application of the back-in provision to expensive discoveries made before its enactment finally persuaded the Trudeau government to offer compensation for about a quarter of the expenditures made.

During the first year of the NEP, foreign ownership dropped from seventy-four per cent to about sixty-six per cent as Canadian companies, including Dome Petroleum and Petro-Canada, made huge buy-outs of foreign-owned properties. The prestigious Organization for Economic Co-operation and Development (OECD), however, ruled that the methods being used violated its resolutions banning member nations from discriminating against foreign-owned companies. In the international community at large, many concluded that the NEP was a key part of a general campaign by Pierre Trudeau's last government against foreign investment of any kind.

The overall consequences for Alberta and Saskatchewan were devastating. The number of oil wells drilled in Western Canada dropped from 550 in mid-1980 to about 120 by 1982. The number of drilling rigs in service across Canada fell from 650 to 450 shortly after the NEP was introduced. Thousands of jobs in Western Canada were lost, mostly in the drilling and service sectors of the energy industry. Proposed mega-projects such as the Alsands plant at Fort McMurray were cancelled. Numerous Western businesses went into bankruptcy. Many careers and families were broken; home mortgages were foreclosed in large numbers.

During the summer of 1982, Britain's respected Economist magazine summed up the NEP in politely brutal language: "The NEP has come close to wrecking an industry that until October, 1980 was drilling like fury finding enormous volumes of gas and much new oil, creating jobs and investment all over Canada and increasingly using Canadian-owned capacity in exploration and management . . . . The NEP drove Canadian exploration and service companies into the United States until only 150 drilling rigs were left, the lowest number since the 1960s de-Canadianization, in effect. Owners of capped-in gas wells had big debts and no cash flow. Oil serving companies in Alberta withered into bankruptcy."

The Ottawa-prescribed low domestic price of oil since the 1970s was calculated by Robert Mansell, a Calgary economist, to have cost Albertans alone approximately $60 billion. Yet the NEP was loathed even by Western Canadians who had no direct daily contact with the energy industry. In the West, it was a major reason for disaffection. It even provided an impetus to separatist sentiments for it blatantly discriminated against two Western provinces, maintained the domestic price of conventional oil and gas resources at about half the world price, and subsidized the consumption of imported oil. It was a Western economic and social nightmare.

1982 Constitution

As a result of the NEP and a long series of other anti-West attitudes associated with the government of Pierre Trudeau since 1968, the overall Western mood was anything but positive by 1981. One opinion survey done in March of 1981 ominously revealed that 61 per cent of respondents in all four Western provinces agreed with the statement, "the West has sufficient resources and industry to survive without the rest of Canada." Between October, 1980 and March, 1981, support for outright regional independence grew from five to seven per cent, and eleven per cent in Alberta. Part of the worsening Western attitude was created by the process and substance of Prime Minister Trudeau's constitutional package.

Following the May 20, 1980 Québec referendum in which a sixty per cent majority rejected sovereignty-association, the premiers of all ten provinces and Mr. Trudeau agreed on a twelve-item agenda to be studied over the summer. In early July, however, the federal government revealed out-of-the-blue a set of new demands for greater powers over the economy if any other legislative powers were to be surrendered to the provinces. Later that summer a memorandum drafted by the Clerk of the Privy Council, Michael Pitfield, a quintessential Inner Canadian from Montréal's upper Westmount, was leaked: it outlined a federal strategy for unilateral patriation of the constitution from Britain by Ottawa.

The political sky darkened even further a few weeks later when the eleven first ministers met. Another memorandum, this time prepared by Michael Kirby, an adviser to the Prime Minister, became public during the conference, causing an uproar among the premiers and later across the nation. In it, it was suggested that Alberta might be isolated on the sensitive issue of control of natural resources if the federal cabinet could make a deal with Premier Blakeney of Saskatchewan. Whether in consequence of this or because of conflicting visions of the national future, the first televised conference ended in stalemate on all twelve agenda items.

At the end of September, the Prime Minister declared he would patriate the constitution without provincial consent and have simultaneously enacted by the British Parliament a Charter of Rights to apply in both the federal and provincial jurisdictions. Joe Clark on behalf of the Official

Opposition denounced these proposals the same day; the New Democrats through their leader, Ed Broadbent, indicated general support for the package, thereby dividing their caucus on east-west lines. Three Western premiers — B.C.'s William Bennett, Alberta's Peter Lougheed, and Manitoba's Sterling Lyon — announced they would join two other premiers in a court challenge to the government's constitutional proposal. Saskatchewan's Blakeney government joined them several months later.

In mid-March, when the cabinet introduced a form of closure in the Commons on its constitutional resolution, Conservative MPs began a filibuster that lasted for two weeks. It ended when the Newfoundland Court of Appeal, differing strongly from the majority view of the Manitoba Appeal Court on the same issues, ruled unanimously that the resolution was unconstitutional. Effectively beaten in its attempt to avoid having the Supreme Court of Canada decide the matter, the Prime Minister agreed to hold off a final vote on its resolution until that Court could decide the issue. By May, a Gallup Poll indicated that two-thirds of both Prairie and B.C. residents opposed the proposal that the British Parliament should be asked to amend the constitution by adding an entrenched charter of rights before returning it to Canada.

At that point, the "Gang of Eight", i.e., all the premiers with the exception of Ontario's William Davis and New Brunswick's Richard Hatfield, advanced a proposal calling for patriation alone, the Alberta amendment formula (which required constitutional amendments to be passed by Parliament and the legislatures of seven of the provinces holding half the population of Canada), and no Charter of Rights. This collided with the amendment formula favoured by Pierre Trudeau which would have provided vetoes to Ontario and Québec alone, whereas full legislative support in three Western and three Atlantic provinces would be necessary to stop a proposal. The Federal-Provincial Relations Office in Ottawa, moreover, conceded to me at the time that it knew of no other federal democracy which assigned, as proposed by the Prime Minister, differing weight to residents of different provinces for constitutional amendment processes. The notion offended Westerners deeply.

In the fall of 1981, the Supreme Court of Canada ruled by a majority of seven to two that the Trudeau package was legal, but six judges also said it violated our constitutional conventions. A first ministers' conference was called for early November in a last attempt to reach an agreement. The famous compromise was reached in a hotel kitchen late at night on November 4th; it proved acceptable to all first ministers except for René Levesque. It quickly passed the Canadian and British Parliaments and was proclaimed by Queen Elizabeth in mid-April, 1982 at a large outdoor ceremony on Ottawa's Parliament Hill.

The overall damage in terms of national unity was high in the West. Even those of us who favoured an entrenched charter of rights on the basis that some rights should be beyond the reach of any legislators were deeply offended by the process. A national government which held our region in barely-concealed contempt had actually tried to relegate all Outer Canadians to second-class status in its preferred constitutional amendment formula. The active role of Saskatchewan's Allan Blakeney and Roy Romanow in the final compromise contributed to the massive defeat of the Blakeney government in the April, 1982 Saskatchewan election. The first separatist MLA in Western Canada, Gordon Kesler, was elected at about that time in a by-election in Olds-Didsbury in central Alberta.

The 1982 Constitution achieved little in terms of a constitutional vision for Outer Canadians generally and Westerners in particular. For example, the decades-old inability of majority parliamentary governments to address real problems of the West was ignored. British Columbia pushed for Senate reform but won little support from the other first ministers. The amendment formula endorsed by the four Western provinces quite understandably reinforced the premiers' view that they alone speak for their respective residents on national affairs because future amendments became exclusively the prerogative of eleven legislatures. Direct citizen participation in the amendment process through referenda as customary in other federations, for example Australia, was blocked.

Another opportunity was lost to restructure Ottawa's institutions so that politicians in our national capital might speak effectively for the regions.

Maintaining CF-18s

Few Inner Canadians, including Brian Mulroney, seem to understand how much the awarding of the maintenance contract for the CF-18 aircraft continues to rankle residents of all four Western provinces.

The issue arose in 1986 when the British-owned Ultramar Canada closed an essentially obsolete Montréal ore refinery. When the loss of 350 jobs in East Montréal caused an uproar in the House of Commons for weeks afterward, Prime Minister Mulroney appointed a committee of ministers, headed by Robert de Cotret, to consider ways to promote growth in the Montréal region. De Cotret soon spotted a pending contract to maintain 138 CF-18 jet fighters purchased from the U.S. as a convenient way of creating some future-oriented jobs in greater Montréal. His problem was that a team of 75 technicians from three federal departments had already concluded that the tender by Winnipeg's Bristol Aerospace was better in terms of proven expertise and about four million dollars cheaper than the competing one by Canadair of Montréal.

In the spring of 1986, de Cotret as president of the Treasury Board simply overruled the officials' recommendation and directed that Canadair should obtain the contract. In October, the full Treasury Board of six ministers, including one from the West (B.C.'s Frank Oberle), so decided.

The reaction to the announcement in the West was uniformly vehement. Had the integrity of the federal tendering procedure vanished? Had Bristol not made a cheaper and technically better bid? The losing bidder indicated it would have to lay off a hundred employees and would probably sue the Mulroney government for the $5 million it had spent to prepare its bid in good faith. Further bad news came when it was revealed that Canadair, in order to do the work, would have to spend $30 million to purchase technology from Bendix-Avelex Inc. of Toronto and the Canadian taxpayer would have to pay. Westerners generally concluded that Brian Mulroney was indistinguishable from Pierre Trudeau on the issue of regional justice.

An Environics Research Group poll done after the decision found that, "84 per cent of Western Canadians — the highest of any area of the country — think the government does not treat all parts of Canada equally." Even the Calgary Herald, at that time and probably still the most loyal booster of the Mulroney government editorially among all Western dailies, observed: "Instead of a national government, we have national decisions made on a selfish regional basis for purely political reasons. There is nothing unusual in that. Just add it to the long catalogue of injustices done to the West."

The NEP and the CF-18 together highlighted for many Western Canadians their continuing colonial status within Confederation. Each of them, severely harming the region's future economic prospects, were made by national governments of different political colours which placed other considerations ahead of the legitimate economic aspirations of Western Canadians.

The New West

Recently, I was told that many Québeckers believe Westerners are still almost entirely people of British origin. The reality is that more than seventy distinct ethno-cultural communities can now be identified across Western Canada.

Between 1880 and 1914, several million immigrants from Europe and numerous other parts of the world settled across the West. They were attracted by the promise of a better life in "the last best West." Literally dozens of communities of diverse ethnic and cultural background arrived in the region, creating a kaleidoscope of languages, dress and customs unique in our country. A visitor first applied the term "mosaic" to Canadians during a 1922 visit to the Prairies.

The Prairie population ballooned from about 400,000 in 1901 to 2.4 million by 1931. A newcomer climbing off a train in Winnipeg just before World War I would meet people on nearby Main Street speaking almost every language then spoken. Half of the Prairie residents at the time had been born in another country; fifteen years later the share was still one in three. By the the 1931 census, Prairie residents who were British by origin had already dropped to about half the Prairie total. Various East European groups, including Ukrainians, Austro-Hungarians, Poles and Russians, numbered about twenty per cent, and West Europeans, German, Dutch and French, including Québeckers, also had about a fifth of the population.

Present thousands of years earlier were a host of Indian tribes which had settled on the Prairies. Later, while the fur trade flourished, French- and English-speaking Métis became the second founding community of the region. A group of hearty Scots helped found the precarious Selkirk settlement in the first decades of the 1800s, but it was not until after the CPR was completed to the Rocky Mountains during 1884-85 that the first of four successive waves of mostly British newcomers began to arrive. The largest group came between 1897 and 1913, bringing almost equal numbers of pioneers from the other provinces, Britain, America and Continental Europe. There were also Icelanders, Mennonites, Jews and other communities.

Immigration to Canada stopped during the First World War. The next large migration arriving during the 1920s was similar to the 1897-1913 one in terms of origin. Immigration was again stopped by Ottawa between 1931 and 1941. The final wave started after 1945 and is still continuing: it consisted of Europeans uprooted by the war and, after 1962, newcomers from most Pacific Rim nations.

Much of the credit for the diversity on the Prairies goes to Clifford Sifton. As Immigration Minister in Laurier's government between 1897 and 1905, he spent large sums of tax money to lure farmers from Europe, Britain and America. His successor, Frank Oliver, increased recruitment in Britain and reduced it in Europe. The government of Robert Borden and Arthur Meighen held the door open to unskilled British immigrants between 1911 and 1921, but continued a Laurier measure which in practice barred most Asians and Arabs. In the mid-1920s, Mackenzie King as Liberal Prime Minister restarted recruiting in Central and Eastern Europe; almost 370,000 Europeans came to Canada before 1931, when R.B. Bennett closed the gates to almost everyone.

The pattern and sequence of settlement in British Columbia differed from that on the Prairies. Thousands of years after the province's aboriginal peoples arrived from Asia came the province's first settlers in the mid-1800s, including a number from south China. Most of those arriving before 1890 came from Britain and it was then that Victoria took on its pronounced British flavour. The 1890-1914 wave included Americans, Britons, Chinese, Japanese, Scandinavians and Germans. People from Central, Western and Eastern Europe comprised the largest numbers of those entering B.C. during the 1920s. The catastrophic impact on the Prairies of the Great Depression caused hundreds of thousands of its residents to move westward. Since 1945, enough newcomers have moved in from virtually everywhere that the province's population is now about three million.

In consequence, the demographics of all four Western provinces were significantly different from Canada as a whole by the time of the 1986 national census. In all three Prairie provinces, less than forty per cent of the residents claimed a single country of origin in Britain or France. British Columbia was slightly over forty per cent, contrasted to Ontario and all four Atlantic provinces where considerably more than forty per cent of residents claim descent from a single family in the British Isles.

Today, and increasingly since the beginning of this century, the West has developed a character that is pluralistic in culture, religion and politics. This has been possible partly because no ethno-cultural community was numerically dominant. Some might say the British were, but no one who knows the history of those islands would group the Scots, Irish, Welsh and English together indistinguishably. In practice, most members of every cultural community, including the larger ones, today believe that all people are of equal worth and that all should have the right to choose their own life-style within the framework of cherished Canadian values like non-violence, civility and respect for others.

Consequently, a pattern of permissive differentiation, not coercive assimilation, emerged at an early date and has set very firmly in the West. More than in any other part of Canada, multiculturalism is all-inclusive. No one's community has been left out, because each one is seen as an integral part of the regional kaleidoscope. Bitter experiences of prejudice and discrimination are gone. The region has emerged confidently from its aboriginal past into a multicultural present and future. A unique mixture of ethno-cultural co-operation now exists.

There is a Western consensus that the survival of all ethno-cultural communities is beneficial to the individual satisfaction and self-development of their members, since it builds a sound climate in which cultural differences do not limit social participation. The preservation of cultural communities also advances and enriches the community as a whole since each of them has a valued contribution to make to the whole. Sustained interaction between diverse groups on the basis of mutual respect and equality is an enriching social experience: each group affects the others, while maintaining its identity.

The various communities can provide wise counsel at a time of national tension and stress. Former Czechs and Slovaks know from experience the dangers of national fragmentation that have long imperiled the existence of their land of origin. Many Flemish- and French-speaking Belgians, Serbs and Croatians from Yugoslavia, and newcomers from Pacific Rim, African, and Caribbean nations also know just how fragile can be the human glue which holds countries together during periods of adversity. Newcomers from Lebanon similarly can tell what happens where one's membership in a particular religion or cultural community is the most important component of citizenship and that Canada must avoid the Lebanese experience at all costs.

Western Economy

British Columbians and Albertans, who constitute just under three quarters of the labour force in Western Canada, did not do well during the economic swings of the 1980s. Recent improvements in both provinces were caused by differing factors: in B.C., rapid interprovincial migration into the province fuelled booms in its construction and service sectors; in Alberta, improved oil and natural gas prices sparked new energy investments and a comparative boom in housing.

The 1990 forecasts for Prairie farmers are poor, due to four previous years of droughts, collapsing world grain prices, high interest rates, the highest dollar value in a decade, and some major international assaults on Canada's supply management programs. In early 1990, Statistics Canada foresaw a more than two-thirds drop in net farm incomes for all three Prairie provinces. European farmers receive $700 a metric ton for wheat compared to the $150 Canadians receive. Prairie grain families are being crushed by the ongoing multi-billion dollar export subsidy battle between Washington and Brussels. By the end of 1990, an estimated one-third of Saskatchewan farmers could face lawsuits from creditors. Overall, despite the excellent Prairie crops indicated for 1990, world conditions remain worse than 1986 and 1987, themselves among the worst since the Depression. Westerners also know that our regional share of jobs in the deeply depressed agricultural sector is virtually twice the national average.

Major adversity in the farm sector invariably leads to difficulties elsewhere. Saskatchewan's population is continuing to drop, urban homes remain unsold in Regina and Saskatoon for long periods (in the late summer of 1990, I observed a home for sale in Yorkton for $26,500), and pessimism returns across the province. The large agricultural sectors in Alberta and Manitoba are similarly affected.

Fortunately, spontaneous diversification is occurring across the West, assisted by a highly-motivated entrepreneurial spirit and a dynamic technical sector. Aerospace, agricultural machinery, petrochemical and construction materials are doing particularly well at exporting. The skills of Westerners in communications, recreation and resource development are well known and many of them are marketable outside Canada.

A major obstacle to further diversification across the West is lack of investment in manufacturing. A recent study by the Canada West Foundation showed that regional manufacturing investment amounted to a negligible six per cent of total national investment. In order to even remain competitive in national resource exploration, Westerners must adopt new technologies such as computer-aided design.

Research and development spending in all four provinces is below the national average. While doing more than half of such spending nationally, the private sector does only just over a third of it in the West. As for the federal government, only nineteen per cent of its research and development spending is applied to the West, though this part of the country holds almost thirty per cent of the national population. Ontario and Québec together receive three-quarters of overall science and technology spending. This makes it more difficult for high-tech manufacturing in a number of sectors to expand in the West.

Is it any wonder that the relative generosity of the Mulroney government toward the West's traditional oil and grain sectors has been compared so negatively to its support for various industries of the future in Inner Canada? The CF-18 contract is a continuing reminder of Ottawa's inability to see Westerners as anything other than wheat farmers, tree chokers and oil wildcatters. The vast majority of Westerners, like other Canadians, are in services of various kinds. The way to a less volatile future obviously points in the direction of processing natural resources, adding value to them and pursuing technological advances. Prairie Canada canola seeds should not be exported in unprocessed form to be crushed into cooking oil in Japan. B.C. logs should not be shipped to Asia for processing into finished plywood.

Canada-U.S. Free Trade Agreement

It is probably too early to measure the full impact of the Canada-U.S. Free Trade Agreement (FTA) on the Canadian economy. Some consequences are already observable: Canada's trade surplus with the States has been reduced, jobs have been lost and plants shut down, companies have relocated to the U.S. or Mexico and pressure from American firms has intensified. The critics claim that 250,000 jobs were lost in the first year; its defenders insist that 200,000 have been directly created.

Two years ago, I supported the FTA believing it was in the best interests of both Western Canada and all other parts of the country. I saw in the agreement a way to reduce the colonialism created by national governments over decades at the expense of Outer Canada in general and the West in particular. Today I am inclined to think that some provisions are hurting parts of the country that can least afford further decline in economic growth.

In the opinion of some economists, the FTA could increase the instability which characterizes the Western Canadian economy because many of our exports are concentrated in very volatile markets and dominated by a comparatively small number of natural resources. Despite the agreement, the likelihood of continuing trade disputes with the U.S., especially in natural resource matters, remains very high unless both nations can negotiate over five to seven years a mutually agreed-upon definition of "subsidy." Some Canadian practices, including provincial Crown ownership of most natural resources, and some non-market pricing rules, are otherwise likely to lead to more anti-dumping and countervail lawsuits to follow the softwood lumber, potash and hog trade ones already completed.

The future of marketing boards across Canada is in issue because rural Westerners, like many people in all ten provinces, see them as essential to the viability of important farm sectors. The agreement requires the elimination of Canadian tariffs on the importation of processed foods from the United States. If this happens on a host of processed foods, the result will inevitably be that much of Canada's very large food processing industry will relocate production to the U.S. and export back to Canada. Our marketing boards would then virtually cease to operate because fewer and fewer processors in Canada would buy their products.

In the matter of ice cream and yogurt, a test case emerged when the Canadian dairy industry learned that the twelve to fifteen per cent tariff on these products was to be phased out. In response, the Mulroney government attempted to replace the tariff with what are termed in trade law as quantitative restrictions on American imports of both products. The U.S. government sought a ruling from a tribunal of the General Agreement on Tariffs and Trade (GATT). It concluded that the use of such restrictions to protect our food processing industry was illegal. The prospects of amending the GATT to allow the use of quantitative restrictions, according to the Ottawa trade expert Mel Clark, are virtually nil. The probable result therefore is that thousands of Western, Atlantic and other Canadian farmers, who have earned a decent living within our marketing board framework, face an uncertain future because of this feature of the bilateral agreement. Many of them who supported free trade in the past, assuming their marketing boards could survive under it, have changed their minds.

The FTA was never intended to be a panacea to Canada's economic problems. I believe it might still assist us to enter the wider global trading arena if GATT succeeds in further liberalizing world trade. Some of its provisions might well have to be re-negotiated if it is to work the way it was intended and before all the hopes Westerners and other Outer Canadians invested in it are completely shattered.

"Rich Uncle Alberta"

The lack of Western diversification doesn't satisfactorily explain the volatility of the Alberta economy. Why were the province's booms and busts since 1980 significantly worse than in Texas or Oklahoma, two American states with similar reliance on oil and agriculture? Why did the province experience a net loss of about 100,000 people between 1980 and 1989? During the decade, home prices collapsed, fourteen provincial financial institutions failed or were forced to amalgamate and approximately a third of the credit unions were placed under direct government supervision. The social and human costs to thousands of Alberta families and individuals were enormous.

The Calgary economist Robert Mansell points out that employment in the province did not return to its pre-1981 recession high until May, 1987, compared to November, 1983 for Ontario, 1984 for Atlantic Canada and June, 1984 for Québec. Contrary to the conventional wisdom in Ottawa that it was a drop in oil and farm prices that caused the most severe Alberta recession since the Great Depression, Mansell notes that the average price for oil and gas producers did not decline until 1986 and farm receipts remained quite stable during the period.

By 1980, Alberta's petroleum industry accounted directly for almost one-third of the provincial economic output, approximately one-half of all construction starts, and about 80 per cent of the provincial government's yearly spending. The growing dependence on the oil industry made Albertans increasingly vulnerable to anything that threatened new investment in the sector, including the NEP and high interest rates. Another important factor was that by 1980 Ottawa's taxation, spending and energy policies as a whole were withdrawing about $15 billion more each year than the national government was injecting into the province through all forms of federal spending. A major consequence of this was the transfer of numerous jobs and incomes out of the province, which severely weakened the provincial economy.

After 1982, the Alberta government increased its spending significantly in an attempt to stimulate the economy. Federal policies, however, were simultaneously more than neutralizing the provincial efforts and creating a major drag on the economy. In short, the lingering post-1981 recession in at least one Western province was mostly induced by discriminatory Ottawa policy rather than caused by over-dependence on natural resources. Ending discriminatory fiscal, monetary and energy policies is essential to restoring prosperity in Alberta.

Albertans wonder why Alberta, and not our largest and richest province Ontario, has continued between 1980 and 1988 to be the only province from which Ottawa removes more in federal taxes than it spends. Why should parts of Outer Canada be the cash cows of Confederation, providing cheap inputs for the industrial heartland? For example, while the Mulroney government continues to spend more in Ontario than it raises in federal revenues, thereby increasing inflation there, his Finance Minister argues that sky-high interest rates are necessary to dampen inflation. In August, 1990, the Prime Minister told his constituents in Charlevoix that the national economy was neither in recession nor approaching one. High interest rates, he declared, were pushing inflation out of the economy. That same week wages across the country went up at a 5.3 per cent yearly rate, prices rose by 4.3 per cent and economic growth was zero.

Some additional data on federal spending and taxation by province released by Mansell in August of 1990 were equally disturbing. Between 1961 and 1988, Albertans contributed $145.7 billion (expressed as 1990 dollars) more to Ottawa's revenues than they received in federal spending and transfers (Fig. 4). British Columbians were the only other net contributors to Confederation during the same period. Ontarians, who might have been expected to have contributed generously to "have-not" provinces, received $24 billion more in spending than they paid in taxes during these years. Most of the national government is located in Ontario and the argument is frequently made that this explains the anomaly. Yet how then to explain that between 1970 and 1979 Ontario made a net contribution to residents of other provinces of about $3.6 billion? Mansell's latest figures also indicate that since 1980 alone Québec received $95 billion from

Ottawa more than it contributed to the national government.

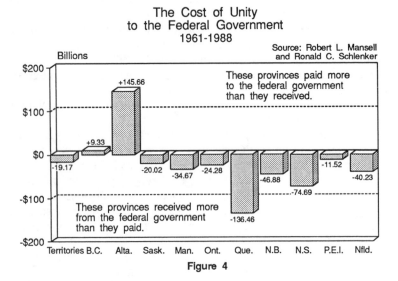

The Cost of Unity
to the Federal Government
1961-1988

Figure 4

Prospects

Overall, the West's experience within Confederation remains a story of buoyancy, optimism and confidence meeting continuous rebuffs from the various agencies of the national government. In consequence, the region has yet to achieve political and economic equality with Ontario and Québec.

Containing approximately 7.5 million residents, who constitute the second largest population grouping in the country after Ontario, Western Canada continues to feel largely overlooked and neglected, frustrated and impotent. The time has clearly arrived for the region to achieve equal partnership with all other regions of the country. Political and economic equality is the only means of ending Western alienation.

FIVE

UP NORTH

The Canadian North is the largest undeveloped region left on a shrunken planet, but mind-boggling though it may be to many futurists, it only sporadically holds southern attention. We take it for granted as part of our national heritage as a northern people and land. The vast majority of us being urban dwellers living within 350 kilometres of the Canada-U.S. border, we often consider our North to be as remote as a small nation in the developing world and about as important.

"The views of the majority of Canadians about the North are unsurveyed, and perhaps unformulated," concluded H.B. Hawthorn in *Science and the North* almost twenty years ago. This view doubtless remains equally true in the last decade of the twentieth century. As we struggle to stay a nation, we can make the last decade of the twentieth century the one of the North. It has stamped our national consciousness deeply and defines our identity throughout the world.

For many, the North is a state of mind; for others, it is more than an area — it is a passion. For still others, the North is, " . . . like an irresistible itch, which implacably drives man to mobility" in the splendid phrase of Professor Louis-Edmond Hamelin of Laval University, an authority on our nordicity. Nineteenth century adventurers, explorers and *coureurs de bois* could not resist the call of the North. There, they had to experience — in fear, in tragedy and in bravery — its awesome and silent power. They had to find escape from monotony and renaissance from subdued spirits.

Among non-native Canadians, we often see the North in a host of localized northern situations: the Northwest Passage, polar expeditions, the Inuit, unimaginable cold, the Klondike, and recently, oil. Two extreme notions about the North clash: the over-idealized and the excessively pessimistic. Pleasant illusions are often ignited by the pioneer spirit; pessimistic ones come afterwards from those disappointed in seeking quick profits. One view claims the North is a hinterland to be exploited for the benefit of southern Canada; another argues the wilderness must be preserved in a pristine condition. Much northern history revolves around this confrontation. Related notions adopted by governments, agencies, industry, interest groups, and so on, continue to shape the affairs of the region, depending on which group is more vocal or dominant.

Southerners tend to ignore a region that holds a fraction of one per cent of our population and has no political and economic clout to speak of. Our view of Canada sometimes leaves off Canada's Far North entirely. At Dorval Airport in Montréal, a large mural depicting Canada represents only southern Canada. To mark the occasion of the Olympic Games in Montréal in 1976, Canada issued a $5 coin displaying a map of the country. Part of the High Arctic was missing.

Even what constitutes the Canadian "North" has undergone considerable evolution since 1870. In the immediate post-Confederation period, anything beyond Lake Nipissing was "North." When we obtained new territories from Britain in 1870, we conferred the name "North-West Territories" on them, but included in this description was land as far south as the 49th parallel. Only after 1912 was the name confined to the parts of Canada lying beyond 60°. Politically, Canada has a federal North, two territorial Norths, and seven provincial Norths.

In assuming control of the new territories in 1870-71, the largest transfer of land in recorded history, the government of Canada developed its new frontiers with little real effort to study or understand the existing situation there, or to adapt its policies to the circumstances of the region. The Red River uprising was one result of this lack of insight, yet, in the historian Morris Zaslow's words, "Canada seemingly learned nothing from the experience of Red River. The bland assumption that the territory, having been paid for (and conquered by) the Dominion, ought to be used for the primary benefit of eastern Canada, continued to characterize her governance of the Northwest."

Our national governments also used authoritarian methods in line with prevailing notions of the Crown as the ultimate source of authority. Decisions were made in accord with national rather than local priorities; boundaries and powers of the resulting new government and territories were set by federal officials, and according to their wishes. Notions of self-reliance typical of the frontier experience in the United States succumbed to general acceptance by residents of authority from outside. Frederick Jackson Turner's frontier thesis found little reflection in Canada's northern frontier movement, partly because Canada's political centre never moved from Inner Canada, and partly because the drive to open the frontier came from groups and forces outside the region, more than from pioneering settlers.

Canadian institutions were clamped onto the Northwest in a rigid and unimaginative way by successive governments in Ottawa. The area continued to be controlled from afar, with its resources exploited in order to ease the burden of the southern taxpayer. Local residents were allowed little initiative. Decisions affecting their lives were to be made in Ottawa by officials entirely out of touch with the situation. The underlying goal of the governments of the day was to settle the region as quickly as possible and replace the institutions of Indian and Métis with social, cultural and political practices from southern Canada. In colonizing the Northwest, Ottawa failed to recognize the urgent problems of aboriginal peoples caught in the vortex of an advancing civilization. In its eagerness to promote development, Ottawa allowed resources to be exploited blindly and for any foreign interest.

Those who live north of sixty degrees are the most isolated of all Outer Canadians. They bitterly resent their ongoing status as political, economic and cultural colonials. Northern Indians and Inuit, of course, see the North neither as hinterland nor as a frontier, but as their homeland, a native land that is held under economic and cultural siege by colonists.

A Regional Colossus

Canada is above all a northern country. One needs only to travel abroad to see how firmly this concept of our nation is endorsed in minds the world over. Hamelin estimates that Canada's North constitutes seventy per cent of our territory, arguing the official thirty-nine per cent merely corresponds to the area of land and fresh water of the Northwest Territories and Yukon: "The Canadian North expresses the concept of vastness almost to excess. By area, the North is the principal component of the country, and in this sense, the North characterizes Canada."

The magnitude of the area is colossal, its coastline longer than our southern two coastlines combined. The Northwest Territories, with 3.3 million square kilometres, and the Yukon Territory, with 0.5 million, contain four-tenths of our national land surface.

The national census figures of 1986 show that the two territories contain less than one-third of one per cent of Canada's population. Of the 52,020 residents of the NWT, fifty-eight per cent report aboriginal origins (Inuit — 18,350, Métis — 3,810, Indian or Dene — 9,370); of the residents of Yukon only 21.4 per cent report aboriginal origins (Indian or Dene — 4,770, Métis — 225, Inuit — 65).

Northern Indians usually refer to themselves as "Dene" except a small group in southwestern Yukon, the Tlingit. Dene leaders insist they can understand the different languages that have a common Athapaskan root and are economically and culturally united enough to become a nation. Although Ottawa forced them to negotiate land claims as a single party with the Dene, the NWT Métis are a distinct cultural group. For historical reasons they tend to share a common view as to the most desirable relationship between the native and non-native communities. The same group in the Yukon does not generally identify itself as Métis and has since the beginning joined voluntarily with Yukon Indians to negotiate land claims.

Canada's Inuit live mostly in the NWT from above the tree line to as far north as Ellesmere Island. For centuries, they were nomadic hunters and gatherers, but today live in settlements close to the sea. A study by Michael Whittington for the 1985 MacDonald Commission concluded that Inuit remoteness from southern Canada has helped them to maintain a tighter consensus on various issues than either the Dene and Métis of the NWT or the Yukon Indian people.

Surprisingly to many southerners, the white population of the North is diverse. The major variable is permanent versus short-term residence. At one extreme are transients who fly in for two-or-three week shifts and have little or no contact with other northern residents. A second group, in Whittington's groupings, are mostly young males, who migrate north by highway to look for work in resource development, mines, and the like. Most return south after a few years. Another group, frequently termed "bush hippies" by permanent white Yukoners, often have university degrees and attempt to experience the North for a few years before drifting back to the South. The "indefinites" include federal public officials, RCMP officers, and bank and chain store employees who usually live in the major urban centres in both territories. Farthest away from transients are those permanently located in the NWT or Yukon. This group, in Whittington's apt language, are for the most part, "whites who have been 'captured by' or have 'fallen in love' with the North . . . those for whom Yukon or the NWT is home."

A central goal of most northerners, whether Inuit, Indian or white, is that their own futures should not be subordinated to the conflicting views of southern Canadians. They are anxious to get rid of overgeneralizations. In fact, differences abound among northerners of the three backgrounds: territorians not only differ in their origins but also in their political, social and economic aspirations.

Ice Trails to Serfdom

"The North can be studied as a society — actually a set of several societies — but it can only be understood as a colony," concluded Gurston Dacks accurately a decade ago. It continues to be an internal colony of Canada, a domestic frontier of exploitation and settlement with a mythical promise of national and personal renewal, where both previous development and current occurrences carry the possibility of growing racial discord, social disorder, and widening economic disparity. Most of the critical decisions affecting its peoples are made thousands of miles south.

Similar patterns of development, repeated throughout the North, illustrate a constant in successive national government thinking about the region: it is Canada's colony to hold, exploit, and develop or not, exclusively as and how Ottawa deems fit. On the other hand, practice frequently conflicts with Ottawa's rhetoric. As the historian Jack Granatstein notes, after one flourish about "what we have, we hold," Ottawa quietly abandoned Wrangel Island, located north of Siberia, to the Soviet Union in the early 1920s. It wasn't until much later that Ottawa began to effectively administer many remote parts of the NWT. Essentially the North remained ours only because no powerful nation thought it worth pursuing.

The Canadian claim to the region is based on the unsuccessful attempts during four hundred years of British explorers, including Hudson and Franklin, to find the Northwest Passage to the Orient. When Britain in 1870 transferred to Canada all lands of the Hudson's Bay Company — essentially everything between Hudson Bay and Vancouver Island — we obtained the North. A decade later, Britain ceded to Canada sovereignty of the rest of the Arctic lands, the archipelago and Baffin Island. It did so largely, it appears, to pass to Ottawa the problem of impending American penetration: Canada was thought better able than Britain to resist Washington's ascendant Monroe Doctrine. The British offer was accepted by a resolution in the Canadian Parliament in 1878. Approval was given on the premise that the region would cost nothing to administer and that the only alternative was control by the United States. It wasn't until 1897, when stories of violence and destruction of Inuit villages reached the south, that the Laurier government bothered to draw boundaries dividing the North into more manageable districts.

The Laurier government's initial efforts to exert sovereignty in the North consisted of six expeditions between 1897 and 1911, to collect custom duties and fees from whalers and to tell residents they lived under Canadian law. By 1907, Senator Pascal Poirier could advance his sector theory which claimed for Canada all land south of the North Pole lying between longitudinal lines drawn from the western and eastern extremities of our two coastlines. This theory eventually won international acceptance after our successful dispute with the Danes over Ellesmere Island. A Norwegian claim to Sverdrup Island was in effect bought out in 1930 by Ottawa for $67,000. A more lively dispute with the Americans began in 1925, when an American scientific expedition to the Arctic commanded by Robert Byrd falsely claimed to have Canadian government permission to enter the region. Subsequent American expeditions respected Canadian law; by 1933, our sovereignty in the North was for the most part established from the standpoint of international law. In practice, however, when World War II began, Ottawa had still to demonstrate a need for the Arctic. When, in 1938, President Franklin Roosevelt pledged to defend all of Canada, he was, as Granatstein notes, in effect "placing Canada under the Monroe Doctrine."

The 1970s saw the first erosion of colonialism in the North. Still, southern factors prevail and dominate northern policies. Northerners remain dependent constitutionally on Ottawa. They elect only three out of 295 members of Parliament and have been represented in only two national cabinets since 1945. Ottawa holds the levers on native claims, political development and economic policy, thus reinforcing the subordinate status of the two territorial governments. Initiatives and serious proposals in these vital areas usually originate in Ottawa rather than in territorial governments, which are forced in turn to react most of the time, thereby diverting available resources from initiating their own long term planning.

The subordinate status of the North is most visible in economic development because southern interests normally determine economic activity. When large-scale economic development takes place in the North, it usually reflects the colonial tendency of providing little benefit to the area affected. Even the local spin-off is not very effective because megaprojects are normally fully supplied from the South. The profits of most projects flow south rather than remaining in the North to finance further economic growth. The relationship between the two dominant northern economic sectors reinforce the colonial character: a large-scale, capital intensive resource sector undermines a small-scale, labour-intensive hunting, fishing and trapping sector. This causes much social and economic dislocation and increases native population dependence on the resource sector.

Traditional Ways of Life

If demographics indicate the importance of not overgeneralizing about northerners, the region's history reinforces the same point. Long before Europeans reached our North, various aboriginal peoples fed, clothed, and housed themselves using wildlife, plants and fish. This way of life was later altered at different times by explorers, fur traders, whalers, and missionaries. The Klondike Gold Rush of 1898, for example, brought thousands of whites into the Yukon for the first time; while most soon gave up and left, a significant number remained. In the eastern Arctic and Mackenzie Valley, however, the earliest white intruders were missionaries, the RCMP, and the Hudson's Bay Company agents, all of whom came "to do something" for indigenous residents. The Inuit in the eastern Arctic were left largely alone by whites, except for the occasional nurse, until as late as the 1960s when most abandoned their nomadic lifestyle and began to settle in larger communities.

The building of the Alaska Highway during World War II caused major changes for natives and whites alike in the Yukon. As hunting and fishing stocks deteriorated along the route, Indians, who were fast becoming a minority, experienced severe social problems, including alcoholism, family breakup and crime. Many of their settlements were relocated to sites along the Alaska highway to facilitate the creation of an essentially welfare economy for them. Their minority status reduced their policy influence on the white Yukon majority.

During the 1960s, economic development in the NWT began with prime minister John Diefenbaker's "roads to resources" program. The building by Ottawa of all-weather roads to a host of remote communities, including Inuvik and Fort MacPherson, produced an effect on the Dene similar to, if less severe than, that of the Alaska Highway earlier on Yukon Indians. Two factors moderated the pattern: greater political sophistication by the Dene and increased sensitivity by southern Canadians to the plight of native people.

In the far North, the building of a network of radar bases and the Distant Early Warning (DEW) Line, along with the coming of frequent airline flights to and from most of these installations, and regular air service to the eastern Arctic, tended to duplicate the Alaska Highway effect. Most Inuit maintained their older way of life for a while, even if families began to live in prefabricated homes with oil heaters. In the case of the inland Inuit of Keewatin, a series of natural disasters among the caribou during the late 1950s resulted in a major famine. Ottawa officials relocated many of them to unfamiliar settlements, including Rankin Inlet, and they became reliant upon social assistance.

During late 1988, any lingering complacency about long term trends for the Canadian Inuit was exploded by the publication of Colin Irwin's report, *Lords of the Arctic: Wards of the State*, which painted a very bleak picture of Inuit society forty years hence. "Most of the Inuit in the Arctic in the year 2025," Irwin predicted, "will probably be second-generation wards of the state, living out their lives in 'arctic ghettos' plagued by increasing rates of crime." Residents with professional or university education will tend to be white and they will continue to dominate the higher levels of management in both the private and public sectors.

Old ways of life were largely lost when the Inuit were moved by Ottawa officialdom into permanent settlements during the late 1950s. A new generation grew up in a cultural environment transplanted from the south and reinforced by a school system that did nothing to enhance pride in native heritage or to teach old values. As traditional skills and language continue to disappear, a new generation of Inuit are neither able to live "out on the land," nor are they well-equipped with employable skills. By allowing destructive and assimilative processes to continue unabated, Canadians as a whole will lose once again an opportunity to preserve a unique and ancient culture as a permanent and enriching component of our cultural mosaic.

The reality of the life north of 60° reflects the dependence on wildlife of peoples who for centuries lived off the land and harvested its wildlife. In their religious beliefs, "wildlife is there for a purpose: for man to make a living off. Wildlife is a gift of the Great Creator. These are the gifts of nature. Wildlife is the fruit of the land." Traditions were established in the past of an Animal Mother who insisted that the carcasses of dead animals be utilized in full; otherwise all would suffer. Today, this essential relationship between aboriginal people and the animals they trap remains an important part of their culture.

The fur trade played a major role in the creation of Canada. It provided the incentive for the exploration of much of the country and remained the economic foundation for Western Canada until about 1870. Today, fur trapping — the oldest land-based industry in Canada — pumps $1 billion into our economy yearly and some fifty thousand aboriginal Canadians rely on it. Wildlife as a renewable resource remains a major component of the northern economy. Hunting and trapping continue to be important for nutritional, economic, social and cultural reasons even though many native northerners are attracted by wage employment available through non-renewable resources.

This is illustrated in a recent survey in which eighty-eight per cent of all Inuit in Chesterfield Inlet were found to have eaten Inuit food the previous day. Store-bought food costs approximately twice as much in the North as in southern Canada so the value of native food is considerable. The product of the hunt represents more than a family's next meal. There are other uses for animals: tools, medicine, jewellery and income. Clothing made from caribou and seal is far superior to southern products in its insulating properties. The meat is shared through the network established by the extended family: older community members, family and friends all receive part of it. Polar bear skins are used to make mitts, soles of boots and pants. Skins can be used in mattresses for sleeping in tents and igloos, and in protective matting for transportation on sleds. Ironically, only those native hunters who have a job can afford to go hunting in the short time spans available. The unemployed cannot afford to go hunting even though they have time to do so — the high capital and operating costs of mechanized hunting (about $10,000 per year for the fully outfitted hunter) restrict hunting to those with cash incomes.

In recent years, the trapping of wild, fur-bearing animals has come under a new and frontal attack by the animal welfare movement based in urban centres. Many Canadians and Americans rallying against furs are only vaguely aware, if at all, of the concept of harvesting rights, or of Inuit nutritional and cultural dependence upon the hunt, and of the scarcity of other economic opportunities in Northern Canada. By forcing natives from the land, these groups would make it possible for major industries to move in, thus causing destruction of wildlife itself — the very thing that these concerned individuals attempt to prevent.

Rosemary Kuptana, vice-president of the Inuit Circumpolar Conference, told Arctic natives that animal rights campaigners are seeking nothing less than cultural genocide against Inuit. Stephen Kakfwi, the Dene Nation president and now a cabinet minister in the government of the NWT, warned his compatriots about the threat and the power of the anti-harvest campaign: "this force is potentially far more dangerous than the threat to our lands posed by resource developers and far more oppressing than colonial governments." Natives, fighting back through the Aboriginal Trappers Association and other organizations, are creating public awareness. There are indications that the general public across Canada now supports the continued harvesting of wildlife by natives.

Finn Lynge of the Inuit Circumpolar Conference Environmental Commission, Greenland, stresses that animal protection movements have a legitimate job to do in sensitizing man to unnecessary suffering, a goal with which the Inuit identify strongly. He adds, however, " . . . my main message from all of us, the Indians, and the Inuit of North America and Greenland, is clear: as far as our right to eat meat, to use skin garments, and to create a modest economy on the surplus of these products we need no colonialistic suppression of our way. ...It is a human right to go and get the food where it is, in a responsible manner, without ruining and depleting the resources around you." I strongly agree.

Aggressive media-oriented campaigns by animal rights groups almost brought the fur industry to an end. The human consequences of the anti-seal hunting campaign to native communities in Greenland and the eastern NWT are well known. In the NWT and Northern Québec, the number of seal pelts sold declined from about 44,000 in 1980-81 to 8,000 in 1983-84 and the value of seal pelts declined from $952,590 to $76,681 in the same period. The government of the NWT estimated that eighteen of twenty Inuit villages lost sixty per cent of total annual community income—a loss that affected 1,500 Inuit hunters and their families. In Resolute, NWT, total income from sealing dropped from $54,000 in 1982 to $1,000 in 1983. A few years ago, Finn Lynge mentioned during a conference on the use of northern wildlife that, on the invitation of the Greenland home-rule government, Greenpeace International had sent two representatives to Greenland to see the conditions in some of the seal-hunting communities in Arctic west Greenland. These representatives extended a public apology to the Inuit people for the damage that Greenpeace has done to them. In general, native trappers find themselves incapable of conducting the high-profile campaigns necessary to counter the crusades launched by well-financed and professionally-organized animal rights movements.

Wolfgang Schroeder, an environmental scientist from the University of Munich, says Europeans need to be shown how important trapping is to the aboriginal way of life. He stresses the need for a broad and thorough campaign about how natives in the Northwest Territories use wildlife and how they will be affected if this centuries-old way of earning a living is seriously threatened. Canadians should have a leading role in increasing this awareness. Our native peoples and their centuries-old heritage, the very thing that makes us different from other nations, is threatened and the cultural fabric of many communities already weakened. If the harvest of wildlife is lost, the fabric may disintegrate.

It is not only the Inuit whose existence, sovereignty, and self-reliance are threatened. The Innu of Northern Québec and Labrador found themselves at the centre of the storm over the low-level flights from the Canadian Forces Base in Goose Bay thundering over the territory they call Nitassinan, or "Our Land." The present 7,000 ear-splitting flights a year would have increased to 33,000 flights a year if NATO had decided to establish a tactical weapons and fighter training centre in Goose Bay. When, earlier this year, NATO sensibly decided not to build a base in Labrador as part of the East-West Peace dividend, Canadians in all parts of the country were vexed when the Mulroney government announced it intends to expand low-level flight tests around Goose Bay. As the spokesman for the 1,200-member Naskapi-Montagnais Innu Association noted, the number of low-level flights could increase from the current 7,000 to 18,000 a year by 1996 under existing agreements.

Thus, until the NATO decision, one of the last hunting-gathering cultures of nomadic people, with a way of life 9,000 years old, was being pressured into "new" lifestyles by industrial development or national interests that did not include them. The results could only have been welfare dependence, alcoholism, malnutrition, domestic violence and suicide. Those Innu who managed to cling to their traditional lifestyle were watching with powerless frustration as their shrinking hunting and fishing grounds were threatened by jet engine noises and a large intrusion of transitory southerners.

Northern Land Use

Land-use is the most emotional issue facing northerners. Land is the basis of life, the source of sustenance, and the origin of material wealth. Northern natives see land very differently from non-natives. Native people call the land their land, for that is the meaning in Nitassinan, of *Nunavut*: "Our land." The Crees call their area *Eeyou Astchee*: "The people's homeland."

The pace of industrial development in the Yukon and Northwest Territories accelerated in the 1970s, bringing with it the need for land-use planning to direct development and conservation of the region's natural resources. A compromise must be reached if land is to be used with care, and resources developed to provide the maximum benefit to the North while satisfying the voracious appetite of the South; this implies northern land use carried out in the North essentially by northern peoples.

The orderly political development of the North depends on significant changes in both the nature and process of land-use decisions. A recent book published by the Canadian Arctic Resources Committee, *Hinterland or Homeland: Land-use planning in Northern Canada*, argues that appropriate forms of planning can make a key contribution to human and economic development in the North and is central to both stable development and to the very security of Canada north of 60°. "The particular mechanisms by which we manage our northern lands will affect everything," says William E. Rees, an editor of the book, "from the fate of that solitary trapper now picking his way along a stony Yukon creek bed to whether Canada has a significant future as a polar nation." A consensus appears among interested parties that land-use planning in the North is essential and that it can be done cooperatively by governments, aboriginal peoples, communities and industry.

Central to it is the need to ensure that the authority to make resource-use decisions be devolved from Ottawa to Yellowknife and Whitehorse. As land claims by aboriginal organizations are settled and enshrined in legislation, the resource-use decisions in the North should reflect the real needs of northerners since they affect the quality of life in the northern third of our nation.

The claims settlements mean in effect opening the door to native participation in decision-making as they will provide aboriginal people with a voice in the management and development of the North's resources. The interests of native northerners will be reflected in wildlife management, environment protection and the use of water and land. For non-native northerners, land claim settlements can speed up devolution by resolving questions of aboriginal title to Crown lands and by creating a better climate for business and industry across the North.

North of 60°, four major groups representing some 40,000 native northerners have engaged in comprehensive claims negotiations. After nearly two decades of negotiation, the Council for Yukon Indians, representing 6,500 natives, reached an agreement in principle with Ottawa and the Yukon government in March, 1990. If ratified, the agreement would give the Indians 41,439 square kilometres of land and $248 million in compensation. The Dene-Métis, comprising two major groups with 13,000 claimants in thirty communities across the Mackenzie Valley, agreed in principle in mid-1990 to a settlement giving them about eighteen per cent of the land in the region or about 121,000 square kilometres and $500 million in compensation. The Dene have since refused to ratify it unless its treaty and aboriginal title provisions are re-negotiated.

The 4,000 Inuvialuit scattered from the shores of the Beaufort Sea to the northern islands in the Western Arctic reached an agreement in 1984 with Ottawa: they were given title to 91,000 square kilometres and $152 million in cash compensation and are allowed to manage the settlement funds and lands and wildlife within the region.

In April 1990, an agreement-in-principle was signed with the Tungavik Federation of Nunavut. It is the largest comprehensive land claim in Canada, representing more than 17,000 Inuit and a land area of approximately two million square kilometres within the NWT. If completed over eighteen months, it would provide the Inuit with $580 million in financial compensation and confirm their title to more than 350,000 square kilometres of land — an area about half the size of Saskatchewan. Other rights and benefits in the agreement include resource royalties, guaranteed wildlife harvesting rights, participation in decision-making structures and dealing with management of land and the environment.

The necessary preconditions to northern growth appear to be within reach as all these agreements become a fact of life.

Northern Development Re-examined

Reviewing the history of the development of the North, one sees three major stages. The first was its discovery and commercial penetration, initially by Europeans and later by Southern Californians. Phase two was the creation of administrative imperialism in Ottawa. The third and current period is characterized by the emergence of industrial production dominated by Inner Canadian-owned businesses and to a degree by foreigners.

The discovery of the Canadian North was probably by Norsemen during the 1200s, but it was mostly the British who were the first European visitors. The dominant fur company in the region became the Hudson's Bay Company, founded in 1670. It supplied its northern forts mostly from London and for many years simply waited for Indians to bring furs to its trading posts. When the more aggressive North West Company, based in Montréal, began diverting business during the 1770s, the Hudson's Bay Company agents began going into the northern interior to get furs. Beaver was the most valuable product so Bay traders largely ignored the Arctic, where no beaver lived, in favour of Great Slave Lake and later the Yukon. Only in the twentieth century did the Inuit enter the fur trade, relying mostly on the Arctic fox.

When the Hudson's Bay Company portion of the continent was bought in 1870, the major prize was clearly the Prairies. Inner Canadians intended to leave the North and its residents undisturbed until southerners determined otherwise. The first flicker of southern interest in the north was the Klondike Gold Rush of 1898. Thousands rushed north to search for gold. A railway was completed with much difficulty from Whitehorse to the port at Skagway, Alaska, in 1900. The first North-West Mounted Police recruits arrived with the miners in the Klondike, and many detachments were later formed across the North. Other officials were sent north to do surveys, research and exploration in order to establish sovereignty more securely. As Peter Usher, a major authority on the North, notes, "Even 50 years after Confederation, there were no publicly employed doctors, teachers, or administrators in the Northwest Territories."

The Northwest Territories as such were only established by Ottawa in 1920; official indifference to native residents, whose land had in effect been seized without compensation, persisted long afterwards. Two treaties were signed with the Dene, but none was attempted with the Inuit. Indeed, accepting constitutional responsibility for aboriginals living in northern Québec caused the national and provincial governments to battle each other to the Supreme Court of Canada in 1939, each seeking to decline any role. Ottawa lost and reluctantly accepted responsibility for Inuit education and health, although in practice both were mostly provided throughout the North by Catholic and Anglican missionaries for long afterwards.

The second phase of Inner Canadian incorporation of the North coincided with a more vigorous exertion of sovereignty by Ottawa, and began with the construction of the Alaska Highway and other northern mega-projects. As world fur prices declined in the mid-twentieth century, the Hudson's Bay Company reduced its credit to trappers and closed a number of posts. Many local natives were forced to approach military and other installations in search of employment, supplies and even food. In the face of incidents of starvation, most notably among the Keewatin Inuit during the 1950s, Ottawa intervened in a number of ways, including the granting of family allowances and old age pensions for the first time. Ballot boxes for federal elections were first distributed in the Northwest Territories during the 1950s.

Federal schools and nursing stations were built throughout the North during the 1960s and 1970s. The downside, again to quote Usher, was "a peculiar form of government totalitarianism in which virtually no facet of native life remains uninfluenced by the state." Severe conditions clearly required major initiatives by Ottawa and the waves of teachers, nurses, doctors and administrators arriving were mostly well-intentioned and dedicated individuals. The health and other programs they administered were unfortunately fashioned solely on Inner Canadian perceptions, and were often applied firmly against the grain of aboriginal culture.

One major consequence of Ottawa's new programs was the end of aboriginal life on the land and the move by many aboriginal families to settlements in Frobisher Bay, Inuvik and Yellowknife. Compulsory schooling meant, in practice, that unless the whole family moved to a centre, parents would be separated from their children. In this sense, many relocations were involuntary.

The third and current phase which began in the 1950s and 1960s, resulted in large measure from the search by American, Japanese and European companies for minerals, oil and gas. One example was the Pine Point mine south of Great Slave Lake in the 1960s, which produced lead and zinc for international markets. Two of the world's largest power stations were built at Churchill Falls in Labrador and on La Grande Riviére in northern Québec; another large hydro-electric project on the Churchill and Nelson Rivers in northern Manitoba. Oil and gas exploration and development has included Alberta's oil sands, as well as the Mackenzie Valley, the Beaufort Sea and the High Arctic. Large amounts of oil and gas have been discovered in the North; more is expected to be found both in the northern and western Northwest Territories and off shore in the eastern Arctic and sub-Arctic regions.

Several proposals have been made to move fossil fuels south, most notably the Mackenzie Valley pipeline from the Mackenzie Delta to the U.S. midwest and the High-Arctic pipeline from west of Hudson Bay to the Great Lakes. By the mid-1980s, only an oil pipeline from Norman Wells south up the Mackenzie Valley had opened. The recently-approved proposal to move $11 billion worth of natural gas from the Mackenzie Delta and Beaufort Sea to California might still begin by October 31, 2000.

Northern mining is a different story, partly because of a continuing long term decline in the world price of many minerals. The only major developments in recent years have been two lead-zinc mines in the Arctic — Nanisivik on Northern Baffin Island in 1976 and Polaris on Little Cornwallis Island in 1981 — and some uranium mines near Uranium City in northeast Saskatchewan. Other mining proposals for Labrador, Baffin Island, northern Yukon, and northern Ontario have not proceeded.

Economic prosperity will, however, continue to elude the North in the 1990s as a number of federal government policies, designed to curb the federal deficit, are undermining an already vulnerable economy. Northern tax benefits, which helped pay for higher fuel and food costs and medical expenses, are to be limited to an area deemed the proper North by a federally-appointed and southern-dominated task force. Thousands of taxpayers will lose these benefits when the eligibility criteria are eliminated which tie the northern living allowance to distances from a major centre. Millions of dollars will not be spent in these northern communities, but will be sent to Ottawa. "Those folks who sit in their ivory towers down south in Ottawa obviously don't know what it's like to live up here," commented Mel Hegland, mayor of La Ronge, Saskatchewan, a northern community that stands to lose the tax deduction.

A decision by Canada Post Corporation and its political masters, the Cabinet, to eliminate cheap rates for food shipments to northern Canada will cause sharp increases in the cost of northern living. The rate hikes, which are to average 32 per cent across northeastern Québec, northern Ontario and the Northwest Territories, will be another blow to northern communities as almost everything they buy is flown in. A grocery bill for a family of five in Pond Inlet, Northwest Territories is expected to rise from $1,300 a month to $1,600. A loaf of bread will cost $4.49 compared with the present $3.45. A five-kilogram bag of flour in small Baffin Island settlements will rise from $11 to $12.50; a dozen eggs will cost $4.20, up from $3.85. In Ottawa, the same amount of flour goes for $5.79 and the eggs $1.55; a loaf of bread between $.99 and $1.60. The unemployment rate in the winter of 1989 for the NWT was thirty per cent for natives, compared to five per cent for non-natives. Many northerners fear the increases on milk, fruit, vegetables and other basic staples will affect the health of native northerners as some families will cut back on these high priced products.

The postal increases, the elimination of the tax credits to certain northern communities, the proposed changes to the unemployment insurance system claims (thus far blocked by the Senate), and the proposed goods and services consumption tax (which taxes transportation costs on all items except food) will hit Northerners much more severely than most other Canadians. The combined effect of these measures by the Mulroney government will affect not only the standard of living of northerners, but also the growing perception that the present government in Ottawa neither understands the realities of life in northern parts of the country nor "gives a damn" about the well-being of northern residents.

Sustainable Development

The North is a resource hinterland supplying the metropolis of southern Canada with raw materials. The northern economy has almost no secondary or manufacturing sector: in 1989, manufacturing in the Yukon accounted for only 7.1 per cent of its economic output. Governments are the largest employers in both territories and in the northern regions of the provinces, accounting for almost forty per cent of all northern employment. Real economic growth in the North, however, depends mostly on non-renewable resource exploitation.

The main source of northern wealth in the early 1990s lies in oil, gas and mining development, but such resources create few permanent jobs. Some say that mega-developments, such as the production of Beaufort Sea oil, would allow the Northwest Territories to offset much of its current federal subsidy. According to John Merritt, formerly of the Canadian Arctic Resources Committee, a confidential federal cabinet document says northern resource development income, even by the year 2000, will amount to no more than a fifth of Ottawa's northern grant. Some federal officials, said Merritt, contend that before the Northwest Territories receive any oil royalties they should pay Ottawa back the billions of tax incentive dollars handed over to oil companies during the 1980s to promote northern drilling. Outer Canadians in some parts of southern Canada can only be thankful that our own provinces didn't have to weather such storms of indifference on our way to provincial status.

Canada's North has been referred to as "the biggest backyard on the planet with untapped potential." The land and offshore waters of northern Canada offer oil and gas explorers opportunities unequalled almost anywhere on earth. The Mackenzie Delta and Valley, the Beaufort Sea and the Arctic Islands cover an area of about 450,000 square miles — an area twice the size of Alberta — and most of it has potential for oil and gas development. The estimated potential reserves in this part of northern Canada are 15 billion barrels of oil and 150 trillion cubic feet of gas according to a recent report by the Geological Survey of Canada. With such promise, the North can be seen as part of the answer to future fossil fuel shortages for Canada, an opportunity to find jobs for many Canadians, and the source of vast export revenues. The resource potential, however, has to be severely discounted because of remote location, high costs, environmental concerns and logistical difficulties associated with most of the North's resources.

Experts say that through the 1990s, the most valuable components of the North's endowment include oil and gas along the Mackenzie Corridor; oil and gas in the onshore and shallow offshore of the Mackenzie Delta; and oil resources in the offshore Delta. The West Beaufort oil opportunities are also likely to be the focus of limited exploration. All this depends very much on future world oil prices, but Northern Canada remains one of the most promising areas in North America in which to explore.

Native peoples in the North have in recent years become increasingly aware of the effects of non-renewable resource development on their lives and cultures, and of the potential benefits for them of such development. The Third National Workshop on Peoples, Resources and the Environment North of 60, held in Yellowknife in mid-1983, heard aboriginal representatives point out that they had not received major benefits through employment in the mining industry and other sectors of non-renewable resources, a view shared by the federal government and admitted generally by the industry.

The desire for more participation in northern development has resulted in specific proposals for equity participation by aboriginal peoples in oil ventures. Political powerlessness among natives generally, and among natives of the North in particular, comes in large measure from a lack of economic power collectively. Native economic companies are instruments that might foster the development of economic power within these communities while minimizing the socio-cultural costs. Michael Whittington argues persuasively that such corporations could be a catalyst for aboriginals to acquire economic power that can in turn be exercised in a manner compatible with their socio-cultural context in order to acquire a greater political power within our national political culture. Native people in the North often lack the necessary training to fill many of the positions in the non-renewable sector. Most of the jobs in the resource-based economy are filled by southerners who return home with the closure of mines and other projects. Since such jobs are usually in urban centres and far from native communities, those with the necessary skills often do not apply because they are reluctant to move from their home communities. The northern non-governmental labour force is thus drawn from temporary and transient individuals: this reality not only makes it difficult for smaller enterprises to recruit their staffs but also reduces the total purchasing power in the smaller communities, itself an essential for successful small business.

The northern economies also suffer from a lack of risk capital. There are virtually no northern financial institutions, especially in remote communities. Small business entrepreneurs cannot normally borrow from chartered bank branches in the larger centres. They must go to larger branches in the south. "The lack of indigenous risk capital and the absence of significant lending institutions in the North is exacerbated by the tendency of southern lending institutions to apply southern standards of credit risk to potential northern investments," concludes Whittington.

In view of the high cost of any northern infrastructure and transportation, development in the future is likely to be dominated by governments and larger corporations because only they have the financial and human resources necessary to operate efficiently under the extreme environmental and economic conditions in the North. For better or worse, both are thus likely to be major players in northern development. However, there must also be room for other types of institutions and other options that will complement large-scale development initiatives and provide fresh opportunities to northerners.

Continued exploitation of the natural resources of the North must take into account and strive to minimize the social and cultural impact on native communities. Those projects which allow employees not to uproot their families in order to take a job should be favoured over those that are based only on southern criteria of cost-efficiency and profitability. Secondary economic goals such as job creation potential in the North, training and skill development for native people, service creation to native communities and stimulation of the local economy, have to be considered as major criteria in an assessment of economic activity in the northern context. Thus, the potential profitability and return on investment must be examined in the context of non-economic costs and benefits. Economic development must be sensitive to the social and cultural milieu of the North, to its unique and fragile natural environment, and to potential positive and negative political impacts.

The Makivik Corporation, with a broad mandate to secure political, social and cultural benefits for northern Québec Inuit, indicates how one native community interprets the economic development in the North. "It is important not to define northern development in purely economic terms," it states. "Rather, we must take into account the significant and complex inter-relationships between economic activity and the social and cultural problems which may result in regard to the indigenous populations." Native development corporations appear to have succeeded as an appropriate vehicle for economic development in the North. They have been springing up since the 1970s, partly as organizations to administer the funds from land claims settlements transferred to the native groups, and partly to allow native organizations to acquire some insight into the Canadian business world.

Increased involvement of native people in economic activities will result in a native middle class with the skills, training, and education necessary to create innovative enterprises capable of accommodating traditional ways with contemporary ones. "If this native middle-class emerges from involvement in native-controlled institutions such as the development corporations," argues Whittington, and I agree with him fully, "it may spawn a new philosophy of development that is different from that of the south and that can establish a place for traditional values within the Canadian economic mainstream."

Northern Environment

Public opinion surveys have repeatedly indicated that the environment remains one of the major issues for all Canadians. Northerners are especially sensitive to environmental issues as the pressures for resource development become stronger. They view the development of their natural environment and economy as parts of the same decision-making process. The sustainable development of northern resources is central to their long-term economic, cultural and social well-being. Industry must thus work closely with northern governments to meet the challenges arising during development of the northern economy. Both must seize the opportunity to learn from past development errors in other regions in order to improve the process in the North. For the time being, the obligation to ensure that the resources of the North are used wisely rests on all of us.

The success of northern environmental protection will be largely affected by political development in the North as territorial governments seek provincial-type responsibilities over their resources. The 1988 agreement-in-principle on the Northern Energy Accord with the Yukon and the Northwest Territories is a positive step toward this goal.

Industry has some essential contributions to make in the development of northern structures, policies and legislation. The greatest are to entrench environmental decision-making into the business base, to improve economic and environmental planning, and to develop a "made-in-the-North" approach to resource management and development. Michael Robinson, Executive Director of the Arctic Institute of America, has identified four generations in the history of environmental practice: the Elders' Generation of the 1960s whose efforts laid the foundation for careers in industry and government; the Mackenzie Valley Generation who through a commission of inquiry contributed to the fostering of Canada's international reputation as an environmentally and socially aware country on northern development; the Mega Project Generation of environmental regulators, industry managers and private and public sector consultants, i.e. the generation of boom and bust of the recession of 1981-82 and the lay-offs of 1986; and finally, the Environmental Technocrat Generation, the managers of the 1980s and 1990s who must deal with the consequences of global environmental change and public demands for strict stewardship and sustainable economic development.

"In Whitehorse and Yellowknife," Robinson predicted, "a new team of regulatory professionals will view environmental and social issues from the perspective of homeland rather than frontier and they will do so with educational experience and qualifications every bit the equal of their industry counterparts. High on their agendas will be project contributions to a sustainable northern economy, free from the boom and bust cycles endemic to southern industries, and detailed concern about project linkages to the northern environment."

Land, water and wildlife have sustained Northerners for centuries. This relationship between human beings and the natural environment is central to native identity and culture. When explorers and scientists first went north, they quickly grew to appreciate it; many would not have survived without assistance given to them by natives. Over the past decade, there has been a growing awareness of the value of the environmental knowledge aboriginal people possess, including their understanding of animal behaviour, and the indigenous systems of self-government which rely on a sophisticated database to provide strategies for conserving natural resources. Everyone now recognizes the need for an economic development that is ecologically sustainable. One way to achieve it is to draw on knowledge collected over generations of observations and to involve local aboriginals in all phases of the management process.

Participants in a fairly recent seminar on the role of the northern community in managing northern resources echoed the concerns of many natives when they referred to "long-term decisions by short-term residents" as hurting the North. Northerners often feel remote from decisions affecting their livelihoods. Decision-makers are usually transient, representing the non-native business sector, and thus fail to understand that native culture places a higher value on the protection of resources than on the potential economic benefits for resource development.

Many speakers commented on the limited ability of northern communities to influence decision-making about local developments. As a consequence, projects are often harmful to the traditional land use and wildlife areas. (For example, the living quarters for Pine Point mine workers are located within the trapping area of residents of Fort Resolution.) The conclusions of these discussions summarized well the role of aboriginal communities in designing future resource development. Northerners now expect to play a major role in decision-making that precedes resource development. Community representatives see their role as encompassing everything from the identification of lands for oil and gas exploration to the negotiation of provisions guaranteeing the use of local business and labour. Native northerners say first consideration must be given to the protection of renewable resources; they are the foundation of northern societies and economies, and northerners must continue to rely on indigenous food. They are determined to make changes that will prevent damage to the environment and minimize hardship during economic downturns.

Tourism in the North

The alluring mystery of the North offers much promise for tourism in a region that could benefit from the industry but could also become its casualty. Southerners seeking unique tourist experiences are welcome for their dollars in the often stagnant northern economy: they are also viewed as intruders, disrupting the nature-determined pace of life of shrinking numbers of native communities and the sensitive northern ecosystems.

Tourism in the North is a recent phenomenon. Prior to 1960, only Dawson in the Yukon could be identified as a tourist centre. At present those who visit the Canadian North annually represent only one per cent of tourists in Canada. While there has been a growing recognition of the importance of northern tourism, the real impact of the industry on the economy and environment is little understood or measured. How the unique flora, fauna and ecosystems of the northern wilderness can compete with southern tourist attractions, such as the Niagara Falls, Prince Edward Island, Vancouver Island or the Rockies, remains unclear. Northern tourism is more nature-oriented and as such will attract visitors prepared to pay high prices to see the mountains of the Yukon and Baffin-Ellesmere, to fish for Arctic char or salmon on the North Shore, to observe nests of migratory birds or species of northern wildlife or just to absorb the fresh air and the pristine environment so quickly and irrevocably disappearing from the planet.

The North has its own culture to offer visitors, one that is not measured by mammoth architecture or magnificent cathedrals, but that reflects the realities of a world in which human beings have little impact on nature. Of considerable interest to southerners are numerous archeological sites, rock paintings, Dene and Inuit communities, and the signs of industrial development in the north, including the White Pass and Yukon Railway and the hydroelectric projects on northern rivers. In the Yukon, a visitor survey showed that 193,700 individuals (most of them Americans) visited the territory in 1987 between June 1 and September 30 and spent an estimated $37 million on direct expenditures.

A 1988 publication by the government of the Northwest Territories attempted to capture the economic impact of the Northwest Territories tourism industry and to determine its potential for development. It estimated the value of the Northwest Territories current travel volume at $119.5 million annually. The sector employed over 3,500 persons both full time and part time. In fact, while the public sector (federal, territorial and local government) is the Northwest Territories' largest employer — almost 40 per cent of the labour force — tourism is the largest employer in the private sector. The industry accounts for almost eleven per cent of the Northwest Territories' Gross Domestic Product.

The best potential for tourism lies in the non-resident pleasure travel market. The key to success, a NWT government document says, lies not in travel volume but in selling good travel products that are unique and are perceived to be high-value attractions to tourists. The same dollar inflow can be achieved here with fewer tourists, and this approach to tourism is more compatible with the uniqueness of the social and economic structure of northern communities. Small communities and fragile ecosystems can neither absorb nor tolerate increased visitor volume.

Eco-tourism, a different approach to tourism in the North, is becoming more popular, as a form of recreation that combines concern for protection of the environment and the enjoyment of wilderness. Bathurst Inlet Lodge, just sixty-four kilometres north of the Arctic Circle, is one of five lodges in the Canadian Arctic providing this sort of product in Northern tourism. Co-owned by non-natives and twenty-five Inuit family members of the

Bathurst Inlet settlement, the lodge provides visitors with some comfort while offering a firsthand opportunity to appreciate the surrounding wilderness and wildlife thanks to the Inuit guides and trappers. For local Inuit this means a stable economic future. They not only assist in the kitchen and with housekeeping, but also act as wildlife guides. When, instead of killing an animal, a trapper tracks it and gets close to it for the tourists to see, he makes a more efficient use of both his skills and the natural resources at his disposal. One local wolf pack or musk ox herd will bring more income from tourists than it will from hides and furs. In this way, eco-tourism could become one of the most important modern economic opportunities for the Inuit.

Politics North of 60°

The Yukon has elected its own government since 1898 and the Northwest Territories since 1967. Yet development of a fully responsible government capable of safeguarding and reflecting the culture and traditions of the region is still only a dream. Increasing numbers of aboriginal and white northerners want to see it realized as soon as possible. Northerners see their region as a colony of the south with its land and resources owned and controlled by southerners. A greater degree of self-government and the gradual transfer of jurisdiction over natural resources are essential to their ability to become more self-sufficient and less financially dependent on the federal government.

Incredibly, both territories were closer to full responsible government decades ago than now. The Yukon was created as a separate territory in 1898 with an appointed commissioner and a six-member appointed council. By 1908, all its council members were elected. The commissioner, council and administration were all located in the Yukon and provincial status was seen as imminent. With the collapse of the Klondike boom, the territorial population declined so swiftly that by the end of World War I the Yukon was run almost entirely by Ottawa's commissioner.

The original Northwest Territories contained the present NWT, Yukon, Alberta and Saskatchewan. After Alberta and Saskatchewan achieved provincial status in 1905, the remnants of the NWT sank back into an unalloyed colonial status: they were even obliged to accept directives from a commissioner and officials living far away in Ottawa. Even the members of the six-member council appointed in 1921 were Ottawa residents. In 1951 the territorial council met in the north for the first time with newly-elected members from the Mackenzie Valley. When the territorial government finally moved to Yellowknife in 1967, the enlarged council still had some appointed members. The first fully-elected N.W.T. council took office only in 1975.

Today, both territorial governments are creatures of Parliament and as such remain in theory subject to federal edict in all their decisions. In practice they are now quite close to achieving the full powers of a responsible government. Since 1979, the Yukon Commissioner has appointed his cabinet on the advice of the majority leader, and must accept the council's advice, thereby functioning essentially as the lieutenant-governor of a province. The Yukon Assembly, dominated by political parties since 1978, operates on the premise that its cabinet must maintain the confidence of the Council to stay in office.

The progress of the N.W.T. Legislative Assembly toward a similar model has been slower. Council members, still elected on a non-partisan basis, choose their Executive Council members, including the Government Leader, and any of them can be dismissed by a vote of the assembly. Assembly divisions tend to be on lines such as Eastern Arctic versus Western Arctic and native versus non-native. In the 1987 election, fifteen of the twenty-four MLAs elected were Dene, Inuit or Métis; aboriginal issues are, accordingly, now at the top of the Assembly's agenda.

In both territories, the local government is responsible for social services, education, tourism and most aspects of renewable resource development. Ottawa maintains jealous control of non-renewable resources and of land use. Meanwhile, federal transfer payments constitute approximately eighty per cent of revenue in the Northwest Territories budget, sixty per cent in the Yukon one. Ottawa provided $825 million in total to both territories during fiscal 1988/89 to cover the gap between territorial spending and revenues. This meant a federal subsidy of about $11,000 for every Canadian living north of 60°. The huge size of the federal subsidy to northerners was presumably what encouraged Bill McKnight, Ottawa's Indian and Northern Affairs Minister of the day, to tell a group of northerners in late 1987 that their political aspirations were "bound absolutely to the ability of the northern economy to generate employment."

In 1988, the Penikett government released a report, Yukon 2000, resulting from an extensive consultation process with residents. It focused on community renewal and economic development. A few months later, Ottawa's Department of Indian Affairs and Northern Development released its own ambitious program for both territories, calling for fully responsible northern governments. It offered to transfer federal programs to their governments, to settle native land claims, to promote economic development, and to enhance Canadian northern sovereignty.

Nunavut — "Our Land"

Another major issue of political development in the 1980s was that of dividing the Northwest Territories between east and west, Nunavut and Denendah. It is closely linked to the settlement of land claims and the establishment of native self-government. The Inuit believe that their economic future and cultural identity can be protected only if they have some control over the government of their area and if they share in the management and the resources of their lands. *Nunavut* — "our land" — is the name Inuit give to their model of self-government and self-determination. "Northern native people want nothing more than to be accepted as part of Canada, yet Canada appears to be saying no to them," concluded the authors of *Nunavut*, a 1989 report published by the Canadian Arctic Resources Committee. Stressing that political, racial, and economic uncertainties plague the North for lack of a political settlement between aboriginal peoples and the Canadian government, they plead for the creation of a new political entity within the Canadian federation: Nunavut. They point out that the Inuit proposal for Nunavut has been specifically conceived to meet the criteria of the two population groups affected. For aboriginal peoples, it would guarantee economic rights, collective cultural rights, and culturally responsive self-governing jurisdictions. For the white population, it would ensure protection for their minority rights, equal opportunity for political participation, and freedom to share in economic development. Since Inuit would constitute about eighty per cent of the population of Nunavut, creation of the new territory would, in effect, establish self-government for the Inuit, concluded the report.

In fact, aboriginal self-government is now supported in principle by most Canadians. A poll carried out by Decima Research in 1987 for the Inuit Committee on National Issues indicated that seventy per cent of Canadians in every region of the country supported the idea of aboriginal self-government. Eighty-two per cent of those polled believed that recognizing the role of the aboriginal peoples in Confederation is important for national pride. A 1989 Southam/Angus Reid poll concluded that more than half of the people surveyed said the right of self-government should be enshrined in the Constitution and that natives should have their own police and justice system.

Nunavut is both a natural geographic region and a distinct cultural community. Canadians who live there should be able to manage their local economies, their social services, their school systems and their way of life according to their systems of values and local circumstances. They should also be allowed to participate fully in the making of national policies which affect their lives.

The Nunavut concept does not call for the creation of an ethnic nation; it invites non-native northerners to share in the future and the culture of the land. Nunavut would constitute a historic step in the development of better understanding between races. Canadians have a chance to demonstrate to the world that old notions of European dominance are gone, and that in our country we see federalism as a way of protecting the identity of minorities. Federalism is practised throughout the world in large measure to protect the identity of minority regions and peoples.

Provincehood

As devolution toward full provincial status in both territories was discussed with increasing frequency during the 1980s, the most widely-resented feature of the now collapsed Meech Lake accord in the North was its requirement of unanimous agreement by eleven legislatures before either territory could achieve provincial status. Yukon premier Tony Penikett noted that the three Prairie provinces were each created by the Canadian Parliament alone after residents petitioned and negotiated with Ottawa. Actually, Ottawa alone negotiated the terms for entry for six provinces between 1870 and 1950. Not one required the assent of any other province. Under the Meech Lake proposal, Penikett insisted, provincial status for the two would have become "practically impossible. Second, it was done without any consultation with us whatsoever."

The architects of the Meech Lake agreement were understandably anxious to end Québec's exclusion from the 1982 Constitution. How could they say "yes to Québec and no to the North?" asked the northern premier who concluded with ample reason, "Other federal democracies, including the United States, India, and Australia require only their federal government and a territory to agree. Alaska, for example, became a state by act of Congress and did not require Rhode Island's permission or consent. Neither should the Yukon or the Northwest Territories require Prince Edward Island's consent." His logic and history inferences are as unassailable as the accord was weak.

Erik Nielsen, the former Yukon Member of Parliament, was equally blunt in his autobiography, *The House is Not a Home*:

" . . . the Meech Lake Accord flies in the face of everything I have fought for throughout my political life. It dismisses the rights and privileges of Canadians living north of the 60th parallel out of hand by denying them the opportunity forever to form one or more new provinces within the Canadian federation . . . and it contradicts the publicly declared policy of the Progressive Conservative Party of Canada as propounded by John Diefenbaker, Robert Stanfield, and Joe Clark, and by formal resolutions adopted by the party itself at successive conventions."

Audrey McLaughlin, the NDP national leader, made essentially the same point: " . . . the Yukon and the Northwest Territories have effectively been cut out of potential future provincehood . . . . There is a very strong feeling in the North . . . the feeling that people have been left out, that they have been treated unfairly and that Canadian justice does not apply to those north of 60°."

What a former Commissioner of the Northwest Territories, Gordon Robertson, has called the northern "holy grail: provincial status," might in fact not be in the best interests of northerners for now. Robertson's 1985 monograph, *Northern Provinces: A Mistaken Goal*, makes a persuasive case. The Nunavut region would have fewer than 14,000 residents and lacks resources to provide employment and development. Denendeh in the Western Arctic would see Indians and Métis residents become approximately a one-third minority in the region. In the Yukon, provincial status is often seen as an ultimate step: a new statute could complete the province-type powers already held by the territorial assembly and council. Most

Yukon Indians, however, appear to prefer another form of self-government which would link resource use and development, the preservation of game stocks, and the environment to their indigenous culture. Finally, concludes Robertson, the legislative and administrative powers of the two territorial governments are already much the same as those of the provinces. There are few other differences relating to health services, criminal prosecutions, specific roads, and, most importantly, to northern Crown lands that are still owned and administered by Ottawa.

It is not clear that a majority of residents in either territory want provincehood, although opinion is clearly more favourable in the Yukon than in the Northwest Territories. Northerners are Canadian citizens and are thus entitled to the full provincial rights and self-determination other Canadians enjoy. The subsidies that northerners enjoy could be paid to two or more new provincial governments in the North. After all, if the Yukon and Northwest Territories administrators today operate as provincial governments, why not extend to them the full constitutional authority of all other provinces?

The North is undergoing complex and far-reaching changes and it will require years before we can assess their full implications. One of the forces that set them in motion was a growing understanding on the part of southern Canadians that decisions about the North must be taken by or with the consent of Northerners. Particularly, native Northerners have for too long been denied any meaningful input in the decision-making concerning their homeland. The North has to be fully integrated into our national union: it will enrich Canada by its diversity and uniqueness.

SIX

CANADIANS SPEAK OUT

In previous chapters I have attempted to examine issues in our past and present that tend to isolate the component parts of our country, that divide it into favoured and disadvantaged regions differentiating two categories of citizens, Inner and Outer Canadians, and, consequently, that create tensions, malaise and division.

The distinction between Outer and Inner Canada is not reflected on any map; nor is it in my experience even a widely-accepted concept yet. "Inner and Outer Canadians," of course, implies dominance by the former and a subordinate role for the latter. The term therefore to some people may seem divisive. Yet, this division is a reality, even if existing only in our national state of mind. It is, therefore, useful to focus on Outer Canada and to bring its concerns and experiences in Confederation out of the shadows in order to help restore a proper national balance and one day, it is hoped, to eliminate the need for any adjective in front of the word "Canadian" that might separate, isolate or patronize.

In other words, by dwelling on the negative aspects of Canadians "living together" my aim was not to perpetuate divisions. My basic assumption is that one cannot build unity unless these frustrations are dealt with candidly as part of a genuine reconstruction process. A denial of regional unfairness, inequality and favouritism within our federal system will not make Canadians change their minds: they know better. A straightforward acceptance of the grievances voiced from distant parts of the country and a genuine effort by national policy makers to remedy them can in my view still succeed in bringing Canadians together on the basis of national justice.

The rhetoric and emotions raised by the acrimonious three-year-long Meech Lake debate and the eleventh-hour negotiations to salvage the deal in June, 1990, highlighted issues relating to our national unity and focused public opinion on them. The process made Canadians fully aware of the high stakes at risk in our unresolved constitutional controversy. Now,

115

Canada faces an uncertain future. No matter what their views on the accord, all residents of the country can share a realization that Canada will never be the same again. New political structures will be necessary to accommodate the constitutional demands of both Québec and other provinces or regions.

Our notions of national unity are bound to be re-examined and redefined in order to reflect new political realities. In this context, I find it of great importance to dampen the feelings of hostility, frustration and indifference, shared by many, to resume or to continue a vigorous national dialogue and to seek to give it a positive direction with the ultimate goal of keeping Canada together.

In making my views known, I wanted to consult with others. This chapter is the result of a dialogue with 110 Canadians, a dialogue conducted in the form of an informal questionnaire that I sent to them. Living in all parts of the country, these individuals by no means constitute a random sample representative of the country, as would be the case in a public opinion poll. I chose them because I knew them to be perceptive and articulate, and was therefore interested in their thoughts. The respondents include leaders of major national, professional and ethno-cultural bodies; academics; scientists; historians and writers. Some are Members of Parliament or Senators, some are members of provincial legislative assemblies, a few are journalists. In short, they are individuals who by reason of their involvement in political and professional life have a good grasp of the major public issues. Those who have requested anonymity have not been identified by name.

Though not designed or compiled in any scientific way, the questionnaires did attract attention to key trends in our national perceptions, attitudes and convictions.

Not surprisingly, many of those who shared their views posed as many questions as they answered, shattered or reaffirmed certain popular conceptions and myths, and in general provided a fascinating look at our national psyche. How should we interpret, for example, a Québec MP listing our national flag as the most unifying factor for Canadians? How should we interpret the reply given by an Ottawa-based journalist who describes the capital's relationship with the regions of Canada as "excellent from my point of view, terrible from theirs"? In the context of the country-wide debate on the Meech Lake accord and frantic attempts to save it, it is interesting that Meech Lake itself was most frequently identified as the most serious threat to our national unity.

By focusing again on national unity, understanding and reconciliation, I run the risk of irritating and embittering readers partly because those notions were so abused recently by politicians and left devoid of much meaning by the rhetoric of the Meech Lake debate. Yet all of us must begin rethinking the country by giving fresh meaning to ideals we all cherish and by providing our own answers to questions that are basic to our badly battered national identity: "What is Canada?" "Who are we?" "What do we as Canadians have in common?" Can we live together, not in grudging acceptance, but by mutual consent and in the realization that respect for our differences makes us better and stronger?

The reader now knows that this book is highlighting those regions where strong convictions of unfairness and bias on the part of our federal system have persisted throughout our history as a nation. It is my hope that we may make these regions and the people living there into full partners in Confederation by giving them the chance to participate fully in decision-making. Despite historical imbalances as to the costs and benefits of Confederation, some recent disappointments, and dire warnings of things to come, this is no time to give up on Canada. This is no time to give up on the grand Canadian experiment.

Defining a Canadian

Much of the world's media attention was captured by events of June, 1990 in Canada when it became apparent to many that a country with so many assets and opportunities might fracture. Until then, the international perception of Canada oscillated between two stereotypes, that of a generous democratic and tolerant haven for refugees and immigrants from around the world and that other cliché of a boring subarctic giant. An early 1990 editorial in Britain's *Economist* magazine, discussing the place of the United States in a rapidly changing political climate, dwelt on America's fate as "stuck between dull old Canada and noisy Mexico." There is in fact little agreement abroad on how to interpret Canada.

Twenty years ago, Jean-Michel Lacroix, a University of Paris professor of English and today one of France's experts on Canada, dismissed our country as uninteresting. "A few acres of snow, Marie Chapdelaine and tensions between French and English," he noted. After two years of teaching in Québec City, he changed his mind completely, and is now convinced that it is a model country of the future. "It's American society with only its positive elements. Canada is fascinating," says Lacroix who considers Canadians to be skilled problem-solvers with lessons to teach the world about bilingualism, multiculturalism and peace.

Canada was created by peoples who had, for the most part, left Britain and France to find better lives for themselves; small in numbers, they paid little attention to the numerous aboriginals who populated the huge territory. It was no love match, but at least offered our nineteenth century forebears an opportunity to profit mutually as a country while maintaining cultural and language distinctions. The national census of 1986 has identified sixty major cultural communities as forming our population today. It is obvious we are not a homogeneous country and must never strive to be one. Cultural homogeneity was never necessary for the creation and survival of a country. Indeed, around the world, a nation with a single culture, or a nation without regions, is a rare thing. India, China, Mexico,

Belgium, Spain, Germany, Italy and Switzerland are only some of many examples of the more common situation. "A country is founded and persists, not because its people share common cultural bonds, but because they agree to common purposes, and accept that these can better be realized together," wrote David Alexander, a Canadian economic historian who had lived in all parts of this country.

Instead of a completed questionnaire, Pierre Camu, the Montréal-born author and vice-president of Lavalin Inc., sent me the chapter he contributed in 1988 to a book entitled, *A Social Geography of Canada*. In it I found these penetrating remarks: "There are some common factors that all Canadians share, irrespective of creed, faith, language or origin, and they distinguish them from other groups of people. They are namely, the notion and feel of winter, the notion of space and distance, the sharing of some unique and distinctive landscapes, the presence of the Federal Government and the proximity to the United States."

Poets, scholars, journalists and writers have attempted to offer an accurate portrait of our national character and have found it extremely difficult. Given the diversity and intensity of the many factors that are moulding our common identity — including the English-French linguistic duality, the rights of those who are neither of British nor of French origin (fully one-third of our population), the long-neglected issue of justice for native peoples, differing cultural and social values, divergent religious and political orientation — all set in the context of a changing political climate both in the country and in the world, this is inevitable. The failure to arrive at some uniform but appealing definition of "Canadianism" should not, therefore, be seen as a sign of weakness, or proof that we are trying to bottle something that does not exist. Twenty-six million of us can feel Canadian for different reasons, identify with different features, and be proud of different traits of Canada. Yet we need a unifying symbol to bind together our diversity and reconcile our differences. The quest for this unifying credo will remain part of the Canadian character.

Stockwell Day, an Alberta MLA from Red Deer, offered a different perspective on defining Canadians: "The greatest tragedy of Canadian unity is our failure to secure our own identity. We know what we are not, but not what we are. This is a function of our regional disparities and our emphasis on mosaics. Our diversity is perhaps our greatest attribute, but it is also the source of our indefinable identity and, under our present system of region muzzling, our greatest threat to national unity. We need to use the strength of our diversity to press towards a 'national vision' which encourages each past, not one which looks to subordinate some regions or individual pasts. Let's stop tearing ourselves up by the roots to see if we're still growing."

What is a Canadian? There are probably as many definitions of what makes us Canadian as there are people in the country. After more than a century of ten-year censuses, we still do not allow "Canadian" as one of the possible categories of ethno-cultural origin. Are the descendants of 1812 Red River settlers still Scottish? Is the thirteenth generation descendant of French colonists still French? Should such people not have a choice to put "Canadian" both as their cultural origin and identity even if it makes life more difficult for analysts at Statistics Canada?

The way we define the concept "Canadian" manifests what is important to us: we are proud of our experiment in nation-building — the founding of a country incorporating many different and distant regions and culturally-diversified people. It has become a fact of life and is world-famous. The replies to "what is your personal definition of a Canadian," one of the questions in my questionnaire, varied from a laconic "me," to "very-very fortunate," to such eloquent replies as that of a Nova Scotia university professor: "One who not only feels a unique attachment to the political state but who also takes pride in that state and its people in all their cultural, religious, ethnic and regional diversity. Someone who desires the continued existence of the unified state but recognizes the need for compromise and sacrifice in order to facilitate the continued unity of a very diverse country. And, someone who can readily recognize what is not Canadian but cannot so readily define what is."

Ray Martin, the Leader of the Official Opposition in Alberta, stresses tolerance and understanding as qualities defining a Canadian and he adds, " . . .recognizing that we are different from the U.S.A . . .we have created a gentler, kinder society, to quote a phrase."

To the same question Québec MP François Gérin, now a member of the Bloc Québécois, replied that a Canadian is "one who loves his region, understands that Canada is composed of different distinct regions and shows understanding of differences of all kinds."

Clarifying what it means to be Canadian, Ken Coates, a West Coast academic, wrote: "It means that we can proclaim, proudly, joyously, that we live in one of the finest, most gentle, most caring, prosperous, progressive societies that has ever existed on this earth. Sadly, it also means that we will not proclaim this self-evident truth and that we will, instead, focus on our shortcomings and point to our continuing weaknesses. May it ever be thus for it is this ability to find fault that has driven our country to become one it is today."

One further definition came from the Italian-born, Montréal-raised, and Ottawa-based cameraman Giancarlo Ciambella: "Someone who has been in the country long enough to understand what this country is made up of and how they can fit in and contribute to it."

Divided Loyalties

David Elkins, a political scientist and interpreter of our national identity, observed in an essay that Canada's history cannot be viewed solely from the perspective of nation-building. "Equally important has been the parallel and contemporaneous process of province-building," he says. Each of the provinces constitutes a "small world" within the wider context of Canada as a subcontinental nation. As a consequence, Canadian citizens have loyalties to their province and region and their perceptions of Canada vary, as Elkins found in his studies. My questionnaire findings indicate, too, that an awareness of Canada as a political concept coexists with a clear awareness of provinces and regions. While I can agree with Elkins that "there is little apparent conflict between these cognitions, though the balance of affectations for one or the other naturally varies from person to person," my own assessment is that this multiple loyalty and affection trait causes many Canadians major concern. It certainly fosters divided loyalties and pride among many of us.

Asked about his definition of a Canadian, Kenneth Pole, an English-born editor and Canadian citizen and resident of Ottawa, replied: "I wish I could answer this! I can say only that I've long envied Americans their national pride and willingness to be identified as 'Americans' without ethnic hyphenation or a parochial bias such as many Canadians seem to have: e.g. 'I'm from B.C., or Québec or Nova Scotia' rather than 'I'm a Canadian,' when asked their nationality."

I've often noticed that virtually the first thing Americans ask each other on first meeting is, "what state are you from?" Contrary to Pole's experience, my own is that Canadians somehow do not tend to ferret out this information quite so quickly. In my judgement, there is not one "correct" hierarchy of feelings or identifications that makes one truly Canadian. Numerous successful federations, through their structures and purpose, require and encourage multiple identities and loyalties. Particular identities develop within the context of a province or state and a country as a whole; an attachment to provinces should reinforce our Canadian national identity. Without Elkins' "abiding sense of place," or attachment to one's province or region, without the pride in one's region, there would probably be much less feeling and enthusiasm for Canada. "I do not know which is correct," states Elkins, " 'I am a British Columbian, and therefore I am a Canadian' or 'I am a Canadian and this makes me part of British Columbia.'"

As to my own loyalties, they are overlapping. Being a Canadian and an Albertan are both important and I'm as much committed to seeing Canada remain as one country as to seeing that Alberta or any other province remain part of it.

Many Canadians are reluctant to answer the question whether their first loyalty lies with Canada or whether they, in the first place, relate to and identify with their region or province. Their doubts and ambivalence vary, however, from region to region. Ontarian respondents mostly tend to identify first with Canada. Respondents from Québec, on the contrary, usually emphasize that their first identification lies with their province. Overall, more than half of the respondents to my questionnaire identified themselves first with Canada, and a third either with a province or with a region. A good number checked off both Canada and a region or province, to ensure they are not seen as disloyal either to Canada or to their province.

In a letter he wrote to me, George Stanley, the respected Canadian historian and former Lieutenant-Governor of New Brunswick, described his own feelings about our country in these terms: "During my lifetime, I have lived in Alberta (22 years); in Europe — England and France (10 years); in B.C. (one year); in Ontario (23 years) and in New Brunswick (26 years). These are rounded out figures and give me an age in actual excess of my years. But the conclusion I have long since arrived at, is that I like New Brunswick best. I am a New Brunswicker by taste and temperament, and certainly by sympathy. But I have had a good experience of Canada. I like the idea of a bilingual country (yes, I use both languages) and I love this country and have no desire to see it Americanized, or absorbed."

The experience of a region in Confederation as perceived by its residents is a good measure of the success or failure of our federal system. Some responses to questions on the grievances of one's province or region with Confederation reflected real bitterness shared by those living in Outer Canada and a dose of both impatience and arrogance from some respondents living in southern Ontario. "We get a little tired of doing all the paying," wrote Toronto MP John Bosley in a manner that would enrage most Outer Canadians.

In a letter clarifying his answers, Doug Tyler, a New Brunswick MLA, doesn't agree with my use of the term "Outer Canadians": "I have stated that the main grievance our province has is regional disparity, and I wouldn't doubt that this has consistently occurred because those in Upper Canada persist in thinking of those outside their two provinces as 'Outer Canadians.' Its implicit message is that while we may be considered a part of Canada, we are not regarded as part of the 'real' Canada . . . only on the fringe. We in the Maritimes do not consider ourselves as 'Outer' in any way other than perhaps in the minds of the politicians in Ottawa. We are every bit as Canadian as any resident of Toronto, Montréal or Ottawa."

Outer Canadians, no matter what other interpretations of the term might be considered, are in my view those who identify themselves with regional injustices and grievances. Outer Canadians feel that they have not been equal partners in Confederation, that Central Canada drains the rest of the country, and that they never receive a fair share of national benefits and progress. They believe successful national governments only care about people in Toronto and Montréal and spend too much time trying to keep Québec happy. The farther from the centre of the country, the less one is listened to, say most Outer Canadians. They feel banished as if in a hinterland. They bring up Macdonald's National Policy of 1879; tariffs and freight rates and transportation policies. They resent financial control at the centre; economic exploitation; cultural ignorance; disparities in allocation of resources, in employment and in development; depletion of resources and the environment.

Québeckers tended to stress other concerns: minority subject to majority domination, lack of understanding between the English-speaking minority and the French-speaking majority of Québec, economic injustice and lack of recognition that Québec is a distinct society within Canada.

Interestingly, respondents from Ontario in general either skipped the question or said candidly: "I don't have any" (grievances) — southern Ontario MP Gilbert Parent; "none" — an Ontario Senator; "The use of taxation to support outer provinces" — an historian from Ottawa, Mauri Jalava.

As to the current grievances with Confederation, respondents from Atlantic Canada often listed monetary and fiscal policy designed for Central Canada, economic dependence, economic colonization within Canada, regional disparity, cuts in our VIA Rail system and centralization of federal government activities in Ontario and Québec.

Westerners stressed financial controls, bilingualism, unfair federal-provincial transfers, Ottawa overspending, high interest rates, lack of knowledge and appreciation of Western Canada, feelings of being ignored, Meech Lake and Ottawa's preoccupation with the constitutional aspirations of Québec alone.

Northerners complained about the fact that the NWT are not part of Confederation, and further mentioned Meech Lake, the North's lack of control over natural resources and Ottawa's poor treatment of native people.

On the present concerns of Ontarians about Confederation, Senator Royce Frith is convinced that "Ontario can have no reasonable grievance with Confederation." Toronto area MP Don Blenkarn has one complaint: "unseemly grousing by regions that are well looked after." Other problems mentioned by Ontarians were free trade, lack of respect for French outside Québec and the unilingual law of Québec.

Under their more recent complaints, Québec respondents mostly expanded on the solitude of French Québec and the lack of recognition for the province of Québec as an equal but distinct partner in Confederation. A Québec MP, Pierette Venne, wrote about her province's "lack of feeling of belonging to Canada."

To the question "How would you describe your own region's relationship with the rest of Canada?" Ontarians generally answered with: excellent, positive and supportive, one of the largest contributors to Canada. Some Westerners and Atlantic Canadians suggested something nearing a love-hate relationship: "tenuous," "strained," "subservient," "supplicant," "poor country cousin of Central Canada." One Haligonian captured well the essence of feelings shared by many Outer Canadians when he expressed "resentment at being regarded as the perpetual 'have-not' region and bottomless pit for financial assistance." Brian Lewis of the NWT Legislative Assembly described his region's experience directly: "Canadians view the 'North' (or 'northerners') as inferior, but whatever use it has is seen in terms of serving metropolitan or national interests."

About the advantages of being a part of the Canadian Confederation, respondents right across the country listed several: a social security system, unity and national identity, being part of a nation, transfer payments, counterbalance to absorption by the Americans, large and relatively barrier-free market, feeling of pride in being Canadian, federal cabinet ministers, agricultural subsidies, a bicultural identity making us different from Americans, access to market. However, Joan Duncan, an MLA from Saskatchewan, stressed "it would be difficult to see any advantage in Confederation if we had to continue to be its victim, sending our raw resources to Central Canada and purchasing manufactured goods on a tariff-protected Canadian market." Finally, let me mention one bitter entry by Brian Lewis from Yellowknife: "The only advantages are those which a 'kept mistress' must feel."

My query on the economic dimension of Confederation indicated most respondents feel they have prospered, relatively, by province. I asked a question about the degree to which the economic potential of the respondent's region/province has been developed. Not surprisingly, the residents of Ontario expressed the opinion that the economic potential of their province is developed quite fully. Those who felt that their region's economic potential is undeveloped or wasted for the most part live outside Ontario and Québec.

Regional disparities have been identified by many, including former Prime Minister Pierre Trudeau, as one of the major causes of regional alienation and probably the major obstacle to building Canadian unity. The responses I compiled generally confirm this assumption. When unemployment rates at a given time vary from 3.5 per cent in some parts of the country to twenty-one per cent in others, this is not surprising. Respondents to the question about the effect on national unity of regional economic disparities in Canada generally agreed that economic assistance and development are operating as a national glue. Similarly, there was a consensus that widening disparities have a corrosive impact on unity, breed discontent, and alienate people from both the federal government and our more prosperous regions.

"The track record is not good. The gap is still roughly the same in spite of spending," wrote Bill Rompkey, MP for Labrador. "Consequently there is frustration mixed with resentment." A University of Manitoba professor, Peter St. John, defines the impact of economic disparities on unity as "devastating." He goes on: "The rich are getting richer and the poor poorer. Manitoba, Northwest Territories, Newfoundland, New Brunswick and Nova Scotia are disadvantaged provinces permanently. Nothing is being done to right these economic disparities, especially by the federal government." Fortunately, Ontarians as residents of our foremost "have" province seem to share the view expressed by many from our "have-not" provinces that economic disparities harm national unity. Even Don Blenkarn wrote,

"They hurt our unity." Sheila Embleton, a university professor from Toronto, said tellingly, "Imagine an upper middle-class family in which there are 10 children and two stepchildren and then try distributing allowances and privileges inequitably, and see how long you last without fights breaking out." "They create jealousy," concurs John Bosley, MP for one of Toronto's most wealthy constituencies. "They harm unity," says an Ottawa-based, well-established but anonymous journalist. "They make the disadvantaged feel like second-class citizens. They cause the advantaged to become smug, and believe their votes equal ten of the deprived." "They empty deprived regions of their most dynamic residents, especially their younger people," commented a Montréal university professor. A few respondents opted for sarcasm when dealing with this question. One Ottawa journalist, explaining that disparities have a "terrible effect" on national unity, quipped, "It turns people into complainers and whiners. It makes them unhappy, they gripe, bitch and quit their caucus if they are Tory MPs."

A clear, overall pattern could be detected from many replies received from Outer Canadians — namely, a bitter sense of injustice. It is based on the conviction that they have been unequal partners in Confederation, suffering from a long succession of economic and political decisions that have subordinated parts of our country and sacrificed important legitimate interests of some regions. Central to the views of most such replies was the strong conviction that Ottawa policies under successive national governments equate our national interest with the improved well-being of Inner Canadians.

I also asked what major changes in attitudes and policies are required to make Confederation work better for all provinces and regions. While knowing that the question was too broad to be answered comprehensively in a couple of sentences, I hoped at least to draw from the replies some indirect answers on how to build national unity. By sorting the replies on a regional basis, I anticipated concerns to be voiced that have been for too long dismissed as extreme, cranky, parochial or irrelevant at best.

Ray Guay, the Ottawa-based editor for the *Regina Leader-Post* and *Saskatoon Star-Phoenix*, born, raised and educated in Hull, with considerable experiences of the country, the Prairies in particular, wrote: "Since coming to Ottawa, I've come to believe one of the greatest detriments to the proper governance of the country is that (a) Parliament itself has become almost an immaterial but costly appendage and (b) individual Members of Parliament don't care so long as they are able to enrich themselves. This has shown itself in many ways: the House no longer looks into the spending plans of government; in that respect, the committees do no more than a superficial job of it, individual MPs being more concerned with their own little bailiwick in questionning ministers and bureaucrats (briefly) and government members would not dare mount any objections. There's nothing wrong with individual MPs supporting their own party, but blind allegiance is harmful to the country."

"You will recall," he went on, "that, after the 1984 election, much was said and written about the 'power' of the West now that the Tories were in government. Not only has this not happened, but policies and decisions that definitely were hurtful to parts of the West were allowed to proceed without a murmur. I've become convinced ministers are so well treated that conscience no longer plays a part in decisions. The very same thing has happened with respect to the Maritimes. Alberta has advanced Senate reform as a means of rectifying this situation. The ultimate solution does not lie with the Senate but with the House. I also believe political parties will not find adequate leadership until such times as they can find the means of overcoming the present mania of selecting leaders only because they have the proper image . . . that of a winner."

Guay's comments are so accurate that any of us, MP, journalist, federal public official, cabinet minister, who have spent more than a few years in Ottawa circles should applaud his candor and insight. That few will do so publicly is, of course, more a comment on our current political culture and the state of executive democracy than anything else. We need more Ray Guays in Ottawa.

Another Ottawa-based, Ontario-born journalist called for "an appreciation that French is an equal language, not a gift Anglos regret giving. A sense of West and the East. A swift kick in Toronto's smug butt." An MLA from Saskatchewan said we need "equal representation by province in the Senate or a similar body, a constitution that would give equal rights in Confederation." John Leefe, Nova Scotia's Minister of Environment, wrote, "The provinces must be treated equally within Confederation in the same sense as the American states are within the U.S. Senate. Neither the Canadian Senate, which was constitutionally intended to do this, nor the federal-provincial conferences, which institutionally were intended to create a balance, have achieved their purpose."

Other respondents across the country called variously for "more balanced regional influence in national policy and administration" (New Brunswick senator); "strong leadership, enhanced national communication, reformed Senate" (Derek Lee, Ontario MP); "a more overt effort by central agencies and institutions to consider Maritime interests and perceptions" (Peter McCreath, Nova Scotia MP); "tolerance towards the English-speaking in Québec, economic diversification and regional programs via Ottawa" (comment from British Columbia); "a major change in attitude to understand and accept Québec and its French-speaking majority — otherwise Québec will demand more autonomy as a means for the survival of its identity" (Québec Senator). Deborah Grey, the Reform Party MP, wrote: "A triple-E Senate — only then will the outer regions have true representation. It is also necessary for Southern Ontario and Québec to quit thinking they are the heartland, everyone else hinterland." Moffatt S. Makuto of Thunder Bay believes that "equality of all cultures — native, Francophone,

English and all others" will make Confederation work better for all of us.

Some Ontarians offered very general remarks: "Forget past mistakes and learn to appreciate what unites us" (MP); "No real changes required in Ontario" (Toronto-based Senator). An exasperated John Bosley, who said he did not finish completing the questionnaire because he " . . . became angry — 'province,' 'province,' 'province,' everywhere 'province,' " suggested one solution to the annoying omnipresence of provinces: "Maybe the only way in this country to create one Canada is to give Ottawa veto power." Many Outer Canadians believe this has been the unstated and unrealized wish of national governments for decades.

Symbols of Unity

To become a nation, residents must share a common sense of purpose and unity. It's usually, of course, through birth that a country becomes a part of one's life, but a common experience can forge common values and create links binding nationals together to become part of a united country. A shared religious faith, a common enemy, a cultural distinctiveness and uniqueness, shared values and convictions, a loyalty to a sovereign — these are some of the factors that make people feel they are part of a nation. In Canada, with our diversity of cultures, religions, traditions and languages, it is a forlorn task to search for a single factor that could be positively identified as our most unifying national force.

One role of a flag is to be a symbol of national pride and a unifying banner. Take the American flag: Old Glory remains a potent emblem of unity in a country that fought for its independence, pioneered its land and gathered a large population from far and wide. It evolved from a rallying symbol into much more for many Americans: their history, their faith, the quintessence of being an American. In our own country, the search for a uniquely Canadian flag twenty-five years ago resulted from the need for a similar symbol. Following an emotional and bitter polarization of loyalties and attitudes, the Canadian Parliament accepted the maple leaf flag now shown with so much pride. At the time, it was a compromise to unity and far from a rallying symbol for many Canadians. A columnist for the *Economist* captured the Canadian emotional distance from the flag still apparent even after a generation: "People seem to become more flagprone when they feel a particular need to say who they are or who they aren't. Canada's maple leaf and Switzerland's white cross are proudly worn not so much to say 'I'm Canadian,' or 'I'm Swiss' as 'I'm not American,' and 'I'm not German/French/Italian.' " Today, I believe our flag has become, to most of us, an excellent unifier across the country.

Many replied to my questions about the events in our history that have had either the most propitious or the most devastating effect on our national unity. Their answers reflect the diversity of a population constituted of immigrants who came from different countries at different times to make their home in twelve provinces and territories. A look at the items listed as having both unifying and destructive consequences for national unity reveals that, apart from several factors and events totally outside our control, there are many initiatives which could be defined as Ottawa-sponsored or promoted. This demonstrates that our national government has played, and can in future play, an effective role in bringing Canadians together by putting far more unity-building policies in place.

More than a third of the responses listed World Wars I and II as the most unifying national experience, with an overwhelming majority of them coming from Western provinces and Ontario. The building of a railway line across the country was the second most identified unifying event; again, the majority of those who mentioned it came from Ontario and the West. Expo 1967 and Canada's Centennial celebrations were the third most frequently mentioned unifying milestones. Others mentioned were: the CBC, the flag debate, Confederation, the Constitution, the Charter of Rights, the Olympic Games, Team Canada's hockey victory over the Russians, and the Canada/USSR hockey series. Sadly, there was also this isolated response from a Western Canadian executive: "The answer to real Canadian unity is to encourage Québec to separate and then work to develop a country with an English-speaking culture that we can all nurture and be proud of."

Among the issues or events considered destructive to national unity, the Meech Lake accord ranked first. On the other hand, it was identified by some Québec respondents as a unifying factor and most of them considered its rejection as destructive to our unity. The July, 1990 *Globe and Mail-*CBC poll concluded that 60 per cent of Canadians outside Québec did not want the Meech Lake accord ratified. Half of the respondents agreed that the failure of the accord will do lasting harm to French-English relations. Yet, the majority of Canadians outside Québec — 80 per cent — want the province to remain part of Canada.

Québec's language laws promoting French unilingualism, in particular Bills 101 and 178, were often mentioned among the dis-unifying factors, which also included: official bilingualism or its implementation, free trade, the Pierre Trudeau era, World Wars I and II, conscription, the 1970 War Measures Act, the awarding of the CF-18 maintenance contract, the threat of Québec separation, and party discipline.

Two Solitudes

A particularly disturbing phenomenon surfaced in parts of English Canada and Québec earlier this year: English-French language tensions led to incidents of intolerance, bigotry and undisguised language animosity. Examples were, English-only declarations — by less than ten per cent of the towns and cities in Ontario — and increased activity by the Association for the Preservation of English. They followed Québec's enactment of Bill C-178 (requiring English only on outside commercial signs), and the suppression for a brief period at some schools in Montréal of languages other than French outside classes. In my opinion, these incidents were fuelled by fears of perceived persecution and discrimination. It is not my intention to explore here the complexities of the English-French language history in Canada, but the subject is so related to our current national turmoil that a brief mention of it is necessary.

With the Meech Lake debate raging during much of the past year, we have seen French-English relations reach a new low. Except for a vocal and small minority anti-French group, English Canadians have generally reached out to French-speaking Canada during the past twenty years. The well-documented efforts by concerned individuals from all provinces across the country indicates our national willingness to compromise on language issues and, above all, to stay together. The enthusiasm for French immersion programs and their success, particularly in the West, is a remarkable tribute to the desire of modern Canadians from all walks of life to accommodate the concerns of their French-speaking fellow citizens. The fact that "Europe 1992" will have nine official languages, including English and French, no doubt helps both our official bilingualism and the expanded teaching of our other heritage languages as well.

One of my questions tried to explore the major issues of difficulty in today's French-English language relations. Mentioned, in order of frequency, were forced official bilingualism or the way it was implemented, Meech Lake, mutual misunderstandings, Anglo bigotry, Québec language laws, the actions of Québec's Premier Robert Bourassa, economic inequalities in stages of development, unequal treatment of English language in Québec, lack of respect of anglophones for the French culture, the reluctance of both groups to learn the other language. A western MP mentioned the problems of "Historically-rooted bigotry in English Canada and historically-rooted fear of assimilation in French Canada (the latter being by far the more logical and realistic)." A respondent from the Prairies wrote, "The English feel that the French language is being forced upon a majority of Canadians that find no need for the second language." A senator from Québec made the other side of the case: "The fact that English-speaking Canada does not recognize that Québec has always been and still is in effect, really a 'distinct society.' "

The Ottawa journalist Daniel Drolet, a franco-Ontarian, wrote of the problem of: "Misunderstanding the issue on the part of English Canada, ignorance of the wider picture on the part of Québec." Another journalist wrote: "Bigotry on the anglophone side. Self-absorption on the francophone. Anglos make no effort to appreciate Québec. Québec makes little effort to explain. The media is as guilty as anyone."

Québec MP Gabriel Fontaine offered his perspective on the issue: "Because our Canadian society is relatively prosperous, some anglophones and some francophones have the luxury of fighting from time to time on language questions." He's correct for most of our language worries, I suspect, but by no means for all.

"The main question that remains," wrote Ken Coates, the B.C. historian, "is what more can English Canada do? In terms of programs, expenditures and new initiatives, I would suspect that the answer is, not much. We can, however, prove that we are serious about integrating English and French perspectives and seek a comprehensive understanding of the French fact in Canada."

The anecdote which, in my own view, best captures our language situation involves an exchange between an English-speaking and French-speaking Québeckers shortly after the Parti Québécois election victory during 1976. The anglophone told the other: "I'm afraid." His francophone friend replied: "We've been afraid for three hundred years."

French-language nationalist poetry written between 1830 and 1855 reflects the ambiguity that many francophone Canadians felt toward their English-speaking co-habitants of their province. Despite writing during a troubled period, Québec poets of the day expressed the feelings of nostalgia for better relations with their anglophone neighbours. The hopes for a better future and for uniting francophones and anglophones are clear in a poem by François-Réal Angers, well known for his nationalist poems:

> Dear old children of Normandy
> And you, young sons of England,
> Unite your energy and form
> a nation:
> One day our common mother
> Will applaud our progress
> And guide fortune's chariot
> Which will guarantee our success.
> Oh land of America
> Be the equal of kings:
> Nature and its laws
> renders you most sovereign.
> — from "The Future," 1836

The co-existence of "two solitudes" today at the centre of Canada and the polyglot mosaic splashed all over the country, are the most vivid distinctions in our collective identity: the desire to stay together and at the same time to keep a certain polite distance from one another as a condition to unity. At the moment, our national cohesion appears to be weak for various well-known reasons, but, like families, we must never give up on any member. A new and happier cycle will emerge. It always has and it always will.

Keeping Canada Together

In my view, the present feelings of insecurity in many parts of Canada over Meech Lake and what it implies come mainly from the view that we all lost something in the process. People in most provinces lacked confidence in both the process and the substance. We all wanted assurances that our own well-defined "territorial" interests were duly protected. Québeckers wanted to be recognized as distinct in order to have more breathing space under the Charter of Rights. The North fiercely opposed any provision that might jeopardize its aspiration to greater autonomy in the future. The West wanted Senate reform to defend itself more efficiently against Ottawa policies tilted sharply in favour of Inner Canadian interests.

Many of us were disappointed that our world-renowned ability for finding solutions to difficult situations through compromise was not evident throughout the entire Meech Lake process when issues of such importance to the country were dealt with. This was as much a result of pressure tactics applied by the federal cabinet, as it was proof of the emotionally held contradicting views on what Canada is really all about and the frustration of Outer Canadians with perpetuating the status quo of regional imbalance.

It is a central part of our national dream to believe we possess a unique ability to maintain harmony among diverse cultural communities. This, undoubtedly, is one of Canada's sterling successes even if it has faded somewhat with some recent incidents of bigotry, intolerance and racism. Long before it was formally recognized as a touchstone for Canadian society, multiculturalism was a fact of life in this country.

The 1986 census indicated that more than a fourth of Canadians are now of origins other than British or French. Some argue that if multiple origins are considered, the figure is nationally about thirty-eight per cent. Whatever the case may be, the percentage will rise as the cultural profile of new immigrants and refugees changes with world political and economic conditions. Countries of South East Asia, Africa, the Middle East, Latin America and the Caribbean are becoming the primary sources of newcomers to Canada. These "third-force" Canadians constitute a particularly dynamic component of Canadian society.

In recent decades, newcomers have not been pressured to believe in any particular Canadian credo and to discard their previous identity. They were instead encouraged to preserve their heritage, roots and culture while enjoying our national values of fairness, equality, and moderation, celebrated throughout the world. "Come to the Last, Best West" boomed Canadian immigration posters during the 1890s, "You may keep your language and religion, just come and till our prairie soil." Fortunately, this remains the essence of our cultural mosaic: by a collage of races, cultures and religions, we continue to build a nation bound by a thread of feelings of belonging to a country, and the understanding that together we benefit from one another and from our respective differences and contributions.

Recent episodes like the active campaign against turbans in the RCMP, an increased number of anti-semitic acts and persisting negative ethnic stereotypes combine with some recently conducted opinion polls to indicate growing intolerance. According to an Angus Reid-Southam News poll conducted in February 1990, one in three Canadians say cultural minorities should abandon their customs and language and become "more like most Canadians"; only thirty-four per cent chose the mosaic model. In my view, Canada is not now the American melting pot and never should be. The United States, in fact, appears to be moving briskly in our own direction as indicated by the fact that Spanish is almost as common as English on exhibits at Florida's Disney World. Nor should people, including Brian Mulroney, rush into concluding foolishly that all those opposed to the turban for use in the RCMP dress uniform are bigots. Many of those opposed only felt the uniform was a national symbol which they did not wish to see changed.

To my question about how to deal with different cultures in Canada, most of the respondents chose the "multicultural mosaic" type; a smaller, but still significant number were in favour of the "melting pot" model; the remainder endorsed neither or opted for a combination of both. The small number of replies to my query cannot be compared with the broadly based and admittedly random sample method of the Angus Reid poll. Yet I believe the discrepancy here reflects the essential ambivalence of being Canadian: We want to be different from others, especially Americans. We celebrate, enjoy and take pride in our differences, yet, collectively we are afraid that these differences could drive us further apart if formally sanctioned and fracture us into cultural ghettos and otherwise dilute our collective identity.

There is considerable pressure on any first generation of newcomers to conform to national norms. Yet on the other hand, people want to maintain their cultural heritage for their own children as a family bequest. In my own experience, the second and third generations of immigrants embody most clearly the process of becoming Canadian and moulding personalities, loyalties and identities. The second generation is often more a part of a new cultural climate, but is still fluent in the language of ancestors and conscious of its own cultural duality in bridging two cultures and two worlds.

No one can say how many generations it takes to become "fully Canadian" because no one really knows what the term implies. Certainly mere "time done" should not determine the degree to which anyone can consider him or herself a Canadian. The moulding of our national identity is an ongoing process, greatly influenced by the overall broad social, economic, political and even geographical context in which it is taking place. Essential to it is that we, as a nation of immigrants, must not exclude any individual willing to participate in the process of building Canada.

"A country, by one definition, is a people with a shared sense of having done great things in the past and eagerness to do more in the future. By this standard, Canada is dying," wrote Jeffrey Simpson in the *Globe and Mail* during the height of French-English tensions relating to the Meech Lake accord impasse. In my own view, Canadians generally were not nearly as pessimistic about Canada's future. Most of us resented deeply the apocalyptic tactics used by many Meech advocates, including the Prime Minister, and wondered what capacity to reconcile or authority to govern remained in elected officials who said, in effect, that Canada would explode if the agreement did not pass.

Are you and I going to stand idly by and watch Canada shatter or are we going to take an active role in attempting to stop this from happening? This might indeed be the best test of our loyalty to a cherished ideal of "Canada." For my part, this book is an attempt to promote unity and an effort to demonstrate that despite our differences and the very uneven flow of benefits Confederation has thus far brought to different parts of the country, the overwhelming majority of us want to continue as one national family.

PART II

FORSAKING THE REGIONS

SEVEN

DEALER'S CHOICE

The lack of a balanced economic growth policy in Ottawa has aggravated regional alienation at a time when Canada's national unity is under severe strain for constitutional reasons. This chapter is accordingly about national unity from a less-commonly heard perspective: that of our regions and our development policies which have a negative impact on national cohesion in Outer Canada. An urgent priority in Ottawa should be to reverse present federal government trends which seem designed to reinforce the hinterland status of Outer Canadians.

Outer Canadians are well aware of the harm done to our districts, towns and cities by many Ottawa policies and by Ottawa indifference. For example, we are aware that numerous federal initiatives, including departmental and Crown corporation procurements, have encouraged considerable overcrowding especially since 1985 within viewing distance of Toronto's CN Tower. The results have included traffic congestion, skyrocketing home prices and rents, increased air pollution, crime, irritability and skill shortages. Many parts of Outer Canada have experienced chronic high unemployment and out-migration during the same period. Quite understandably, Metropolitan Toronto became the goal of many of those hurt by these circumstances and looking for a job.

Few Outer Canadians think Ottawa's exorbitant interest rates and expensive Canadian dollar are motivated by real concern for our problems. When the Governor of the Bank of Canada and the Finance Minister stolidly defend an interest rate level five percentage points above that in the United States, they maintain it is indispensable to combat inflation. In reality, they are alarmed by price-hikes in Toronto. They should recognize that Ottawa's procurement practices, its research funding and many other of its policies are aggravating the trend. Yet, Michael Wilson implies that increasing bankruptcies across Canada are necessary to wring inflation out of the economy — as if they contribute to it significantly.

High interest rates cannot effectively fight inflation without first bringing on a serious recession. Speaking to several groups of students and business people this year in Edmonton, I couldn't find a single individual who thought otherwise. We Outer Canadians know from past experience that the recession John Crow and Michael Wilson are creating with corrosive interest rates will have the most serious and lasting impact on the outer eight provinces and the North. We also know that a major reason for the present interest rate level is an attempt to keep the Canadian dollar at a level acceptable to foreign holders of Canadian government bonds, mostly Japanese and American institutional investors.

Job creation across the country remains in large measure a function of federal government spending activities and legislation. A more inclusive national vision would pursue balanced economic, social and cultural growth as a major national goal. This would have important short and long term positive effects on the regions.

In a host of ways, successive national governments have perpetuated economic disparities, uneven growth and unequal career opportunities for Canadians on the basis of their province of residence. The 1879 National Policy of John A. Macdonald planted manufacturing firmly in the core of Ontario and Québec. Subsequently, Ottawa's transportation, banking, communications and other policies enhanced the dominant roles of Toronto and Montréal. The AutoPact provided an enormous stimulant to a manufacturing sector located almost exclusively within southern Ontario and metropolitan Québec. The National Energy Program of 1980 was intended to weaken western private and provincial government dominance over one of the few sectors that were not yet dominated by Inner Canadians.

Regional differences are key facts of Canadian federalism. It is federalism that ensures that our diversity can be maintained in Québec, as well as in nine other provinces and two territories. As disparities among various provinces persist and grow, a number of economists and political scientists have become concerned, however, with the question of "who gets what" and "whom does the political system serve."

The benefits of any federal union are much more subtle and intangible than can be represented by any arithmetic on dollars won or lost. The advantage of belonging to a much envied country, which unites French and English or Atlantic and Western Canadians, should never be translated into money alone. Equally, no price tag or penalty should be placed on one's loyalty to a province or region. Much of the time, the evaluation of benefits and costs of Confederation to a region or province is a matter of opinion, perception and evaluation in the eyes of the beholder. The perceived distribution of benefits might have little to do with dollar transfers or material gains, but, more importantly, be seen in the sphere of attitudes and subjective or symbolic injustices. The long-held Outer Canadian symbol of the milk cow of Confederation — with its head grazing in the pastures of the West, its teats being milked in Central Canada, and the hind end dumping on the Maritimes — originates from a subjectively perceived popular analysis of the benefits and costs of Confederation. In large part, these perceptions are based on economic matters and the feelings of under-representation for residents of most provinces in national decision-making.

John Hotson, executive director of the Committee for Economic and Monetary Reform, offers this metaphor to characterize the Canadian economy: "Canada is like a ten-room house with one hot room and nine cold ones. People are crowding into the hot room where they can find a job, but not a place to live, causing real estate prices to explode." Residents of the "cold rooms" are likely to agree with Hotson when he says that more imaginative and fairer national policies would spread the heat so that more Canadians could find jobs from Newfoundland to Vancouver Island.

According to some preliminary Statistics Canada data on provincial economic performance released in mid-1990, Ontario and Québec accounted for almost two-thirds of Canada's gross domestic product at market prices in 1989 (Fig. 5). Although British Columbia had the highest growth rate in the country during 1989, it did not alter the basic trend of the 1980s — the continuing dominance of Central Canada in the national economy. It was beyond any doubt another decade for Inner Canada.

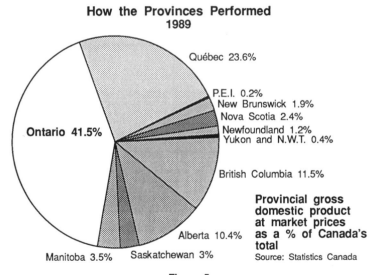

How the Provinces Performed
1989

Québec 23.6%

P.E.I. 0.2%
New Brunswick 1.9%
Nova Scotia 2.4%

Ontario 41.5%

Newfoundland 1.2%
Yukon and N.W.T. 0.4%

British Columbia 11.5%

Provincial gross domestic product at market prices as a % of Canada's total
Source: Statistics Canada

Alberta 10.4%

Manitoba 3.5%   Saskatchewan 3%

Figure 5

Other national governments have been much more successful in stimulating balanced economic growth. Within the United States, Florida led all fifty states in growth during 1989. Orlando, in central Florida, with approximately a million residents, ranked fourth nationally during the same year in attracting new business facilities and expansions of existing ones. The top five metropolitan areas in new plants and expansions — Dallas, Portland, Atlanta, Orlando and Los Angeles — are located in five different American states. The best-performing ten states under the same criteria were Florida, California, Alabama, North Carolina, Texas, Ohio, Pennsylvania, New York, Virginia and Georgia. Not all regions are represented in this group, but balanced regional growth clearly means far more in the United States than in Canada.

Australia, a vast land, sparsely settled with just over 15 million inhabitants, is often portrayed as a "region-less" nation. From data assembled by the Australian Bureau of Industry Economics in the early 1980s, it is evident that disparities in unemployment by state and regional income differentials in Australia were smaller than in the United Kingdom, Canada or the United States. Regional problems certainly exist in Australia and policies designed to divert population and economic activity away from the major centres have not worked as expected. Nonetheless, regional fairness is constantly on the agenda of Australian cabinets.

In Australia, the national government has major fiscal functions such as revenue raising, but state governments do undertake much of the spending. As with Canadian provinces, they exercise a wide range of powers affecting economic activity.

Section 99 of the Australian constitution orders the federal government to favour no state, or any part of one, over another state or its components. Another section bars favouritism on tax matters either between states or within regions of them.

After World War II, tax concessions were offered to the Australian mining industry, which benefits non-metropolitan areas. Concessions similarly were extended to petroleum exploration and development companies which had a positive impact on remote areas such as northwestern Australia. Personal income tax concessions are also available for inhabitants of remote regions. These areas have received special assistance when their industries have encountered difficulties. Various forms of aid are regularly offered to primary industries in rural areas for product research and development, restructuring and marketing. Finally, special projects play a role in decentralizing policies: irrigation schemes, railway and wood construction, the placement of military and educational institutions, and the development of the national capital, Canberra, away from metropolitan Australia.

In Japan during the 1989-90 fiscal year, the national government allocated 300 billion yen for grants known as the "furusatososei," or creation of home towns, to revitalize regional economies. Three thousand cities, towns and villages, including a tiny island village 367 kilometres off the coast of Tokyo with only 210 residents, will receive a special grant from the government up to an amount of one hundred million yen (approximately $900,000 Can.). Such communities will spend it to attract young people to "come home." The Japanese ministry responsible for carrying out this project, while conceding that 100 million yen will not be enough to revitalize all regions, stresses that the real objective of the project is to get people thinking about how to revitalize their towns and regional economies. Political scientists in Japan say the "*furusato* program" will have a positive effect in boosting morale in many regional communities across Japan by sending a message that the government is henceforth watching out for "country folk." In Canada, efforts to create such a "caring image" in the regions have rarely been a priority of our national governments.

Is it any wonder that the perception of Ottawa indifference and remoteness persists among Outer Canadians? The government's tendency to abandon the regions is contrary to the spirit of the Japanese "furusato programme." Instead of attracting people and keeping them employed in small communities, it favours the already overpopulated metropolitan centres and lets the small communities die.

From Ottawa's Department of Regional and Industrial Expansion (DRIE) figures for 1986-87 and 1987-88, it is obvious that our largest, most diversified and industrialized provinces, Québec and Ontario, received the major portion of regional grants: 60 per cent of the total in 1986-87 for both of the provinces, and 71.5 per cent during 1987-88. A closer look at regional development funds reveals astonishingly that they tend to benefit major urban centres, not small remote and underdeveloped communities as anyone would expect. "For one thing, they appear to have ended up favouring the major urban centres where much of the development would probably have occurred in any case; for another, it was costly," said the 1989 Report by Canada Employment and Immigration's Advisory Council.

In May, 1990, the Mulroney government announced with much fanfare that $584 million spread over five years would be spent to revive the fishery, diversify the Atlantic economy and create more employment in the troubled Atlantic region. Whether the program, still short on details, is going to accomplish all these goals in four severely depressed provinces, the amount of the package was low relative to federal regional development funds going to Québec and Ontario, our two provinces with the most diversified economies. For example, during 1988-89 alone, these two large provinces received fully $633.9 million in grants and contributions from DRIE, now "the lead department for regional economic development in Ontario and Québec," in the wording of the 1988-89 annual report of DRIE and the new Department of Industry, Science and Technology.

Economic development in the West and Atlantic Canada is in future to be the sole responsibility of the Western Diversification Department, with a budget of $1.2 billion spread over seven years, and the Atlantic Canada Opportunities Agency, with $1.05 billion spread over seven years. Their budgets, though considerable and much needed in both regions of Outer Canada, do not compare favourably with the financial help Ottawa provides each year to Ontario and Québec filtered through a host of different programs, departments and subsidiaries. In fact, these funds, including the half a billion dollars provided for Atlantic programs over five years, contrast with the $1.3 billion the Etobicoke North riding in the greater Toronto area received in contracts awarded by the federal Supply and Services Department during 1987 alone. If the eight outer provinces received a fair share of the goods and services bought each year by the federal departments and Ottawa's crown corporations, special economic development programs would be unnecessary.

In their editorial comments on the government's aid program for Atlantic Canadians, two Inner Canada newspapers, in effect, invited Ottawa policy makers to treat them as fodder for Toronto's labour market. *The Ottawa Sun* considered that "a good many more Maritimers and Newfoundlanders should be thinking of relocating in Central Canada where, right now, there's a shortage of labour." In like manner, *The Globe and Mail* observed: "The government cannot continue to support indefinitely Canadians in communities with little hope of employment." Both newspapers would apparently prefer every Atlantic Canadian to resettle in the Toronto area. Do they really want twenty-six million Canadians to live in Metropolitan Toronto?

While national governments in other countries attempt to spread economic activity more evenly, Outer Canadians see the historic pattern of power and wealth concentration in Central Canada flourish. Personal income per resident for Canada as a whole averaged about $18,070 in 1987, for example, but it was only $12,400 in Newfoundland (Fig. 6). The highest provincial income in the land was not far off twice the lowest.

Personal Income Per Capita by Province
1987

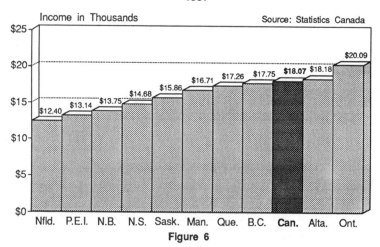

Figure 6

140

Across Canada, during 1989 and into 1990, there were 144 businesses started which already employ more than fifty individuals. Eighty-five of them — sixty per cent — are located in Ontario and Québec; 52 are in Western Canada; only seven are in the four Atlantic provinces. None is in the North. According to the Financial Post's 1989 ranking by sales or operating revenues, 365 of our largest 500 companies — 73 per cent — have their head offices in Ontario or Québec (Fig. 7). An even greater percentage of the largest financial institutions — four-fifths — are based in Ontario and Québec, leaving eighteen per cent for the West and a pitiful two per cent for Atlantic Canada. Toronto itself houses the head offices of forty-five of our large financial businesses, with nineteen in Montréal, three in Québec City, seven in Vancouver and two in Edmonton. The head offices of all six of the major chartered banks are located in Toronto or Montréal. Such head office concentration might be understandable for London or Paris in the case of relatively small Britain or France. In the United States it does not exist to nearly the same extent.

Head Offices of Top 500 Companies

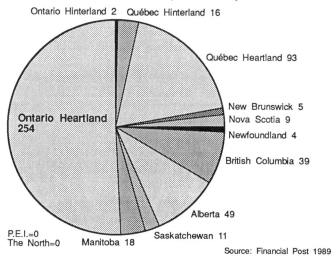

Source: Financial Post 1989

Figure 7

A strong argument can be made that our private sector must be free to locate corporate and head offices where it chooses and to expand where it is most cost efficient to do so. On the other hand, when Northern Telecom expanded to the United States its senior management was told informally that to be considered a responsible national company it must locate manufacturing facilities in different regions of the country. Northern Telecom complied, building its American manufacturing facilities in five regions. To its credit, it has done so in Canada as well. American-based companies, involved in manufacturing in various parts of the United States as responsible corporate citizens at home, should spread their Canadian subsidiaries across Canada, instead of concentrating them in Canada's Main Street.

During 1988, of the fifty fastest growing Canadian companies, two-thirds were Ontario or Québec companies. Only fifteen were in the West and only two called an Atlantic province home. Even more significant perhaps are the figures for the so-called companies of tomorrow. They include the up and coming along with some which have slipped out of the 500 largest, such as B.G. Checo International of Montréal, dealing in electronics, and Simplot Canada of Brandon, a fertilizer company. Only three per cent of these businesses now have their head offices in Atlantic Canada, twenty-four per cent in the West, and seventy-three per cent are in Ontario or Québec (Fig. 8).

"100 Companies of Tomorrow"-Head Offices
By Region

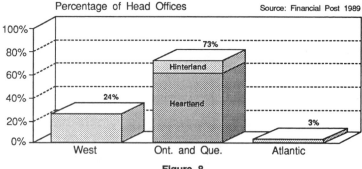

Figure 8

Despite some deficit reducing measures undertaken by the Mulroney government, Ottawa handouts to large businesses continue. Hundreds of private-sector companies, some very prosperous, receive billions in tax-payers' money each year as unnecessary subsidies. It is estimated that Ottawa today spends $8 billion annually on subsidies to promote exports, industrial expansion, research and development and related activities. This figure does not include a host of very large federal tax breaks and loan guarantees. For example, among eight companies from the 1988 list of beneficiaries, seven were headquartered in Ontario or Québec and one in Calgary. One of them, Noranda, with a net income of $603 million, received approximately $22 million in grants from federal taxpayers.

Between September, 1984, when the election of the first Mulroney government was elected and January of 1990, approximately 1.6 million jobs were created across Canada, virtually all by the private sector (Fig. 9).

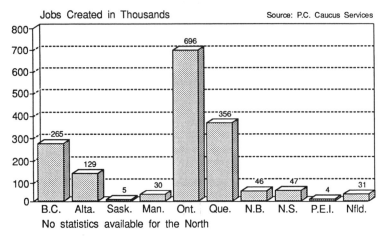

Figure 9

Approximately 8 per cent of the jobs created were in Atlantic Canada, 24 per cent were in Western Canada, and 65 per cent were in Ontario and Québec. As of December 1989, almost 80 per cent of the manufacturing jobs were in Ontario and Québec (Fig. 10). A common excuse from manufacturers in southern Ontario as to why they do less and less manufacturing in Outer Canada is that it lacks population from which employees might be recruited. However, a spokesman for one manufacturing company told me

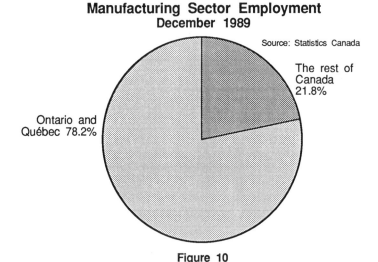

Figure 10
143

recently that they face on-going difficulty in hiring enough people for their three plants located within Metropolitan Toronto.

Regional Unemployment

The opposite side of this coin is the regional breakdown of unemployment rates. The Economic Council of Canada noted in its 1977 study of regional disparities that "Unemployment in some areas of Canada continues to be a national disgrace." Today, thirteen years later, the situation has not improved and in some locations has actually grown worse (Fig. 11).

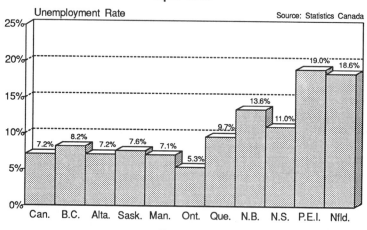

Unemployment Rates
By Province
April 1990

Figure 11

The difference among regions in unemployment rates of as much as eighteen percentage points shows that our recovery since the 1981 recession has been the most uneven of modern times. For example, in March 1990, the average unemployment rate across Canada was 7.2 per cent. In the same month, the unemployment rate in the Gaspé region of Québec was 23.1 per cent; in the Port-aux-Basques area of Newfoundland, 21.3 per cent; and in the New Brunswick counties of Northumberland, Restigouche and Gloucester, 20.6 per cent, while in the Toronto and Ottawa-Carleton regions the rate was 4.8 per cent.

The spring 1990 issue of Statistics Canada's *Canadian Social Trends* carried an article by David Gower, a Statistics Canada analyst, on regional unemployment in Canada. He concluded his analysis of the 1985-88 regional unemployment rates by saying that regional inequality in unemployment is growing, and the gap between the areas of high and low rates is widening. Statistics Canada figures reveal that almost all of our ten areas with the highest unemployment rates during 1988 were in the Atlantic provinces and peripheral parts of Québec. Non-metropolitan Newfoundland experienced the highest unemployment rate of any region in Canada in recent years: 19.2 per cent during 1988. Two hinterland regions in Québec, the Lower St. Lawrence and Lac St-Jean-Cote Nord, had the second and third highest unemployment rates in the country during 1988 with 13.8 per cent and 13.1 per cent respectively.

Gower concludes that in general, between 1985 and 1988, unemployment rates decreased about forty per cent in our ten highest employment regions, compared with a twenty per cent decline in the high unemployment ones. In the 1988 survey of forty areas across Canada, every one of the 10 areas with lowest unemployment rates came from Ontario with nine of those ten in southern Ontario.

As the Economic Council of Canada noted in its 1990 study of our national service sector, *Good Jobs, Bad Jobs*, "virtually all recent employment growth has involved either highly skilled, well compensated and secure jobs or unstable and relatively poorly paid jobs." By this, it meant that a computer programmer in a head office has a good service job and a bright future whereas a postal worker in a Newfoundland outpost has a meagre income and doubtful prospects. The growing division of service employment across Canada into "good-job" and "bad-job" sectors during the 1980s and 1990s will increase disparities between our regions because good jobs tend to be concentrated in large cities — the dominant centres of service growth — which are disproportionately located in the more developed communities within Ontario.

How are Ottawa's myriad agencies, departments and crown corporations doing in an age of instant communications in providing regional leadership to our private sector? Only five of forty of our largest or best-known national crown corporations have their head offices outside Inner Canada. Not one of the five is in Atlantic Canada. The five in Western and Northern Canada are: Canadian Wheat Board — Winnipeg; Cameco (formerly Eldorado Nuclear) — Saskatchewan; NWT Power Commission — Yellowknife; Petro-Canada — Calgary; and Canada Harbour Place Corporation — Vancouver. The other thirty-five are all located in either Ottawa or Montréal. Some seem especially out of place there given the nature of their activities and the locale of their clientele. Why, for example, do the St. Lawrence Seaway Authority, Farm Credit Corporation, Canada Ports Corporation, and Canadian Dairy Commission need to be in Ottawa-Hull?

Newcomers

In the crucial area of immigration as a stimulus to local economies, congested Inner Canada continues to be the disproportionately dominant destination of most newcomers to Canada. There are also concerns in Outer Canada that the proposed Ottawa-Québec City agreement on immigration in the wake of the collapse of the Meech Lake accord will mean in practice that Québec must receive twenty-five to thirty per cent of all future immigrants to maintain its present share of our population. This might well translate into a reality that nine other provinces are held back in the numbers of newcomers they can have in order to maintain this population ratio if Québec has difficulty in attracting its allotted share in a given year.

Between 1946 and 1986, approximately 3.5 million immigrants arrived in Canada. Nearly two million of them settled in Ontario. During 1988, the largest share of all categories of immigrants understandably went to booming Ontario: fifty-six per cent of the family class, fifty-five per cent of the independents, and fifty-four per cent of refugees and designated classes of newcomers. In the same year, 83,000 persons, or fifty-two per cent of the total number of immigrants, settled in three cities: Toronto, Montréal and Ottawa-Hull.

During 1988, approximately 4,000 business immigrants arrived in Canada (Fig. 12), with two-thirds going to Ontario and Québec, eight per cent to the Prairies, twenty-five per cent to British Columbia and the Yukon, and only two per cent locating in Atlantic Canada. It is estimated that entrepreneurs and self-employed individuals arriving during that year brought with them approximately $3.4 billion available for investment. Ontario and Québec received about half of this total. In Outer Canada, in fairness, British Columbia benefited from about $1.3 billion in new investments from immigrants.

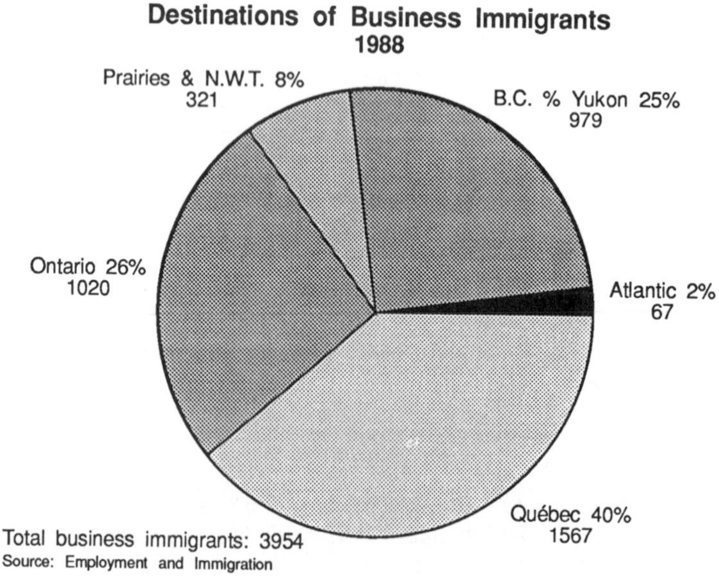

Destinations of Business Immigrants
1988

Prairies & N.W.T. 8%
321

B.C. % Yukon 25%
979

Ontario 26%
1020

Atlantic 2%
67

Québec 40%
1567

Total business immigrants: 3954
Source: Employment and Immigration

Figure 12

The "investor" group of immigration categories, which allows in people with $250,000 or more in cash, does not require that the investors live in the same province as their investment. A recent policy change authorizes such newcomers to invest $250,000 in Alberta, Saskatchewan, Manitoba, the Yukon, the Northwest Territories and the Atlantic provinces. Immigration policy-makers in Ottawa are in short so unfamiliar with business opportunities across Outer Canada that they actually believe that the specified areas could not attract new investment if the amount of $350,000 necessary for Ontario, Québec and British Columbia was maintained for the "boondocks."

Ottawa Spending

In advanced industrial democracies, government purchasing policy has long been recognized as an important instrument of economic policy in advanced industrial democracies. In Canada, Ottawa's regional procurement favouritism generates on-going federal-provincial conflict. Outer Canada governments claim with good reason that federal purchasing policies actively contribute to the growing concentration of industry in Ontario and Québec. "They are correct . . ." said Donald Savoie, an authority on regional development, during 1986. "About eighty per cent of all federal contracts are placed with firms in Central Canada." Professor Allan Tupper of the University of Alberta, in his *Public Money in the Private Sector: Industrial Assistance Policy and Canadian Federalism*, wrote in 1982 that Ottawa's Department of Supply and Services "seems rather resigned to the continuing pre-eminence of centrally-located firms" and concluded "Ottawa does not appear to have consistently employed purchasing policy as a regional development tool." There seems to be little sign of improvement since that time.

Always a factor in Canadian political decisions, the "numbers is politics" reasoning clearly prevails in the present pattern of Ottawa spending. This is at any rate how it is perceived by some provincial governments. They tend to interpret every discrepancy in the allocation of spending as Ottawa's regional bias. Frustrated with their recent experience in Confederation, they draw balance sheets showing they are losers in dealings with the federal government. If this federal government were to adopt regional criteria in allocating its overall procurement of goods and services, its large role as employer and purchaser would make it an efficient instrument to achieve greater regional fairness.

Government facilities, varying from armed forces bases to post offices, are scattered across the country. Where such facilities are built, where Ottawa turns for its supplies, where it hires and employs people, and where it establishes and maintains defence bases has important effects on the regional distribution of benefits. Its practices here also create an impression of regional fairness or unfairness. During the fiscal year 1987-88, total federal government spending on goods and services amounted to $9.6

Federal Government Procurement
By Province
1987-1988

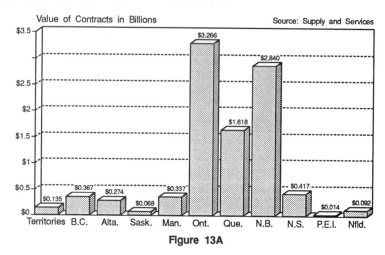

Figure 13A

billion (Fig. 13a and 13b). By total tax dollars spent, Québec and Ontario received 51 per cent of the government's purchases. The four western provinces got 10.9 per cent. Atlantic Canada's total of 35.2 per cent was much higher than normal because of the award of the patrol frigate contract to the Saint John dockyard. For the 1986-87 fiscal year, the numbers were even more distressing: Central Canada — 76 per cent, Western provinces — 11.5 per cent, and Atlantic Canada — 7 per cent.

Federal Government Procurement
By Region
1988-1989

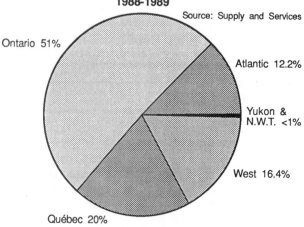

Figure 13B

Individual federal government departments and major federal crown corporations often display the same dreary pattern as far as their expenditures on goods and services are concerned. The chart "Spending on Goods and Services" graphically shows the procurement practices of some selected federal government departments and agencies (Fig. 14)

For example, Ottawa's Public Works ministry bought $106 million in goods and services in 1988-89. Eighty-three per cent was obtained through its offices in Ontario and Québec. During the same year, Labour Canada bought an astonishing ninety-three per cent of its goods and services within Ontario and Québec, including the National Capital Region. The Canada Council, which specifically denies any role for regional justice in its cultural mandate, purchases less than one per cent of goods and services beyond Toronto-Ottawa-Montréal. During 1988-89, the Ottawa-based International Development Research Centre placed orders with suppliers in eighteen different countries, including Ethiopia, Botswana, Sri Lanka and Panama. At home, however, during the same year a breathtaking ninety-nine per cent of its orders were awarded to suppliers in Ontario and Québec.

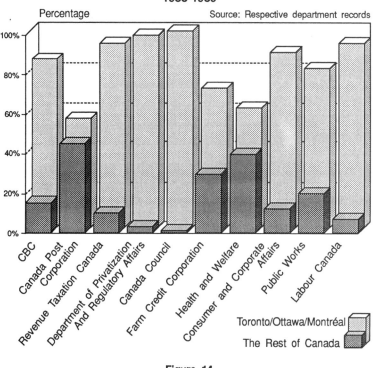

Spending on Goods and Services
1988-1989

Figure 14

149

One model of what national agencies might be, a clear exception to the norm, is the Federal Business Development Bank (FBDB). Eighty-five per cent of the FBDB regional and branch office supply expenses are made outside of the Toronto-Ottawa-Montréal triangle. It currently employs 1,250 persons across Canada: fifty per cent of the total number in Central Canada, thirty-six per cent in the West and fourteen per cent in Atlantic Canada. On a provincial basis, as of March 1988, the FBDB's loan portfolio included over 7,400 customers in Central Canada; 6,100 in Western Canada and 2,175 in the Atlantic provinces. This is a federal agency attempting to enfranchise every part of the country.

Defence Dollars

It is occasionally argued that defence spending should not be considered a regional development tool because of efficiency and vaguely-defined security considerations. Other NATO countries, however, have been more successful in stimulating local economic development in stagnant areas through the awarding of defence contracts and the location of bases. In Britain, where the southeast is already overcrowded with military research laboratories and facilities, there is growing pressure to move such facilities and service personnel to other regions of the country. Michael Heseltine, a possible Conservative successor to Margaret Thatcher, in his book, *The Challenge of Europe*, stresses the need to give the whole of the country a fair share of wealth-creating potential. Tim Sainsbury, the junior British Defence Minister responsible for procurement, set out the Thatcher government's position when he announced the transfer of 1,500 jobs from London to Teesside, in northeast England.

In Canada, as past statistics indicate and the April, 1989 federal budget reinforces, the trend is to concentrate defence-related activities within Inner Canada. A determined federal government as the principal customer for Canada's munitions industry could have major influence on where that industry is located. Despite its dependence on Ottawa for its so-called modernization grants as well, more than ninety per cent of the 3,000 jobs in that industry are within Ontario and Québec. According to Supply and Services unofficial departmental statistics for the period of April 1988 to February 1990, Central Canada received ninety per cent of the value of munitions contracts awarded ($333 million) (Fig. 15). The four western provinces received only eight per cent of the contracts, and the Atlantic provinces 1.3 per cent.

Defence-generated spending in the aircraft and parts industry also benefits Ontario and Québec virtually exclusively. For example, during the 1982-83 fiscal year, it provided Ontario and Québec with 75 per cent of available jobs. Offset contracts associated with our two major aircraft purchases, the CP-140 and CF-18, also go mostly to Ontario and Québec.

Under Ottawa's Defence Industry Productivity Program (DIPP), which is designed to assist high technology firms in the defence sector, ninety per

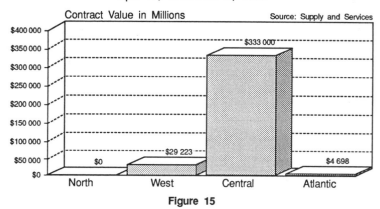

Munitions Contracts
By Region
Apr. 17, 1988-Feb. 6, 1990

Figure 15

cent of the payments in dollar value went to companies in Québec and Ontario during the fiscal year 1987-88. No-one in PEI, New Brunswick, Saskatchewan, Yukon or the NWT received a thin dime of this tax-payer-funded work. During the 1988-89 fiscal year, Québeckers and Ontarians received ninety-five per cent ($213.3 million) of the money available in the program. The four western provinces got four per cent and Atlantic Canada a mere $400,000.

In reply to my letter of inquiry about the DIPP's blatant regional unfairness, H.G. Rogers, the Deputy Minister of Ottawa's Department of Industry, Science and Technology, conceded in an early 1990 letter: "As you correctly stated, the majority of the money is spent in Québec and Ontario . . . . DIPP assistance is forthcoming in response to industry investment intentions. As most of the industry, and hence most of the new investment by industry is located in Central Canada, the majority of DIPP funds are also expended there." In other words, the ministry provides no guidelines to encourage using tax money paid by all Canadians to achieve even the tiniest degree of regional fairness on defence matters.

Even the Toronto *Globe and Mail* admitted editorially that "DIPP is really another regional development subsidy spreading federal money mostly in Québec and Ontario. Almost all of these companies can obtain financing through normal commercial means." Those receiving the funds are well-known names in Canada's aerospace, defence and high-technology industries, such as Spar Aerospace Ltd., Canadian Marconi Ltd., CAE Electronics Ltd. and Canadian Astronautics Ltd., but also privatized crown corporations such as Canadair Ltd. in Montréal, now owned by Bombardier, and De Havilland Aircraft of Canada in Toronto, a subsidiary today of Boeing. Bombardier received a $43 million loan to develop a regional passenger jet and De Havilland, $50 million to produce a series of its Dash 8 commuter plane.

According to the *Statistical Abstract of the United States 1989*, the American federal government in contrast allocates defence contracts in all fifty states. These cover military awards for supplies, services and construction. The total budget for 1987 was more than $131 billion. Of this total, fifteen eastern states received approximately thirty-four per cent of the contract funds; seventeen western states received approximately twenty-seven per cent; and eighteen central states received a third. Seventy-two per cent of the fifty states each received over half a billion dollars in defence contracts, and fifty-four per cent of the states received over a billion dollars. The average appropriation for defence contracts in each state was $2.6 billion. In short, elementary regional justice was done for virtually every corner of the country. According to our own Department of National Defence statistics for the fiscal years 1985-86 and 1986-87, a breathtaking seventy-seven per cent and sixty-six per cent respectively of the dollar values of contracts were awarded in the Montréal-Ottawa-Toronto triangle. The department says it did not keep records of financial activities by specific urban areas before 1985.

Analysis of the 1988 Public Accounts list of contracts awarded by DND by a specific area of specialization shows a less than equal distribution of contracts in Canada's regions. In 1987, for defence engineering services, Western Canadians received only eight per cent of the total allotted budget amount. In training and education, the Atlantic provinces received fourteen per cent of the contract but only 8.6 per cent of the funding by dollar amounts. For computer services, Central Canadians received no less than ninety-seven per cent of the budget. For scientific services, Central Canada received 96 per cent of the available contract funds.

The Department of National Defence study on its estimated spending in each federal constituency for the fiscal year 1988-89 did it little good in parts of Outer Canada. For its regular military and civilian staff then numbering 112,000 persons, only 8,400 were based in the three poorest provinces of Atlantic Canada. The cutbacks announced since then will reduce this number even further. The "have-not" Western provinces of Manitoba and Saskatchewan together included only 7,350 military personnel among their residents and these modest numbers will also shrink with the cutbacks at places like Portage La Prairie. In terms of defence spending on items other than salaries, the study is equally uninspiring from the standpoint of the hinterland. Atlantic Canada that year received about 17.3 per cent or some $793 million of such spending, but closer examination reveals that two-thirds of it went to Saint John for the frigate contract. Toronto's Etobicoke North riding alone received almost $500 million in the same year. In the West, Saskatchewan received a pitiful $16 million.

Obviously, such patterns can be reversed only through a new and iron-willed government direction. New defence spending policies which focus development on our Western and Atlantic provinces will not only help their economies but will also stimulate migration to these areas, which in turn will stimulate spin-off economic activities. It will also strengthen national unity and the sense that Ottawa is for once acting like a national government. As demonstrated in the United States, government spending can generate development in isolated areas. It can also promote a common national direction and teamwork among Canadians everywhere.

Research and Development

Research and development (R & D) is usually defined as creative work undertaken on a systematic basis to increase the level of scientific and technical knowledge and the use of this knowledge in new applications. If, on the world scene, Canada in general and our outer regions in particular do not want to be again relegated to roles as hewers of wood and drawers of water in the coming century, our R & D activities need to be assessed carefully. Spending on R & D is an important indicator of the national effort to stimulate creative activity, and is directly linked to technological innovation and economic growth. As the federal government is one of the major funders of R & D in Canada, the level and the distribution of such expenditures shows where Ottawa is concentrating its development efforts.

Ottawa, Toronto and Montréal are the three major "nodes" of science and technology within Canada. For example, more than 25,000 Ottawa-Hull residents work in high-technology firms or government labs. A quarter of the 1987-88 federal budget for R & D was spent in the National Capital region alone. The Western provinces received twenty per cent of the $2.3 billion our federal government spent on research and development

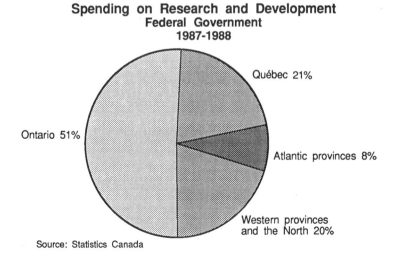

Spending on Research and Development
Federal Government
1987-1988

Québec 21%

Ontario 51%

Atlantic provinces 8%

Western provinces and the North 20%

Source: Statistics Canada

Figure 16

153

during 1987-88. Ontario got a little more than half; Québec approximately twenty per cent; and Atlantic Canada, eight per cent (Fig. 16). The Mulroney government is spending hundreds of thousands of public dollars to relocate the Space Agency from Ottawa to a community near Montréal, but declines to spend a greater share of Ottawa's R & D money across Outer Canada.

Much of Central Canada's dominance in research and development is because of the concentration of federal government scientific establishments in the region. In this regard, the recent decision by the Minister of Energy, Mines and Resources, Jake Epp, himself a Manitoban, to close a federal surface mining coal and oil sands laboratory at Devon, Alberta, the only such facility west of Ontario, is the opposite of regional justice, especially when his department already has three such labs in Ontario, one in Cape Breton and one more proposed for Québec.

Ottawa Mandarins

"There can be little doubt that Canada has been dominated economically since Confederation by Ontario and Québec and particularly by a relatively small group of people and companies located in Montréal and Toronto," concluded David Walker of the department of geography, University of Waterloo, when analyzing Canadian regional development policy in 1983.

A continuing conviction shared by Outer Canadians is that we are chronically under-represented in the public service of our country. Atlantic Canadians protested soon after Confederation about this; francophones have long complained that they are under-represented at more senior levels. Kenneth Kernaghan concluded in a 1978 study that middle levels of the pubic service were more representative of the country as a whole than were senior ones in terms of both birthplaces and geographical regions.

Two years later, Dominique Clift wrote that a disproportionate number of top officials were from Ontario. The journalist Jeffrey Simpson revealed during 1981 only one deputy minister and three of 198 assistant deputy ministers were Albertans. Roger Gibbins points out in his book, *Regionalism: Territorial Politics in Canada and the United States*, that as of 1982 provincial origin was not, in the mind of the Public Service Commission of Canada, a factor at all relevant to recruiting federal officials. By my own inquiry it has still not become one.

Toronto, Ottawa-Hull and Montréal together contain almost half of the more than 200,000 federal employees. About one third of federal government employees live in the National Capital Region. In the United States, the equivalent figure for Washington, D.C. is only twelve per cent. The new national Liberal Leader, Jean Chrétien, revealed during the early 1980s that only one out of seven senior executives in the federal public service lived outside Ottawa-Hull. Chrétien also noted that as many as seventy per cent of senior government policy makers in Ottawa had little or no regional experience and that as many as half of them never worked outside Ottawa during their entire careers. There appears to be a clear consensus now among federal mandarins that there is no such thing as a parallel career for their colleagues "in the regions." Job classifications, salaries and a host of other factors make it clear to everyone that the best careers are ones which begin and end in Ottawa.

Data on the regional or provincial composition of federal officials are difficult to find because, unlike linguistic and gender data, they are rarely recorded. My own survey of the 220 most senior individuals in twenty-eight federal departments and agencies in mid-1989 indicated that only about ten per cent were born and educated in Western Canada. Four per cent were from Atlantic Canada in both education and birth. Senior executives who were both born in and educated in either Ontario or Québec hold seventy per cent of the highest posts. Eight per cent of the top job holders were born outside Canada, but all of them had received at least part of their education in Ontario or Québec. None of these high-achiever newcomers to Canada had completed any post-graduate education outside Inner Canada. None of the officials surveyed was born or educated in the Yukon or Northwest Territories. The remainder were persons born in Outer Canada who later either moved to Ontario or Québec or completed their education there.

The experience of a Manitoba-born friend seems relevant here. Applying in Winnipeg for a professional position in the public service several years ago, she was shown only a small number of those available in her own province even though she was willing to relocate. She moved to Ottawa and shortly afterwards applied to the Public Service Commission where the list of available positions seemed endless. She quickly had an interesting position in the capital. Is this justice for all or only for those who can afford to move without first having a job?

During 1989, there were eleven senior executives in the Prime Minister's office (PMO), influential advisers in our system of unreformed executive democracy. My research that year showed that by location of birth and place of post-secondary education used to establish a criterion of regional origin the following breakdown applied to the PMO: of the eleven individuals, nine were both born and educated in Central Canada. The one person of the group who was born in the West was Don Mazankowski. There was no representation in the PMO from the North or from the Atlantic provinces. One, the Prime Minister himself, was educated at St. Francis-Xavier university in Nova Scotia.

The same basic regional composition of the PMO applied during 1989 to the twenty-five senior executives in the Privy Council Office. Of the twenty-five, all of whom were appointed with the exception of Don Mazankowski, sixty per cent were born in Ontario and Québec, and seventy-six per cent were educated there. In this group, who speaks for Outer Canada?

Information on the province of birth of employees in the management group is not readily available because selection in staffing is presumably based on merit and because candidates do not generally provide this kind of information. The provincial distribution of post-secondary degrees obtained may therefore serve as a rough indicator of the province of birth. Accordingly, as of December 1988, the regional breakdown of the overall management category of most but not all of the federal public service was as follows: Atlantic Canada — 6.9 per cent, Central Canada — 60.2 per cent, Western Canada — 14.4 per cent.

Reform of the Senate is currently at the centre of the growing national debate on how to provide better representation for regional interests in the major institutions of our national government. However, our federal public service and its ability to respond to legitimate regional aspirations has been largely ignored. One of the reasons why, as Donald Savoie suggests, may be the fact that so few academics across Canada understand the workings of our Ottawa public service. In Savoie's words: "Many people still cling to the belief that politicians set policies and public servants simply administer them and carry out ministerial directives." In reality, appointed Ottawa officials play the key roles in shaping most policies and in the decision-making process. Having served as a parliamentary secretary to four different cabinet ministers, this is certainly my own conclusion. Often, ministers in the Commons question period and elsewhere only mouth policy phrases prepared by their ministry officials.

Major policy decisions are normally made at the middle and senior levels of departments — often by an associate deputy minister for policy. Cabinet ministers are rarely in a position to have much influence on the first draft of a policy position paper or cabinet document. The aphorism in Ottawa, "who controls the first draft controls policy," carries considerable and probably increasing weight. Officials prepare the groundwork for the introduction of new policies and it is they who are, in practice, expected to reconcile regional interests while defining new programs and initiatives. It is therefore vital to look at the federal bureaucracy from a regional perspective in order to see who are the usually faceless personalities behind policies which affect Canadians in every corner of the country.

Our national government is a highly centralized organization with a disproportionate number of its key-decision makers originating from Inner Canada. The organizational capacity of our federal government to represent regional circumstances is both inadequate and showing very little improvement.

A new threat to regional balance among Ottawa mandarins, which Roger Gibbins and others have pointed out, has emerged from attempts to create a more linguistically balanced federal officialdom. During the 1970s and 1980s, the Public Service Commission designated numerous senior positions in many departments as mandatorily bilingual, thereby requiring persons filling them to have a relatively good command of both English and

French. Over a decade, this was coupled with good on-the-job language training which allowed unilingual officials to learn the other official language. The reservoir of bilingual people in and around Ottawa today is now sufficiently large that unilinguals in either official language are less likely to be hired or, if hired conditionally, to hold their positions if they fail what I'm told by officials is an increasingly difficult periodic language examination. Applicants from parts of Atlantic Canada as well as Western and Northern Canada and Québec, where only one official language is normally used, therefore face a growing language obstacle to a career in Ottawa. I agree with Professor Gibbins that the federal public service is therefore likely to become in future even less representative of Canadians generally than it is now.

Regional Policy Impotence

It is usually at the level of national policy making that Outer Canadians lose to politically-powerful Inner Canada. Some recent deficit-reducing programs have demonstrated a disproportionately stronger negative impact on Outer Canada.

The North is facing some very real new hardships as the Mulroney government proceeds with cost-cutting measures in selected programs. The new mail rates for northern commercial shipping went into effect on November 13, 1989. The average increase in postal rates is roughly thirty per cent for the entire North. Some of the immediate effects of the increase will be at least $300 more on family grocery bills; children going without fresh fruit and vegetables and the possible return of an old Arctic enemy — scurvy; the soaring cost of shipping essentials such as medicine and spare parts and even rifle shells; the potential for local disaster if some villages have to stop bringing in fresh spring water and go back to their old polluted wells.

On October 27, 1989, the task force on tax benefits for northern and isolated areas reported to the Minister of Finance, recommending massive cutbacks to a program which until now has tried to address basic needs of Canadians who live in the north — in short, insensitive measures by a government driven by the demands of its more vocal and influential southern business constituency.

The two most recent federal budgets, the VIA Rail cuts, and the goods and services tax, if analysed from a regional perspective, clearly hit parts of Outer Canada harder than Inner Canada.

For example, Atlantic Canadians, who were the largest per capita users of VIA Rail services, suffered most from the recent cutbacks. With ninety-one per cent cuts of the sixty-six weekly return trips in the Maritimes, only six are left: two tri-weekly long-haul trains. Fully sixty-three per cent of the VIA staff in Atlantic Canada were cut and the century-old regional headquarters in Moncton was closed. Overall, the cutbacks eliminated over three-fourths of the intra-Maritimes routes and reduced the frequency of all others by over fifty per cent. "Does Ottawa think Canada ends in Montréal?" asked John Pearce, the president of Transport 2000 Atlantic Branch, during an address to a rally on Parliament Hill opposing the cuts. He went on to ask about the disappearance of Prince Edward Island's bus service, and the end of all VIA trains to Cape Breton and connections to Newfoundland. The answers to his questions are suggested in the title of this chapter.

The number of seats offered by VIA Rail in the West was cut by 80 per cent. It was impossible to book a cross-Canada sleeper during the next six months, observed Darrell Richards, Transport 2000 national president. He also commented on a bizarre new VIA policy that bans the sale of tickets between Edmonton and Jasper within three days of departure — a move to limit the number of train-travelling Albertans to free more seats for bigger-dollar transcontinental passengers. The new restriction also affects passengers travelling on the Canadian train on two other stretches: between Capreol and Foleyet in Northern Ontario, and between Farlane, Ontario and Winnipeg. According to Alberta government estimates, $1.2 billion was injected into the Canadian economy by tourists and travellers on the transcontinentals operated in 1989. Reducing their capacity by eighty per cent is expected to eliminate about $900 million in badly needed economic activity.

Some of the 1989 budget measures have a major impact on rural communities across the country. Dismantling VIA Rail was felt hardest in small communities which lost one of their few major transportation links. The Canadian Forces bases to be closed were not in urban areas but in such communities as Summerside, Prince Edward Island; Mont Apica, Québec; Sydney, Nova Scotia; Portage La Prairie, Manitoba; and Port Hardy, British Columbia. As a cost-reducing measure, Canada Post is closing 1,500 rural post offices. Unlike urban centres, these smaller communities do not have other sources of economic development, and the losses in jobs and local business are unlikely to be absorbed easily by vulnerable local economies. Large cuts planned for the crop-insurance and regional development programs also target rural communities whose resources supplied Central Canada's manufacturing needs and now often need coherent development assistance urgently. "Ottawa is laying siege to rural life in Canada," commented Gerald Hodge of Simon Fraser University.

In a historical perspective, the natural and people resources of rural communities were indispensable; they still are in building a sprawling urban Canada. It is a matter of deep national injustice to continue with policies which hurt the most vulnerable and fragile economies of rural Canada.

The recent changes to unemployment insurance benefits under Bill C-21, passed by the House of Commons, have been widely seen as abandoning our most hard-pressed regions. The majority of witnesses who appeared before the Special Committee of the Senate on the bill shared an opinion expressed by Earl McCurdy of the Fishermen, Food and Allied Workers union, that the legislation is " . . . an attack on small communities; it is an attack on underdeveloped areas; and it is an attack on the basic decent foundations of our country. Bill C-21 is a classic case of blaming the victim." Under proposed changes, the claimants in a region such as St. John's, Newfoundland, with an unemployment rate of 12.4 per cent, would lose up to eleven weeks of benefits and would require three additional weeks of work to qualify for benefits. The analysis of the proposed benefit structure shows, the Senate Committee says, that the maximum duration of benefit entitlement would be reduced in the regions with high unemployment rates. For example, claimants in Central Nova Scotia, Hull, Sudbury, Northern Ontario, Southern Manitoba, Regina and the upper Fraser Valley would lose up to thirteen weeks of benefits. Some of these places have an unemployment rate higher than ten per cent. Claimants in Halifax, Calgary and Vancouver would lose up to twelve weeks of benefits.

One of the anomalies of the change in the duration of benefits, the senators say in their final report, is that regions such as St. John's, with 12.4 per cent unemployment, Montréal with 8.5 per cent and Northern Alberta with 9.3 per cent would all lose up to eleven weeks of benefits, while three regions with unemployment rates below four per cent, Toronto, Oshawa, and London, would lose a maximum of only three weeks of benefits. "The only other regions where the maximum loss would be limited to three weeks would be those with an unemployment rate in excess of sixteen per cent," noted the Senate report.

It is also our smallest and poorest provinces that might have lost in the decentralization provided for by the opting out clause in the Meech Lake agreement. In a looser Confederation, if larger provinces had opted out to run their own programs, the federal government might well not have been able to afford national programs, including hospital and medical care, which Manitoba, New Brunswick and Newfoundland could not finance themselves.

All in all, the Mulroney government is seen virtually everywhere throughout Outer Canada as having abandoned peripheral Canadians on a host of issues. In the 1988 national election, it lost most of its Atlantic MPs, all of its Northern ones and some of its Western ones. More than ever, Brian Mulroney is perceived as a prime minister of, by and for some Inner Canadians alone.

EIGHT
PRESSURE POINTS

The mood across Outer Canada during the summer of 1990 was anything but supportive of our present model of top-down democracy in Ottawa. We agreed with Inner Canadians on many issues, ranging from wanting lower interest rates to the need for stronger national leadership, but, unlike these fellow citizens, we urgently require changes to make our national government representative of all Canadians. Such changes relate to various fields: grants to cultural agencies, constitutional commitments, the handling of the taxation system. In each of them the pressure on national unity has increased: thus these issues deserve a closer look from the standpoint of Outer Canadians.

Culture and Communications

Cultural disaffection among Outer Canadians is a growing problem with national unity implications. The Canadian Broadcasting Corporation, a national crown corporation whose television and radio services are used by an estimated twelve million Canadians daily, is a major culprit. It should be a major unifying vehicle providing a broad cultural highway of national self-expression. It should allow Canadians everywhere to share a cultural heritage that reflects our full national diversity.

Neither the English nor the French television network of the CBC currently provides an adequate contribution with respect to regional and cross-cultural communications. This vein was first documented officially during 1977 when the Boyle Commission of Inquiry concluded that virtually all regular network CBC English television series were produced in Toronto with Ottawa providing some political programs. As for the rest of the country, said Harry Boyle, then chairman of the Canadian Radio and Television Commission (CRTC), the Prairies and Atlantic Canada provided virtually nothing, although British Columbia contributed more significantly (e.g., the recently terminated *Beachcombers*). The Commission concluded glumly: "The regions of English Canada, from sea to sea, exist chiefly during the summer vacation."

In the case of the French language Radio-Canada, based in Montréal, the presentation of the regions of Canada outside Québec was so extremely limited that the two solitudes were encouraged in the structures of the corporation. A content analysis of major national television and radio newscasts of the corporations done for the Boyle Commission in mid-1977 indicated the extent of the problem. The estimate of the common ground in the sampled English and French media was approximately 15 percent. More than half of the time used by Radio-Canada on Canadian news focused on Québec events, whereas on English news only 17 percent of the air time was devoted to Québec. The enforced separation of the two solitudes continues to be virtually total. For example, the television drama series *Lance et Compte* (*He Shoots, He Scores* — Radio Canada 1986) was extremely successful in Québec; its English audience was minimal. Some say this was because the English version was censored, but it certainly indicates important cultural differences. The 1977 drama by Radio Canada, *Duplessis*, was watched by two million Québeckers, a quarter of the population; in English Canada, the series attracted less than 5 per cent. CBC's television series, *The Nature of Things*, produced for twenty-seven years and sold to 30 countries, has never been shown in French in Canada.

Both the English and French CBC television networks give little attention to Outer Canadians. A study for the Boyle Commission revealed that Radio Canada and CBC devoted less than 1.3% of their sampled news time to British Columbia. To the four Atlantic provinces, Radio-Canada news allotted no time and CBC English television news devoted 3.2% of its time during the period surveyed. The Prairies received 13.6% of English television news time but only 2.8% of the French television time. The North got 13.6% of English television but only 1.3% of French television news time.

Toronto, Ottawa, Montréal and Québec City were the sources of 73 percent of both the television and radio news. Four of the larger cities in Outer Canada, Halifax, Winnipeg, Edmonton and Vancouver, could each muster just between one and two percent of the news items. All other communities in Outer Canada presumably failed to register at all on what the CBC editors thought was newsworthy during a ten-day period in our ongoing national story. Understandably, Harry Boyle's 1977 reporting letter to Prime Minister Trudeau stated that, "the CBC has thereby, in the commission's view, failed in its very important responsibility to 'contribute to the development of national unity' ". Both Outer and Inner Canadians will have to assess for themselves whether it's doing significantly better today.

The president of the CBC at the time, Al Johnson, conceded that the corporation had failed to adequately reflect English Canada and French Canada to each other. I am unaware of any independent or content analysis since 1977 which demonstrates substantive improvement on the television news side. It is my sense that things have improved only very little since the Boyle report of 1977.

The late-1989 study by the Fraser Institute's National Media Archive still chided the trend of our national media for unbalanced regional coverage. Based on an analysis of six topics (free trade, the federal election, labour, health care, privatisation and abortion) the study revealed that news from Ontario dominates media reporting, with nearly two-thirds of the CBC's and a little over half of the *Globe and Mail*'s coverage focusing on Ontario. The Atlantic provinces and Québec received minimal coverage from both media: 1.4 per cent and 9.7 per cent respectively. Prairie provinces took 22 per cent of the *Globe and Mail*'s coverage and only 8 per cent of CBC time. British Columbia did better with 18 and 22 per cent respectively. The North hardly attracted any story at all on the six issues analysed — 0.2 per cent.

A spring 1990 study by the same National Media Archive revealed that 90 per cent of the CBC stories on the GST originated in Ontario. The only other province that attracted attention was Alberta, where opposition to the GST is the strongest because of the absence of a visible provincial sales tax. Over half the coverage on CBC and two-thirds on CTV on the issue originated from Ottawa and more than one-third of the coverage on CBC came from the Toronto studio. The voice of Outer Canada, the region most adversely affected by the GST, was virtually absent.

The 1989 coverage of the Meech Lake accord by CBC was also highly Toronto-centred with almost 80 per cent of all statements coming out of the Toronto studio. None of the stories about Clyde Wells or Newfoundland, according to the National Media Archive, were broadcast from Newfoundland, and only 3 per cent of CTV's stories were.

On the CBC English radio news side, an internal corporation analysis suggests an exemplary record in reporting regularly from many centres across Canada. Radio news is clearly much more portable than television news, but even so it appears to deserve high marks as a vehicle for having Canadians speak to each other across often vast distances. An independent analysis of four major CBC AM radio programs, *As It Happens, Sunday Morning, Morningside* and *The House*, performed in 1985 by Professor Barry Cooper of Calgary, concluded that 78 per cent of the sampled items originated in Central Canada. This suggests that the current affairs section of CBC radio has yet to catch up with the Boyle Commission's recommendations.

A large part of Atlantic Canada's present difficulties are the put-downs it receives constantly from our national media. As a national institution concerned with national unity, the CBC should make an effort first to understand the region better, including its potential, and then to minimize the number of insults broadcast about the region. Why, for example, are CBC English television stations in the region (as elsewhere) only permitted about an hour daily for local news and current affairs in contrast to its English radio, which has seven or eight hours daily in prime time for local programs?

The standard argument of CBC English television against the charge that it constantly trivializes Atlantic Canada in particular and Outer Canada in general is that television costs more than radio. But Atlantic Canadians pay taxes too, and a lot more could be done if the Canadians-talking-to-Canadians part of the network's mandate was taken more seriously by both its senior management and federal cabinets. Why should CBC staff in Toronto be permitted to indulge Inner Canadian prejudices and in all likelihood their limited understanding of Atlantic Canada in choosing virtually everything that is shown on *The National*, *The Journal* and almost everything else appearing on the English network? Presumably the privately-owned CTV and Global television networks would improve their overall treatment of the region if our public network provided better leadership.

Harry Bruce's excellent book about Atlantic Canada, *Down Home*, provides another perspective on the CBC from Canada's east coast. In the mid-1960s, Jack McAndrew was based in Halifax as Chief of the Outside Broadcast department for the Atlantic region of the CBC. Increasingly he resented, in Bruce's words, "the cultural imperialism of his superiors in Toronto. The Maritime stories they wanted seemed always to be clichés, features about Anne of Green Gables, Highland games, national parks, and fishermen in slickers and rubber boots. When he suggested more original stories, CBC headquarters in Toronto insisted they were 'not representative of the region' . . . . They wanted only the most stereotyped stories from down here. If you didn't have a seagull shittin' on the lens, they just didn't want it." A man of real principle, McAndrew later turned down the best CBC job in the Maritimes, that of regional director, because it might have appeared that in accepting it he was endorsing its policy of gutting regional creative production. He quit the CBC in Toronto and with his family relocated to Charlottetown.

McAndrew complained that in the late 1970s under its former general manager, Peter Herrndorf, the English branch of the CBC sacrificed music, drama and variety programming in favour of becoming "a purveyor of information": "I say you find the soul of a nation in its artists, not in panel discussions on freight rates and free trade," he argued. Also the Boyle Commission noticed that the rare television adaptations of English novels about Canadian life tended to be "completely reshaped from within the CBC."

The Caplan-Sauvageau Task Force on Broadcasting Policy, after hearings across Canada, noted in 1986, "a widespread feeling that our broadcasting system, like so many other Canadian institutions, reflects reality largely as it is understood in Toronto and Montréal. Similarly, there is strong belief it also reflects the mainstream elite of central Canada. As a result, Westerners, Easterners, Northerners, women, natives, ethnic groups and minority groups in general feel that Canadian broadcasting neither belongs to them nor reflects them." Participants in a follow-up series of forums on broadcast policy, sponsored by the Canadian Association for Adult Education, reinforced this same message about helping, not hindering, the regions to develop voices on the national scene. Fil Fraser of Edmonton, a former CBC broadcaster, described CBC regions today as "a sham. The regions are not producing programming because they have no access to the network schedule and they don't have any money to produce with."

Yet a third volley from Outer Canadians was presented to the House of Commons Committee on Communications and Culture during 1987 in St. John's. Robert Paterson of the Canadian Union of Public Employees, objecting strongly to a recommendation of the Caplan-Sauvageau Task Force that all CBC television production in Atlantic Canada be done henceforth in Halifax, pointed out that the proposed regional centralization "cuts some regions out of the national dialogue . . . . Newfoundland and Labrador, along with the other regions of Canada, need to preserve their ability to present themselves to other Canadians and tell them what they think."

In Halifax, David Colville, on behalf of the Nova Scotia government, lamented that "the problems of gaining either regional or national network time and money must be resolved in CBC head office in Toronto. The standing joke here is the $500 cup of coffee." He looked forward fondly to a day when regional and national programming would be decided together. In Halifax, Alexa McDonough, leader of the Nova Scotia New Democratic Party, spoke of her province's "wealth of real, long-established cultures . . . . Nova Scotians do not want a broadcasting policy that enables us to be more like Torontonians, no disrespect intended to Torontonians. We want a broadcasting policy that helps our unique Nova Scotian character to grow and flourish on our terms, as well as maintaining healthy ties with our fellow Canadians."

In Moncton, New Brunswick, Liane Roy of the Acadian Society made the point that the Radio Canada national news received in New Brunswick "often concerns Montréal and does not reflect the situation in New Brunswick." Claude Thériault, president of the Canadian Artists' Representation, made essentially the same point to the same hearing: "the programs produced by la Maison de Radio-Canada in Montréal do not reflect the reality of the French language community throughout Canada." Going on about his problems in obtaining more regional programming, he complained, " . . . every time we try, we are told that programming is the responsibility of headquarters. Headquarters is either in Montréal, in terms of decision-making, or in Toronto. And in both cases what you get is a reflection of those provinces. You do not get a reflection of the Canadian situation."

In Northwestern Ontario, David Wright told the Communications Committee that his region consists of over 100 counties and is the size of France but must obtain its local TV news from CBC Winnipeg. "The alienating affect of this is hard to overestimate until you live here and realize your community is never mentioned on any national network and no sporting event in your area is ever covered by a local reporter . . . . Our area is, by default, portrayed as an accident-prone 'empty quarter' rather than in its true colours as a fascinating and diverse territory . . . . Only a disaster or a federal or provincial election will draw a TV crew."

For years, the CBC has not troubled itself much with discharging its legislated mandate to be a cultural link between our diverse cultures and with regions. A regional consensus appears to exist across the country that our private television broadcasters are even worse.

The proposed amendments to the Broadcast Act as specified in Bill C-40, now at the report stage in the House of Commons, might result in the phrase presently in the CBC's mandate that it "contribute to the development of national unity" being removed in the new act. Replacing it is the requirement that the CBC "contribute to shared national consciousness and identity." In view of the reality that the CBC in its own interpretation of the unity mandate has quite often been dangerously close to becoming a voice for the government of the day, and perhaps never more so than in its coverage of the first ministers' meeting in June, 1990, I believe that relieving CBC of its national unity mandate in the area of news reporting should result in fair, unbiased and accurate journalism. However, in other areas of broadcasting such as public affairs, entertainment, special events, sports, etc., the CBC should continue to remain a vehicle of Canadian unity by reflecting regions of the country and by explaining Canadians from urban and remote communities to one another.

The performing arts grants by the Canada Council for support to the arts go disproportionately to Inner Canadians. The grant figures over a period of years indicate that cultural groups in the Toronto region and in Montréal get more than half of the Council's grants to metropolitan areas. Spokespersons for the Council insist that regional fairness is not part of this mandate. It is self-evident that Toronto and Montréal have both more industrial and corporate patrons of the arts and larger populations to fill theatre seats.

The experience of the Canada Council's exploration grants programs in recent years may be representative. The program was established to provide federal support for projects in fields such as theatre, film, writing, music, dance and other visual arts. The regional breakdown of the contracts seems reasonably fair on a population basis, but again, bearing in mind the economic state of the various provinces, the Council should direct more of its grants to Outer Canadians and fewer to the Toronto-Ottawa-Montréal based artists. Generally speaking, Outer Canadian artists need more help, whereas some of their counterparts in the favoured cities do not. Ottawa's excellent Little Theatre, for example, has operated successfully for many years without a nickel of federal, provincial or municipal money. It is now almost impossible to obtain a ticket to its plays shown during the winter season.

The federal government spent more than two-thirds of its 1987-88 expenditures on culture in Ontario and Québec; the Atlantic provinces, having about 9 per cent of our population, received a mere 6.3 per cent of the money and the Western provinces and the North, having approximately 30 per cent of the population, received 15.4 per cent.

Telefilm, the national film and television production agency in Montréal, has a strong Central Canadian tilt. When, during a Commons Communications and Culture committee hearing in the summer of 1989, I confronted its executive director, Pierre DesRoches, with the fact that most of the movie and television projects it had supported in recent years had been in the Toronto-Ottawa-Montréal triangle, he replied that regional considerations are not a factor in allocating funds. One of the problems with Telefilm is that its notion of Canada appears to stop at the limits of Toronto and Montréal.

Newspapers and magazines are influential cultural forces. They are read by millions of Canadians and inform them on a wide range of topics, from professional sports to economics. Public opinion is at least partly fashioned by the print media. A survey of national reader habits done by Statistics Canada during 1978 found that 62 per cent of those surveyed about what they read in newspapers said they "read usually" local and regional news. Another 18 per cent said they read such news "sometimes." A study done for the 1981 Kent Royal Commission on newspapers found that more than two-thirds of readers said they were very interested in local and regional news. Such information should accurately and fairly reflect the communities across the country, including their full range of opinion, attitudes and perceptions on issues of community concerns.

At the turn of the century, 114 daily newspapers were published across Canada. Eighteen cities each had more than two daily papers. A further seventeen communities published two daily papers. By the start of World War I, there were 138 dailies and 138 publishers. Today, there are 110 dailies and only seven Canadian cities have two or more daily papers in the same language and under different ownership. Competition is healthy in only four cities of Outer Canada: Edmonton, Calgary, Winnipeg and Québec City. As a rule the dailies in Outer Canada are owned and managed by Inner Canadians.

In Western Canada, a number of historically proud regional voices have been humbled in recent years, including the *Vancouver Sun*, *Victoria Daily Colonist*, and *Victoria Times*. *The Winnipeg Tribune* was closed. Today, as Vancouver's George Woodcock notes, "an independent press has ceased to exist beyond the Rockies. Every word printed every morning and afternoon in British Columbia appears on sufferance of powerful combines whose headquarters are in Central Canada or even farther away." In Alberta, the Toronto-based Southam and Sun publishing companies own the competing dailies in both Edmonton and Calgary. In Saskatchewan, the Armadale Corporation owned by the Toronto-based Sifton family owns the only daily newspapers published in Regina (*The Leader Post*) and Saskatoon (*The Star Phoenix*). In Manitoba, there appears to be a strong consensus among both readers and journalists that the 1980 passage of the *Winnipeg Free Press* into the hands of Toronto's Thompson chain weakened its traditional position as an independent and strong Prairie voice, at least outside its editorial pages. Three large companies dominate 90 per cent of the market in Québec: Pierre Pladeau's Québecor, Paul Desmarais's Gesca, and Jacques Francoeur's UniMédia. In the overall English-language market across Canada, the Southam and Thompson chains control 59 per cent of the circulation between them and the Irvings in New Brunswick control another 15 per cent.

The recent purchase by Ottawa's National Gallery of "Voice of Fire" by the American artist, Barnett Newman, generated much public outcry over the $1.8 million spent on one addition to the Gallery's collection. Cultural institutions in Outer Canada already envy the $3 million yearly budget of the National Gallery. Many Canadian artists from different parts of the country, moreover, are seriously under-represented in the Gallery's collection. The "Voice of Fire" incident, among other things, has reinforced the view that national cultural agencies financed by all the taxpayers respond mostly to the tastes of a small elite in Inner Canada.

Meech Lake Mayhem

The Meech Lake accord was widely seen in the outer eight provinces as an accommodation of political and business elites in Inner Canada. Few Outer Canadians were surprised that the three reluctant assemblies were all in peripheral provinces. When Elijah Harper, an Indian member of the Manitoba legislature, deftly used the rules to kill the accord, Outer Canadians were generally very supportive. Clyde Wells of Newfoundland has been the real scourge of the Meech Lake defenders. The Prime Minister denounced him when the Newfoundland legislature rescinded its earlier accord approval and when he refused to hold a vote after Harper stopped it in the Manitoba legislature.

The road to these incidents in the Manitoba and Newfoundland legislatures began with the 1980 Québec referendum on sovereignty-association, which was lost by the Parti Québécois by approximately 40 per cent to 60 per cent. During the emotional campaign that preceded the referendum, Prime Minister Pierre Trudeau promised that a "no" victory would bring renewed federalism. Many Québeckers concluded he had in mind the more decentralized model advocated by then Québec Liberal leader Claude Ryan. Trudeau never went out of his way to correct this impression. Real bitterness grew in the province when it turned out during the constitutional wars of 1980 and 1981 that this was not his concept at all.

Following months of terribly divisive wrangling, all the first ministers except René Levesque signed a compromise constitutional package containing a popular Charter of Rights that was proclaimed by the Queen in Ottawa on April 1, 1982. No one had any doubt that the provisions of both the old and the new constitution applied as much to Québec as to any other part of Canada. René Levesque himself recognized this by invoking the notwithstanding clause of the 1982 Constitution Act to declare that all Québec statutes were to be expressly excluded from the federal Charter of Rights.

In late 1985, when the Québec Liberals defeated the Parti Québécois, the resurrected premier, Robert Bourassa, put forward five conditions for his government to sign the 1982 Constitution: recognition of the province as a distinct society; a veto for Québec on constitutional amendments; a larger role for the province in immigration; a provincial role in appointments to the Supreme Court of Canada; and limitations on federal spending power. At the time, these principles offended few Canadians, including the premiers of the day. Presumably, most believed that no one's rights anywhere would suffer by respecting them.

During the next ten months, Brain Mulroney, who had been Canada's prime minister since September, 1984, and Qubec's premier Robert Bourassa lobbied the other premiers. Following a 19-hour bargaining session in an elegant cottage beside Meech Lake in Gatineau Park, and to the astonishment of many, all eleven signed an agreement on April 30, 1987. The accord achieved the very important goal of bringing Québec amicably to the constitutional table. However, when the fine print was later examined, nothing in recent Canadian history, including the 1980-82 patriation of the Constitution and the Canada-U.S. free trade agreement, revealed deeper differences among Canadians.

Both major Québec political parties — the Liberals and the Parti Québécois — and probably a majority of French-speaking Québeckers had rejected Pierre Trudeau's 1982 Constitution, a fact that was of grave concern to anyone who sees Canada as essentially a family. Nor can anyone minimize the potential appeal of nationalist voices in Québec now the Meech Lake accord has failed. The August 13, 1990 win of the Bloc Québécois candidate Gilles Duceppe in the East Montréal by-election with 68 per cent of the votes is a clear indication of the mood in a post-Meech Québec. Unfortunately, the Québeckers speaking up then and now for the province as a continuing part of Canada were neither as numerous nor as articulate as Canadians generally expected. The Parti Québécois, which won approximately four in ten votes during the 1989 provincial election with an openly separatist platform, clearly wanted it to fail. Robert Bourassa's comments about the need for a new government "superstructure" if the Meech Lake accord expired and statements afterwards about the need for full political sovereignty disturbed many non-Québeckers. Equally troubling were various opinion polls indicating that a majority of residents of the province judged that failure of the accord to win acceptance would significantly increase the likelihood of independence for Québec. The prime minister of Canada, moreover, strongly reinforced the "either-or" view, presumably as part of his win-at-any-cost strategy to obtain support from all ten provincial legislatures before June 23, 1990.

Arrayed against these factors were major defects in both the process and substance of the accord. Eleven first ministers reached an agreement in secret meetings. They were able to ram their private deal through their legislatures untouched later on, relying on what is probably the most extreme party discipline in the democratic world. How could they presume to exercise exclusive control over constitution-making? Why was there no real participation of the ordinary citizen in this process through the convening of a constitutional assembly or some other means? Why were Canadians not even afforded the opportunity to approve or reject what amounted to a new constitution in a subsequent national referendum? One of the original Meech Lake group, Richard Hatfield of New Brunswick, had earlier rejected any notion of allowing Canadians to express themselves on constitutional issues: "I am opposed to a referendum at any time for any purpose. Any referendum is an attack on our superior system and should never be encouraged." It appears that Hatfield was not in touch with his province on this and other matters. In his first rendezvous with voters after his participation at Meech Lake, they elected only Liberals, led by Frank McKenna, to the New Brunswick Assembly.

Examining the Meech Lake accord during the summer of 1987, the House of Commons-Senate Committee conceded that its public hearings were little more than a charade. It noted in its report that, in future, both "legislators and the public must be encouraged to participate in the process of Constitutional change before and not after First Ministers meet to make decisions." Outer and Inner Canadians alike agreed it was unacceptable democratic and constitutional practice for provincial premiers to arrogate to themselves alone the right to remake the constitution.

Constitution-making Elsewhere

Other democracies have updated their constitution with full democratic legitimacy. The United States did it two centuries ago after winning independence from Britain. Most of the American states were then behaving like independent republics, with seven of the thirteen issuing their own currencies and showing mostly indifference to the fate of the larger union. A number of national leaders in the War of Independence responded to a growing paralysis by meeting during 1787 in convention at Philadelphia to devise an improved system of government.

Fifty-five delegates from all but one of the American states refashioned the American constitution, albeit behind closed doors, in meetings which lasted four months. At the end, thirty-nine individuals signed the document, a safe majority. It included George Washington, who said it was about as good as could be expected and could be corrected later by amendments. Federal and constitutional laws were to override all conflicting state ones. No longer would the union be "a firm league of friendship" among the states. A new national government was to be established by the American people as a whole. Each state, large or small, got two senators with six-year terms as all states were nominally equal. The voice of the people in the House of Representatives, based on population, would be heard frequently through biennial elections. Both chambers were equal on most legislative matters, although initially only the House could originate tax measures.

A system of checks and balances, so absent in Canada's national government, was established by placing each of the executive, legislative and judicial branches on a separate basis of authority. Voters were the ultimate source of power, but the delegates wished to minimize the risk of one political party capturing the entire government, presidency, House of Representatives, Senate and federal judges, in a single election. The House and Senate were to balance each other in legislation and Congress and the President were to check each other. Members of the federal judiciary, having the final word on what the new constitution meant, were appointed for life to provide them with the necessary independence. Both they and the president, however, could be ousted for cause by the Congress through an impeachment process.

For constitutional amendments, the Americans dropped the rule of the earlier articles of Confederation which required the consent of every state. Instead, amendments could be proposed by a two-thirds vote in each house or upon application from the legislatures of two-thirds of the states for a constitutional convention. Amendments proposed by either method would go into effect when ratified by the legislatures or conventions in three-fourths of the states.

The constitutional proposals were sent by the Philadelphia delegates to Congress for approval with two recommendations: first, it should be returned to each state for approval at special conventions to be chosen by state voters, and, second, it should be ratified by nine states among the thirteen before going into effect, leaving dissenting states, if any, without any national roof. A furious national debate followed, but conventions were elected in all states to assess it. By mid 1788, nine states had ratified. By 1790, the rest had come on board. The victors in seven of the states had agreed to enact a bill of rights through amendments to the constitution, which was done the following year. The American people early on pointed the way to constitutional change on an essentially democratic model.

Following World War II, West Germany provided a modern example of democratic constitutional renewal that might have considerable appeal to Canadians for a post-Meech Lake reform of our constitution. Like Canada today, the regions of Germany which became the Federal German Republic faced a major crisis in 1948 when the Soviet Union withdrew from the four-nation occupational government. A constituent assembly was convened with sixty-five delegates being chosen on a population basis from each state. In fact, the delegates were chosen by the various state legislatures and were mostly members of them. Mirroring closely the strength of the various political parties at the time, delegates met in a series of committees for five months before producing a new constitution.

Subsequently, the assemblies of all states except Bavaria approved the proposals and the first national elections were called under its provisions in late 1949. On the promise that the Basic Law was a creation of representatives of the entire population, the refusal of the Bavarian parliament to approve it was considered unfortunate but legally insignificant. Bavarians in fact have participated as fully as any residents in the Federal Republic since its inception.

"Distinct Society"

The text of the Meech Lake accord eventually attracted even greater criticism than its elitist and secretive process. Naming Québec as a distinct society in an interpretation clause rather than in the preamble or in a substantive provision created uncertainty about its scope. The province is clearly distinctive, linguistically, culturally and demographically, but many of us worry that this provision, as worded and placed in the accord, would have allowed the language and other rights of non-French speaking Québeckers to be adversely affected by future Québec legislation designed to enhance this distinctiveness.

Multicultural, women's and aboriginal communities were sceptical about the protection, if any, afforded them under the Meech Lake agreement because their rights to equality were not included, as well, even within the interpretation section. Women's organizations contended that the accord placed their Charter of Rights-based equality rights in serious jeopardy. Ethno-cultural communities worried that the "linguistic duality — distinct society" provisions might be used to weaken the present constitutional position of the eight to nine million Canadians having their origins in nations other than Britain or France. Aboriginal leaders resented that their excellent claims to distinctiveness and constitutionally-recognized self-government were not even mentioned in the accord, itself completed only a few weeks after the Aboriginal-First Ministers Constitutional Conference concluded with nothing substantive achieved.

The immigration provision was a particular sore point in some of the outer eight provinces. Why should the constitution of Canada provide for immigration agreements between Ottawa and provinces which appear likely, on the basis of the current Canada-Québec agreement, to guarantee that Québec would receive one quarter of all immigrants coming to Canada each year? How could a better population balance among the provinces ever be reached without increased immigration to the outer ones? The federal-provincial agreement already in effect on immigration appeared to explicitly prevent this from happening.

In the spring of 1990, Angus Reid-Southam News conducted an opinion survey which found that opposition in Outer Canada to enacting the Meech Lake accord in its original form was 73 per cent in British Columbia, 64 per cent in Alberta, 74 per cent in Saskatchewan and Manitoba and 65 per cent in Atlantic Canada. Specific objections in Outer Canada to the Meech Lake accord came from aboriginal peoples, women, linguistic minorities, most ethno-cultural groups, northerners, and many of those favouring a Triple-E Senate.

In Manitoba, Howard Pawley, who had signed the accord, was replaced as premier by Gary Filmon with a minority Conservative government, before it could be ratified by the legislature. Following the passage of Qubec's law banning English on outside commercial signs, Filmon angrily withdrew the accord from his assembly. Afterwards, he, Manitoba Liberal leader Sharon Carstairs and NDP leader Gary Doer, maintained one of the tightest all-party alliances in Canadian history until the recent Manitoba election was called. Until the dying moments of the first ministers' June meeting in Ottawa, they held firmly that the agreement could not be passed without prior substantive amendments. Manitoba public opinion remained so strong in support of this all-party position that whichever of the three parties broke from the consensus seemed likely to lose most of its seats in an ensuing provincial election.

In Saskatchewan, Grant Devine's Conservative government pushed the accord through quickly with little legislative opposition or public debate. The Social Credit majority in Victoria also passed it with minimal scrutiny. Nonetheless, one clear lesson from the regional debate was that Westerners were no longer homogeneous on constitutional issues. Alberta Premier Don Getty managed to obtain passage in the Alberta legislature without public hearings, but ones held by the New Democrats heard 150 groups and individual presentations which were sharply critical.

One of the submissions came from Eugene Forsey, Newfoundland-born and probably Canada's leading constitutional scholar, who excoriated the proposal. He was confident that the effect of the unanimity feature of Meech meant that every province would have an absolute veto over most future proposals involving constitutional amendments. He saw the implications for the territories as a "gratuitous buffet in the face for the Yukon and the Northwest Territories, and delivered by a body in which they were not represented and which, as far as I know, gave them no chance to be heard." For aboriginals, Forsey expressed regret that at the very least the list of matters to be discussed at First Ministers' Conferences should have included aboriginal rights. On the distinct society, he argued that its presence in the interpretation section of the accord meant that the courts were being directed to interpret the constitution in a manner consistent with the principle of Québec being a distinct society. Would the position of

English-speaking Québeckers deteriorate if this occurred? He also concluded that the principle of language duality, as worded and located in the Meech Lake accord, would amount to "sheer humbug" for French-speaking Canadians in the other nine provinces. The clamour for changes in the agreement soon mounted, led in large measure by the new Liberal premier of Newfoundland, Clyde Wells.

First Ministers' Meeting in Ottawa

Many Canadians noted the seven-day first ministers' meeting in Ottawa and most were offended by its secrecy. Even the participants were distressed enough to agree to consider at the next constitutional conference using mandatory public hearings before adopting future constitutional amendments. What fools they thought Canadians if they believed anyone could now believe such self-serving nonsense. Their sudden reformation was weak and tardy.

The Prime Minister revealed his personal agenda the following week during a *Globe and Mail* interview. The entire first ministers' exercise, he boasted, was deliberately timed by him to bring the impasse down to eleventh-hour negotiations. He had told his advisers a month earlier when the meeting would occur during the first week of June. "That's the day we're going to roll the dice." He also expressed no regrets — "none whatsoever" — about the absence of public debate on the constitutional negotiations, contending that the private talks followed the precedent set by Canada's founding fathers. "This is the way Confederation came about. There was no public debate; there was no great public hearings. It became a kind of tradition." This was, of course, historical illiteracy. There was intensive public input and debate before Confederation. The *Confederation Debates* which records the various proceedings is a volume of 1,032 pages and is known by anyone who has ever looked seriously at our history.

According to Michel Gratton, Mulroney's former press secretary, after the *Globe and Mail* interview was printed the prime minister telephoned Clyde Wells to persuade him that his schedule was simply too full to hold the first ministers' meeting at any other time. Senator Lowell Murray's travels across the country to meet with all ten premiers in search of sufficient consensus to call a meeting was a farce. The prime minister knew he'd be convening a conference even though he had protested repeatedly there would be no meeting if it was doomed to failure. In short, outright deception is a perfectly acceptable practice in Brian Mulroney's Ottawa. The meeting, when held, was almost identical in form to Montréal labour negotiations held during the 1960s.

First Ministers' Agreement

Substantively, the first ministers' doomed agreement in June 1990 on the Meech Lake accord was essentially a worthless bauble for all who had concerns about features of the accord.

For example, a federal-provincial-territorial commission, appointed by the three levels of government, was to hold hearings on Senate reform and make recommendations to a First Ministers' Conference to be held by the end of 1990. Given that there have been eight or nine official studies on Senate reform, a further one was clearly unnecessary, but at least this one was to report quickly. If the Meech Lake accord had passed, any substantive Senate reform would have required the unanimous agreement of eleven legislatures, a prospect unlikely, in practice, to disturb the status quo.

To create new provinces out of the Yukon and Northwest Territories, the first ministers agreed that future conferences should address options for their provincehood, including the only reasonable one (to Outer Canadians) that they should become so exclusively by a joint representation of Commons and Senate. This was useless because the Meech Lake accord, if passed, would have afforded a veto to every provincial legislature on giving the two territories provincial status. The agreement threw the territories only two very small sops: discussion on any issue that the prime minister exclusively decides affects them, and a non-binding promise that once the Meech Lake accord was ratified the role of the two territories in Senate and Supreme Court of Canada appointments would be a subject of future constitutional amendments.

A three-paragraph legal opinion from six lawyers was attached to the first ministers' agreement, which the Prime Minister and some of the premiers claimed ensured that the distinct society clause would not be used as a sword to reduce rights within Québec. Most Canadians are immediately skeptical of anything said by lawyers in three paragraphs. More seriously, the best known of the jurists, Peter Hogg, was so identified with the pro-side of the Meech Lake debate that the legal objectivity of the opinion was suspect to many. Nor was the thrust of the opinion as helpful as Meech Lake defenders might wish. For example, it said that the protection of the Charter is "not infringed or denied" by the distinct society clause, but then added that it "may be considered, in particular, in the application of section I" (which says that rights are "subject only to such reasonable limits prescribed by law as can be demonstrably justified in a free and democratic society"). The opinion also conceded that the clause could be considered by courts in determining whether a Québec measure fits within the legislative authority of the province.

I agree with John Whyte, dean of the law school at Queen's University, that the opinion was "confusing in intent, substance and effect" and that under the surface it described a process by which the rights of Canadians living in Québec were probably going to be diminished. Like so much in the hurried agreement, it was also legally irrelevant. Instead of referring the distinct society and other controversial clauses to the Supreme Court of Canada for an opinion, as could have done at any time during a three-year period, Brian Mulroney persuaded most of the premiers to attach a letter with little legal weight. It was neither signed by any of the premiers nor adopted as sound by them. No court can give weight to a legal opinion bearing only a very thin veneer of government sanction and neither confirmed by legislative resolution nor endorsed by government resolution. Legal mayhem would otherwise result. The lawyers' letter in essence constituted a sordid little manoeuvre to attempt to convince the first ministers and Canadians generally that the Charter of Rights would apply in all provinces to the same degree.

Apart from the constitutional guarantee of equality the agreement gives to both official languages within New Brunswick, linguistic minorities in the other nine provinces and territories received nothing substantive. Changing anything in the important area of languages would require either the unanimous consent of all premiers or a constitutional amendment, which could be vetoed by any legislature.

The agreement promised that at first ministers' constitutional conferences held every three years, representatives of aboriginal peoples would be invited to participate in the discussion on matters of interest to them. An amendment of the constitution, presumably in relation to the constitutional rights of aboriginals, would be sought from provincial and federal legislators. The overwhelming opposition to the passage of the Meech Lake accord by aboriginal peoples across the country was thus understandable. They received nothing from the agreement except a commitment to discussions once every three years.

The agreement noted various failed efforts over two decades to draft a statement of constitutional recognition, a "Canada clause," and said all drafts might be submitted to a Special Committee of the Commons. Following public hearings, it would report to the first ministers at the end of 1990. Unfortunately for Canadians interested in substance, given that the Meech Lake accord would then have been the central part of our constitution with a unanimity rule, this was nothing but more warm air from our first ministers.

Many who were familiar with the practices in other federations worried that the Meech Lake accord's requirement of unanimity by all provincial legislatures for constitutional amendments would, in practice, make them impossible. The first ministers' agreement again bound no first minister to anything except further discussion at constitutional conferences. In short, the first ministers promised Canadians "peace in our time" in a way very reminiscent of Neville Chamberlain's pledge to Britain after the Munich agreement of 1938. The public participation in the process was so minimal and the crisis atmosphere created by supporters of the agreement so blatant as to repulse any Canadian democrat. The only substance to the first ministers' agreement was the entirety of the 1987 Meech Lake accord. Something far too important to be left to well-meaning or scheming politicians — the constitution of the country — would have been usurped by them except for a courageous Outer Canadian, Elijah Harper.

Goods and Services Tax

Few policies of the Mulroney government since 1984 have provided more outrage among Canadians generally than its proposed goods and services tax (GST). In parts of Outer Canada, however, the opposition to the tax continues to be the strongest. An Angus Reid poll published in early 1990 found, for example, that 77 per cent of Alberta residents opposed the seven per cent proposal. In British Columbia, 65 per cent opposed the tax; in Manitoba and Saskatchewan, 72 per cent; in Atlantic Canada, 68 per cent. The weakest level of opposition was in Ontario (62 percent). A survey completed by Decima Research for Ottawa's Finance department in January, 1990, concluded that only 14 per cent of Canadians generally were in favour of the GST. Reid's regional samples may have been too small to be statistically significant.

The goods and services tax intended to take effect in January 1991 plays very clear regional favourites, hitting most severely the residents of our national family who can least afford further tax burdens. The Atlantic Provinces Economic Council, for example, was clear on the regional effects of the proposed tax: Atlantic Canada contains more low income Canadians than most parts of the country so the inherently regressive nature of consumption taxes will hit residents of Atlantic Canada harder than most Canadians (tax credits which are not fully inflation indexed do not overcome this overall regional impact).

As some of the dust began to settle from the Meech Lake process in late June, 1990, a *Globe and Mail*-CBC survey asked Canadians across the country if the Senate should pass the GST as passed by the House of Commons. Sixty per cent said "no," compared to only 29 per cent who said "yes," and 10 per cent who were undecided or did not have an opinion. A full regional breakdown of the replies was not provided, but an accompanying story indicated that Québeckers were much more favourably inclined to the proposal, with 39 per cent wanting its passage by the Senate, compared to 26 per cent elsewhere. The lowest support for the measure, it went on, came from the Prairies.

How the GST became such a disaster for the government says a good deal about how little Outer Canada counts in current Ottawa policymaking.

The best insight I can obtain from a senior Ottawa official and from others is that the GST proposal sat on the policy shelf in the Finance department for many years. Attempts were made to sell it to each of the Liberal Finance Ministers during the various Trudeau governments, but each of them, including Marc Lalonde, could see economic and political catastrophe in it. Michael Wilson, a former Bay Street bond trader and firm believer in the trickle-down economics of Ronald Reagan, swallowed the proposal when he became finance minister in 1984. He then sold the concept to the Prime Minister and presumably to the cabinet before it was announced in detail to the government caucus long after the votes from the 1988 general election were safely counted.

To say, as some GST defenders do, that the government outlined the essential features of the GST before the 1988 election is sheer nonsense. What little was said about the GST by ministers before the election — and it was as little as possible — bore virtually no resemblance to the substance of Wilson's technical paper tabled in the Commons in mid-October 1989. The Minister promised in mid-June, 1987, that the tax would meet five broad objectives: "fairness, competitiveness, simplicity, consistency and reliability." No-one today except government MPs would ascribe these qualities to the GST as passed by the Commons in April, 1990.

Equally serious in terms of the Finance Minister's earlier reputation for honesty are his continuing assertions that the GST will be revenue neutral. In other words, it will not, at the 7 per cent rate at least, cut a nickel from the deficit. Virtually everyone I've spoken to who supports the proposal does so in the belief that it is necessary medicine to reduce our federal government deficit and mammoth national debt. If this is representative of the 14 per cent who now appear to favour the GST, it suggests that what little support exists is based on the conviction that the Finance Minister is intentionally misleading Canadians.

Some of the earlier media ads by Wilson's department, presumably approved by him, would make the average snake oil salesman blush. They were finally stopped when John Fraser, the Commons Speaker, commented adversely on them in the House. In the current fiscal year, however, his department is spending approximately $14 million on what it terms policy development and advertising. Most of it currently appears designed to cajole or bully more than two million small businesses and others — Ottawa's designated unpaid collectors of the tax — into registering. The general cynicism about both the measure and its government defenders, anecdotally and in opinion surveys, appears to be increasing everywhere outside Québec.

Senate Hearings

The Senate Finance Committee hearings held over the summer of 1990 on the GST vented the opposition of representative Outer Canadians. In Edmonton, for example, an alderman said the tax, being applicable to city-operated services such as telephones and electricity, would add $20 million to city taxpayers' yearly bills. To collect the tax, he estimated, would cost another $1 million annually. A retired school teacher, who spends half of each year in New Zealand and half on the Prairies, testified that he believes much of New Zealand's current unemployment and inflation problems relate to the introduction of the GST in the mid-1980s.

The Alberta publisher, Mel Hurtig, told the committee that the GST would further burden individual Canadians while allowing companies to continue as the least taxed among all industrial democracies, including the

U.S., Japan and West Germany. During 1989, he stressed, individuals paid 88 per cent of all income taxes and companies about 12 per cent. Since Michael Wilson began his tax reforms in 1986, Canadian corporate taxes rose from $14.4 billion to $15.3 billion, whereas yearly personal direct tax receipts went from $85.3 billion to $112.8 billion. Between 1980 and 1987, our chartered banks paid income taxes at the rate of 2.48 per cent. With many other Outer Canadians, he asked, "Is it justifiable to now transfer billions of dollars of additional tax burden away from corporations onto the backs of families and individual Canadians?" The withdrawal of the manufacturers' sales tax (MST) and its replacement by the GST are, of course, designed to do precisely this.

Hurtig avoided the usual government charge that he had no alternative to the GST. Among his proposals to the committee were higher effective taxes on large companies, a wealth tax equal to the average among OECD member nations, progressive but small inheritance taxes, a two per cent reduction in interest rates (which would save $7 billion in government debit charges over four years), and additional taxes on expensive houses, cars and other luxury items. My sense is that most of the opposition to Hurtig's approach to tax reform would come from a few thousand people in Toronto and Montréal.

The submission by Lawrence Alexander, a thoughtful Edmonton businessman in his seventies, represented another frontal attack on the GST. He saw the measure as a blueprint for a far-reaching change in the Canadian way of life. How, he asked, could the advocates of the GST argue that the purchase of items such as gas and heating oil are discretionary? How would taxing air tickets build national unity? Replacing the MST with the GST was simply adopting a remedy which was much worse than the disease. Better, he argued, to increase the income tax without setting up an onerous new system. This would disturb the economy the least and would entail the least administrative cost.

During the summer of 1990, many other points also came to light. The chairman of the Don't Tax Reading Coalition pointed out that although 1991 subscriptions to Canadian magazines are to be subject to the tax it would be unenforceable against many foreign publications. A spokesman for one of the three Prairie wheat pools declared they could not change their computerized accounting system by January 1, 1991 because Ottawa officials had been unable to provide enough details. The president of the Canadian Real Estate association pointed out the unfairness of applying the GST to some real estate fees but exempting stock market brokerage fees. Renters would also be hit because many landlords would find a way to pass on to them the GST they must pay on plumbing and other services. A funeral home chain concluded that pre-paid funeral arrangements bought after September 1, 1990 would be subject to the tax. The head of the Saskatchewan Federation of Indians estimated that the GST would cost natives in the province more than $45 million yearly. Indians across

Canada are exempt from provincial sales taxes and consider that their treaties exempt them from such levies.

A persuasive letter carried during the summer of 1990 in Vancouver's *West Ender* newspaper walked readers through a day off work in the life under the GST of a resident (admittedly one with a relatively high income) who could not qualify for a tax credit. Virtually everything she bought during the day — newspapers, meals, taxis, stamps, art gallery tickets — was subject to the tax, causing her to pay out $7.65 on the tax in a single day. During one year, the writer estimated that the tax would cost the hypothetical woman an additional $2,792. On no item she bought did the price drop because of the removal of the MST.

Large groups of Outer Canadians hit to some degree at least by the GST are farmers and fisherman, performing artists, tenants of commercial realty, owners of owner-operated businesses, charities and non-profit organizations. All Outer Canadians will be hit harder than Inner Canadians both as consumers and producers because of the application of the tax to transportation services. Food transportation would also be hit, as a trucking expert pointed out, because you rarely can separate food from other items in a load of merchandise. Most consumer products are made in southern Ontario and the cost of moving a refrigerator from there to, say, Nanaimo or St. John's would be taxed on the distance involved: the farther one lives from Toronto the more tax one pays. The new levy on transportation also hits producers hardest according to how far they live from the population centres in Ontario and Québec where most products are consumed. A small tax advantage which remote makers of finished products enjoyed under the manufacturers sales tax disappears under the GST.

The Regina-based Western Canadian Wheat Growers, representing 11,000 Prairie grain farmers, concluded that the GST would "significantly reduce farm operating margins." Three reasons: non-family members buying farms will pay seven per cent on land and be required to carry finance charges until the rebate for items other than carrying costs is received; farm implements, not now taxed at point of sale, are expected to rise three to four per cent because of the inflationary impact of the GST; farm purchasers would only receive a portion of this back as a GST rebate.

Tourism is one of the sectors that will be hardest hit by the GST. An industry that generates $24 billion in gross revenues per year, and $11 billion in tax revenue for all levels of government, will lose, according to the Tourist Industry Association of Canada, $1 billion per year and 25,000 jobs by 1993. Joe McGuire, an MP from PEI, noted during the debate on the GST in the House of Commons, that the effects of the GST will be particularly devastating for the Atlantic provinces. About half of the tourists to the region come from Central Canada. With the GST in place they may opt for American destinations.

Some major resource industries in Outer Canada, which for the most part now escape the MST, are also caught. Mining activities will now be taxed on their sales at 7 per cent. Similarly, natural gas sold domestically will be taxed for the first time at the federal level. Forest product companies, much of whose input is not currently taxed, will be hit by the GST both on domestic sales and on expenses such as transportation. Finally, provincial taxes, including sales taxes, are to form part of the value on which the GST is imposed. The residents of hinterland provinces with larger-than-average provincial sales taxes will thus pay more.

The GST will also contribute to the worsening of existing regional disparities and its impact will be most harmful in the provinces with the highest provincial tax rates. For example, in Prince Edward Island, there will be a total of 17 per cent charged through the GST and the provincial tax system as the 10 per cent provincial tax will presumably be added to the cost of the item plus the cost of the GST. A farmer on the island will pay more for farm equipment than one in Ontario because of increased costs in transportation.

As this book goes to press in September, it remains unclear what the Senate will ultimately do with the GST bill. Constitutionally, the senators are fully entitled simply to refuse to pass the measure on the basis that it is both sufficiently important to the national economy and radically different from anything hinted at by the Prime Minister and his party candidates during the 1988 election. Our unreformed and unloved Senate is paid — and paid well — to be a chamber of "sober second thought." If ever another measure warranted the forcing of an election, as the Senate did with respect to the proposed Canada-U.S. free trade agreement, the GST is an ideal candidate. If, however, the Prime Minister takes the view that in order to achieve passage of the measure as is, he is solely entitled since the failure of the Meech Lake accord to fill the present vacancies with Tory *apparatchiks*, and does so, any real Senate reform will become significantly more difficult to achieve.

Appointing new Conservative senators would still not produce a Tory majority because the Liberals still have 52 of 104 seats. This would leave only Section 26 of the British North America Act, which in theory allows a prime minister to appoint four or eight additional senators in case of a genuine deadlock between the two chambers. As no prime minister during 123 years has successfully applied this provision, our highest court could conceivably decide that its use now by a desperate first minister violates our constitutional conventions. Section 26 has atrophied. The public reaction to such constitutional sharp practice would be negative and would presumably reduce support for the government party even further. The only senator with democratic legitimacy, Stan Waters of Alberta, who was appointed in the period between the June first ministers' meeting in Ottawa and the collapse of the Meech Lake accord, says that any use of a s.26 by Brian Mulroney to force passage of the GST would be the political equivalent of dropping a nuclear bomb on the Canadian electorate.

PART III

TOWARDS UNITY

NINE

KICKSTARTING DEVELOPMENT

Almost from the first months following Confederation, Ottawa's programs affected some regions more positively than others. All provinces did not share prosperity equally; this pattern of regional disparities has persisted and probably worsened in recent years. Initiatives designed to reduce existing disparities and promote economic development in poorer regions were introduced in rapid succession following the late 1950s when national politicians first grasped the large differences in levels of regional prosperity, and accepted responsibility for removing them.

Billions of tax dollars have been spent since by way of regional development and regional fiscal adjustment measures. Yet, no single economic theory exists to explain regional disparities; nor is there yet much agreement on even the best theoretical approach to the problem. One reason for the lack of a coherent overall policy may be that the debate over regional development has been left largely to politicians. A former senior official of Ottawa's Department of Regional Economic Expansion admitted, "Regional development is sustained almost entirely by politics and by a political commitment." In Ottawa, where regional economic considerations are often equated with partisan politics, programs that are formulated under a "national" label are intended to benefit provinces with heavier political clout. As a result, regional jealousies, feelings of frustration and even anger are built up, while economic disparities between rich and poor provinces, most notably those in Atlantic Canada, are perpetuated.

It is probably on the rocky field of economics that the friction between Outer and Inner Canadians continues in its most acute form. Evidence, both anecdotal and statistical, is abundant. A family left southeast Edmonton in the mid-1980s to return to Toronto from where they'd come in the late 1970s. The continuing flat Alberta economy after the 1982 recession meant there was no longer sufficient work in the husband's realty consulting field. They finally managed to sell their Edmonton home for about $85,000 and to acquire a smaller one in a Toronto suburb for $215,000 in 1985. Their new home is, of course, worth far more now. Many other Outer Canadians left their homes to establish themselves in one of our largest cities. In doing so, they lost their entire equity. After selling their homes as prices in Outer Canada were sagging, they are now paying rent in Toronto or Ottawa.

A central issue of Canadian unity has to do with income levels across the country. During the most recently surveyed decade, 1971-81, residents of Atlantic Canada had a per capita market income which varied between about 54 per cent (PEI) and 69 per cent (Nova Scotia) of the national average. There is no reason to believe that this state of affairs has since improved for Atlantic Canadians; it has probably worsened significantly over the past few years. A number of government programs, combined with positive factors such as a lower cost of living, mercifully do improve the overall Atlantic picture. The personal disposable income per household in three Atlantic provinces today is about 80 percent of the national average. The overall economic "penalty" for remaining an Atlantic Canadian remains in the 20 per cent range.

It is still true, as a Special Senate Committee on Poverty reported almost twenty years ago, that most low income Canadians are concentrated in Québec and Ontario. It is also true that family incomes for poorer Canadians are generally higher in Atlantic Canada and Québec and lower in the Prairies and Ontario. Average family incomes in Outer Canada, however, are well below those in Toronto, Montréal and Ottawa.

Regional unemployment rates are another important dimension of the economic issue. In recent years the level of unemployment in several provinces is much more than that of Inner Canada. The average Ontario unemployment rate during 1988 was 5 percent; for the same year the average for Newfoundland was 16.4 per cent, PEI — 13 per cent, Nova Scotia — 10.2 per cent, New Brunswick — 12 per cent, Québec — 9.4 per cent and B.C. — 10.3 per cent.

Earned income per capita may provide a more accurate measure of a region's economic performance than per capita income. Earned income excludes relative gains resulting from interregional transfer payments and thus better reflects the overall economic prospects of a province or region. According to this indicator, regional disparities are even more pronounced, and disparity narrowed only slightly between 1961 and 1981.

Another interesting measurement is the total amount of government spending in each province as a percentage of the province's gross domestic production. In 1981, the national average was 39 per cent, but it was 69 per cent in PEI, 81 per cent in Nova Scotia, 72 per cent in New Brunswick, 63 per cent in Newfoundland, 47 per cent in Québec, 35 per cent in Ontario, 41 per cent in Manitoba, 35 per cent in Saskatchewan, 23 per cent in Alberta, and 32 per cent in B.C. In 1987, combined federal and provincial government spending equalled almost two-thirds of the economy of the Atlantic provinces — almost twice its significance in Ontario (37 per cent).

In Saskatchewan, the government share in 1987 soared to 64 per cent from 35 per cent in 1981. In Alberta, government spending amounted to 38 per cent of the provincial economy the same year compared with 23 per cent in 1981 when the province was far less dependent on the public sector to sustain its economy.

No doubt, this public spending has allowed residents of our poorer provinces to enjoy a higher standard of living than would have been the case without transfers. Yet, provinces where the percentage of public spending is very high are becoming almost financial wards of Ottawa. The well-being of their residents is to a substantial degree dependent on the inclinations of the federal government. In the long run, moreover, their development may actually be hindered by transfers since the adjustments required for greater economic self-sufficiency are less likely to be made.

One major consequence of the stress created by these economic conditions over the decades is that larger numbers of Outer Canadians are emigrating to southern Ontario and elsewhere in search of better futures. The 1986 national census documents point out this pattern: that year approximately 1,000,000 Canadians lived in different provinces than they had five years earlier. During the 1976-81 period, the four provinces of Western Canada overall gained about a quarter of a million inhabitants through inter-provincial migration and about 200,000 more through immigration from outside Canada. Following the economic recession that hit the Western economy in 1982 and lasted several years, the region gained a few thousand people through inter-provincial migration. The four provinces did manage to attract 150,000 newcomers from outside Canada. These newcomers — often bringing children, and usually very hard-working — helped to fill our schools, provided impetus to construction, assisted in finding new markets for our exports and generally boosted the four economies. They also enriched many communities culturally and intellectually.

For Atlantic Canada, the demographic trend was uniformly bleak. In each of the four provinces, more Canadians were leaving than moving in during the 1976-81 period. Newcomers from abroad were too few to offset the losses. The pattern improved slightly in the 1981-86 period, but not enough to significantly alter the region's or any of its provinces' share of our national population. It continues to be about 9 per cent of the total.

Québec's post-1971 experience is similar to that of Atlantic Canada. Between 1976 and 1981, its overall loss of population to migration within Canada was a little over 140,000 people. A little more than half this number settled in Québec during these years as immigrants from outside Canada. A low provincial birth rate was another blow to its hope for an increased share of the national population. In the five years up to 1986, 63,000 more Québeckers were leaving the province than moving into it from other provinces. Only 72,000 moved in from abroad. Many Québeckers fear that their share of Canada's population is bound to drop below 25 per cent before the turn of the century. This fear has became grist for the independence mill.

From 1976-81, Ontario lost about 78,000 residents through migration almost entirely to B.C. and Alberta. During the next half-decade, Ontario's net interprovincial migration alone more than offset those losses. Moreover, the province received another 221,000 immigrants from outside Canada for an overall gain in newcomers alone of more than twice the population of Prince Edward Island.

Regional Disparities

The statistics show that economic disparities have persisted despite efforts by a series of federal governments. The contrast has been most evident between Central Canada — southern Ontario, in particular — and the Maritimes, parts of Québec, Northern Canada and Western Canada.

Acknowledging the differences in the regions, Liberal and Conservative governments since the late 1950s have attempted to equalize funding, programs and opportunities for Canadians. They endeavoured to develop an effective policy approach after breaking the elements of regional inequality into a number of broad categories: the natural endowments of a local economy, such as geographic features that provide economic benefits, e.g., oil; the inequity of certain federal or provincial actions where disparities can be most successfully reduced; market imperfections caused by local monopolies; particular consumer preferences in a region, etc. The Walter Gordon Commission in the 1950s examined this subject and the Trudeau government, elected in 1968, established a series of programs beginning with the creation of the Department of Regional Economic Expansion in 1969. The Department of Regional Industrial Expansion followed in 1982-83.

In the early 1980s, an Industrial and Regional Development Program was announced and the Department of Industry, Science and Technology was created. The Mulroney government founded three regionally based agencies: the Atlantic Canada Opportunities Agency is to spend a $1.05 billion budget over five years on developing the economy of the Atlantic region; NORFED was established for Northern Ontario with a budget of $55 million over five years; and the Department of Western Diversification was launched for the four western provinces with a five year budget of $1.2 billion.

Yet, despite a host of government efforts and repeated reorganizations of the departments over the years, regional disparities have not been reduced significantly. Equally important, regional disparity in public attitudes have remained at high levels. Outer Canadians in 1990 feel disenfranchised from their national government in a general sense according to how far they live from Ottawa.

Dissatisfaction has led to periodic and at times almost comical reorganizations of federal efforts, often reflecting the desire of various ministers and cabinets to put their own mark on regional development policy. Numerous regional initiatives sought to create jobs; but they didn't achieve the changes in the structure of provincial economies needed to ensure long-term opportunities for sustainable growth. Creating new jobs usually implies that growth has occurred. Growth alone should, however, not be confused with economic development as it may not mean any improvement in the region's future prospects. A greater scope for self-sustaining growth in a given area — a fundamental change in its ability to create its own wealth — is required before we can speak of economic development.

The persistence of regional economic disparities is widely recognized as a major threat to national unity. According to Donald Savoie, a national authority in the field of regional development, extremely powerful and costly countervailing forces would be necessary to change existing development patterns and abolish regional disparities. "The burden that would be imposed on the 'have' regions would be so large that it might well be unacceptable and could threaten national unity quite as much as would persistent and pronounced regional disparities," he says.

Many Outer Canadians want regional disparities in Canada to be re-assessed and a new set of regional development objectives to be adopted. Those applied in the late 1960s are still seen as sound by too many in Ottawa and some provincial capitals: they must be revised. The goal of reducing regional disparities as traditionally defined by income and employment levels is today unrealistic.

I do not intend to assess past policies and programs that have been tried in Canada's regional development efforts or to assess their success in alleviating regional disparities. Nor is a solution offered that would bring a dramatic breakthrough in the field. Inspired by a persuasive example of new and better thinking, the recent monograph prepared by Dirk de Vos, an Ottawa official associated with the Research Centre for Technology Management at Carleton University, I'll attempt to put regional development into a new perspective in the following section.

Regional Development: A New Look

Canadians, says De Vos, have ample resources for sustainable regional economic development: space, capital, location, people, materials, knowledge, markets and means of communication. The resources we do not have we can get abroad. And yet, in various parts of Outer Canada, residents face essentially three options: "get smart, get poor, or get out." Residents have to decide whether their region will compete on skills and quality of effort (get smart) or to reduce their standard of living to compete on cost (get poor) or simply lose population (get out). This is what one might call the Atlantic Canada syndrome.

The heart of the issue is the ability of a region to manage what it has got or can get. National and provincial governments can do much by way of removing barriers and constraints — whether fiscal, regulatory or trade-related — but the key question remains: can a province manage its actual and potential resources?

No community anywhere in Canada or across the earth is without resources. Singapore's resources consist of people and location — nothing more. Hong Kong has no land. People without markets for their products have gone out to create them. A remarkable feature about the Japanese economic miracle is that, contrary to conventional thought, they have often done things backward. The Japanese tend to first create or capture a market for exports, using borrowed money and borrowed technology. Once they "own" the market they invest equity and profits in further research and development in a major way. Canadians across the country might try to copy this Japanese approach in the markets of the Pacific Rim.

In contrast, Canada's regional development efforts have followed the traditional way of thinking. Federal and provincial governments alike have sunk billions of dollars in first building up infrastructure and subsidizing research and development. The idea was that the public sector first invests in bricks, mortar, roads, airports, harbours, schools, shopping centres, industrial parks, production lines, tourist facilities, dams, power lines and all sorts of "growth poles." Then the governments subsidize research and development — the magic process of creating new science and technology. Canadian scientists loved it, and so did many participating companies — mostly large and foreign-owned — who walked away with the write-offs and the credits considered to be the second-most generous in the world.

It was hoped that these two types of infrastructural investments — hardware and research — would sooner or later create business and wealth in the fashion of a production process. The Americans, for example, have statistics showing how until 1980 on a per capita basis, incomes across the United States continually converged, i.e., tended to become more equal.

Canadian governments made similar claims. Regional disparities, for one reason or another, tended until 1980 to become less pronounced. Around 1980, however, a basic change took place: the gap between regional per capita incomes and the average national per capita income was widening. In many cases, this pattern could be attributed to well-known forces such as the collapse in commodity and energy prices, low labour-cost competition from developing countries, the Japanese onslaught, the glut in the world automobile markets, or the formation of regional trading blocs. Simultaneously the ability of Ottawa and other central governments to control the impact of external forces had weakened. Governments manipulated income taxes, exchange rates, interest rates, and money supply to bolster or cushion their economies. They also borrowed to the hilt, or beyond it in the case of Canada, but such methods are now running out of steam. The economists' computerized economic models simply no longer work. As if in desperation, national governments, including Canada's, began to shift responsibilities and spending burdens back on to the shoulders of regional or provincial governments. These, in turn, are leaning more heavily on municipalities which in many instances must absorb mounting social assistance costs.

At the other end of the spectrum, there is another pervasive force at work: the increasing globalization of economic activity, which, in many cases, ignores, or to a certain extent neutralizes, national boundaries. The Canada-US Free Trade Agreement and the Single European Market of 1992 are only two of many dramatic examples of this world-wide trend. Meanwhile, regions are re-emerging as economic actors within a globally competitive world. Within nations, pronounced regional disparities are appearing once again — for example, between the southeast and the rest of Britain; the south and the north of Italy; the east and the west in Australia; between Bavaria and parts of the Rhineland and the rest of West Germany; and also within the United States. Our country is no exception to this trend. Some of these regions are quite small; some of them straddle national boundaries. Examples of integrating such regional economies abound: along the north-eastern and north-western coasts of North America, around the Great Lakes, in the basin of the Rhine River.

What can be done for, in, and by a disfavoured region in Outer Canada to build greater economic viability? A region can do nothing about where it is located nor can it do anything about the resources within its borders. Yet it has the ability to control what it does quite aside from its infrastructure or the amount of research and development performed within it.

Most conventional economists fall back, time and again, on the availability of the so-called factors of production — land, skilled labour, capital and technology. They speak about comparative advantage as a kind of automatic benefit created by the particular configuration of these factors of production in a given region. They assert that if you have land, skilled labour and capital, but lack the technology, then you must create technology or go out and buy or rent it. Hence the new battle-cry: "R & D and technology will save us." We live in an information-intensive economy; therefore we need more information. The Fraser Institute in Vancouver has gone so far as to assert that a country or a region can now be viable and wealthy merely on the basis of an information-intensive service economy. This is a very dubious proposition.

Other economists say that a region should focus on particular sectors in order to be competitive, whether agriculture, transportation, pharmaceuticals, or telecommunications. They argue that competitiveness and productivity vary from sector to sector and that some sectors are better than others. If there is a slump or oversupply in world markets, we must quickly get out of the steel industry, agriculture, shipbuilding, textiles, footwear, automobiles or whatever. Indeed, everybody should be into computers, biotechnology and new materials. This is true to a degree, but the essential point here is that many development experts also stress the importance of a region's ability to change and adapt to external circumstances.

What is often overlooked is that in each of these sectors there are regions and businesses that are not adversely affected by the changes. The so-called sunset industries remain successful and profitable while other regions and companies fail miserably in the so-called sunrise sectors. More seems to depend on who is doing what than on what is being done.

Approximately four years ago, the Commission of the European Community examined this phenomenon. It produced a report entitled *Sectoral Productivity and Regional Policy*. Having looked at productivity trends across various sectors and regions in Western Europe, it concluded that "productivity disparities are greater among different regions in the same sector than among the various sectors within the same region." The sectoral composition of these regional economies holds very little explanation on the levels and the growth rates of productivity, the study concluded. Nor did it make sense to classify sectors as being advanced or backward.

Others who have looked at economic performance differences among nations noted that it did not seem to depend on what kinds of business some nations were in. The Japanese, to their credit, appear to make a success of almost anything they tackle from electronics to mandarin oranges. Why have the Danes been so much more successful than the Dutch in the industrial exploitation of the dairy industry? What distinguishes the brilliantly successful Swiss pharmaceutical industry? Why is Sweden far ahead of Canada in the technological and design exploitation of wood and metals? Why are the Finns so far advanced in applied technologies in the forestry sector? It has little to do with the resource endowments — cows or pastures, forests or mines — little to do with their location or the size of their economies.

First, regional productivity depends less on endowments and particular sectors and more on something else. Second, competitiveness is not a function of having or providing land, skilled labour, capital and even technology; nor does the secret lie in "comparative advantage." Third, external forces are important but they are not conclusive. For example, even after a 100 per cent appreciation of their currency the Japanese have achieved an annual current account surplus of U.S. $80 billion and the profits of more exporting Japanese companies have soared. Many have also adapted well to the environmental needs of the day by reducing the amount of resources used in their manufactured products.

We must therefore look again at factors that are internal to regions and capable of being controlled. The brutal message is that in the long run, if a region is incompetent it will remain uncompetitive, whatever its level of endowments and whatever sectors it tries to exploit.

The more pertinent question, of course, is: what and whose competence or incompetence do we have in mind? Numerous signs now point in De Vos's view, which I share, to the issue of managerial competence, the skill of local politicians and bureaucrats as much as of the managers of enterprises, whether large or small. This competence has to do with two distinct spheres of activity: the management of individual enterprises, whether public or private, and the management of the linkages between or among enterprises, public or private.

One should not equate management with investment. In the final resort it is not a question of physical infrastructure and plant and equipment and raw materials or even of generating or acquiring technology. Nor, in the first instance, does the burden rest on employees and labour skills. As for the technologies, even companies that spend 12 per cent or more of their sales on research and development agree that technology is not the problem. The technology of the humble zipper was available thirty years before its successful marketing. Some entrepreneurs even shun the opportunity of being "first to market" because of the well-known problem of the "liability of leadership." In fact, few major innovations have been developed by their originators.

What counts is the management of technology and the management of enterprises and of the linkages among businesses at the regional level almost regardless of the types of technology or the industrial sectors in and around which the activities take place. In a broad sense, the issues are social, not economic or technical. They have to do with organization. More specifically, they focus on the organization of linkages both within an enterprise and among enterprises. These linkages are not only vertical between, say, suppliers and users and horizontal among similar players but they also depend on feedback loops within systems.

This is the real secret of Japan and of the regional productivity gains identified in Europe. A successful region or enterprise is one that is able to add value to almost anything by integrating its activities through the management of linkages. What we are looking for is not so much the management of technology, albeit a crucial matter, as the technology of management. In fact these two interact with each other. Mastering the technology of better management by committed local people is where regional development policy should now focus not only our attention but also our resources.

Governments and business in Outer Canada must concentrate on improving local managerial capabilities and functions. A region is much better placed than any other geographical or political entity to master and practise the art of exploiting linkages. First, a region is geographically confined; sooner or later spatial factors assert themselves despite all the talk about the global village and electronic networks. This is why many sensible economists are economic geographers; they have their feet on the ground. For this same reason, engineers are such useful people — they deal with the real world. Perhaps the best thing the American General Douglas MacArthur did after the war was to put Japan's industrial resurgence in the hands of engineers, after he had fired most of the economists, especially the ones who preached comparative advantage.

A region also has a degree of social or cultural homogeneity, which helps to enhance the quality of communication, the essence of linkages.

Residents of Cape Breton share the same history; so do those of northern Saskatchewan. Also, regional loyalties can be quite strong and command a high degree of commitment and self-interest. A region can redefine itself, an important aspect of the ability to adapt to change, to survive and to prosper. The new linkages that are forged will also help to redefine the region. Thus a region can become more flexible and more innovative as it develops new internal and external alliances. In fact, it may become part of a different region for different purposes. Linkage is a creative process, but it has to be managed.

A country or region or enterprise can no longer wait for these things to occur haphazardly. Technological and market windows of opportunity appear and pass quickly, so one must be organized in advance to be able to seize them when they open up. Japan can apparently jump on to any passing train. Hong Kong and Singapore prosper in the same way. They are able to gear up an existing organizational infrastructure on very short notice.

The need to be able to manage technology rather than simply relying on capital subsidies or research and development incentives has finally caught the attention of people in other countries and regions. The first major American conferences on the management of technology took place in early 1988; the first important European conference on the subject was held in Belgium in mid-1989. In June, 1989 the Department of Industry, Science and Technology organized in Ottawa its first in-house pilot introductory course on the management of technology for the benefit of departmental officers who deal directly with business people usually in Outer Canada.

Technology management is a multi-faceted art, not easily taught or learned. Just as in the field of computing and communications the emerging emphasis is on the software, on programming, rather than on the hardware; and just as in the management of technology the focus shifts from the technology to its management, so, on the managerial side, more attention must be paid to the organizational aspects of management. Innovation as well as production and marketing depend more and more on designing and exploiting linkages.

Consider the ongoing problem of technology transfer within companies, among companies, among universities and businesses, and within and among regions and countries. It boils down to the nature, quality and extent of vertical and horizontal linkages and their management. Outer Canadians in particular can no longer take a hands-off attitude to these processes. Linkages themselves are an engine of growth, which can be harnessed for profit, if not economic survival. Thus, in both our public and private sectors, and between them, managers must develop a better capacity to understand, use and exploit various forms of co-operation, whether we call them strategic alliances , partnerships or joint ventures.

These have been practised very successfully over the years in particular fields such as oil and gas exploration in Western Canada and elsewhere. Prairie farmers do not have to be convinced about the value of cooperatives and agricultural extension services. Such reservoirs of experience could form a good foundation for the more sophisticated modern approaches to the art and science of inter-community linkages, particularly when they involve technology. Indeed, an impressive consulting service for businesses in Australia was directly modelled on agricultural extension services despite the added difficulty that business people, unlike farmers, are often in direct competition with one another.

Speaker after speaker at conferences on the management of technology arrive at similar conclusions, namely, that the crucial difference lies in organizational structures and processes and their design and management.

Considering the complaints of many Outer Canadians, the fact that regional supply factors are more important than national demand factors is as staggering as the fact that sectoral factors are relatively unimportant. What matters most is the deep interdependence among the actors and sectors in the same regional economy. And surely, this is a management problem. What we do not need are more institutions, more "centres" of this, that or the other kind, more bureaucracies, more studies and reports, or probably even more borrowed public money to be dumped into the black hole of conventional regional development notions. Western Diversification, for example, prides itself on its funding to date of more than a thousand enterprises. All Westerners hope the long-term success rate will be high. I worry when I hear accounts such as the one only a few months ago from a local manufacturer in Edmonton who came to my office to complain that a competitor generously subsidized by Western Diversification was threatening to put him out of business.

Equally important is the realization that regions, and quite often small ones, now interact directly with the global economy and no longer necessarily through or by the grace of the central or federal authorities. For example, the state of Texas has an observer in meetings of the Organization of Petroleum Exporting Countries (OPEC). Regional interests often straddle national boundaries as demonstrated by the recent meeting of two Western premiers with the governors of several Western states.

Ottawa must rethink its regional development programs in fundamental ways. Likewise, Outer Canadian leaders must redefine their strengths and concentrate on the areas where those strengths are greatest. As usual these kinds of change can be either a threat or an opportunity. At the very least, they put regional development into a new perspective.

The new challenge will bring out the best or the worst in Canadians everywhere. We have a splendid developmental opportunity. We could start by mastering such difficult things as the ability to exploit linkages where the actors compete and co-operate at the same time. Simultaneous competition and collaboration within partnerships and among businesses is one of the apparent contradictions that can now be put to work for the benefit of both Outer and Inner Canadians generally.

TEN

RECONCILABLE DIFFERENCES

A decade ago, the Carleton University school of journalism asked 1,300 voting age persons across the country, "Where does your first loyalty lie — with Canada or with the province in which you live?" Approximately 74 percent of them said Canada, while 26 percent chose their province. The percentages for the Atlantic region were 66/34; for Québec, 53/47; for Ontario, 90/10; and for Western Canada 80/20. Roger Gibbins, a University of Calgary professor, conducted a national survey on the same topic in April, 1983. Nationally, 73 percent of the respondents said that they thought of themselves first as Canadians; 17 percent first as provincial residents. Eight percent refused to choose or stated an equal preference, and two percent did not have an opinion.

Again in late 1989 a Decima/Maclean's magazine survey of 1,500 adults in all provinces on whether they considered themselves first as Canadians or as citizens of their province, gave the following results:

Percentage of respondents who indicated first loyalty to:

	Canada	**Province**
All Canada	73	26
British Columbia	83	17
Alberta	74	24
Saskatchewan	83	16
Manitoba	84	15
Ontario	90	9
Québec	44	55
New Brunswick	75	25
Nova Scotia	63	37
Newfoundland	47	53

RECONCILABLE DIFFERENCES

Few Outer Canadians would be surprised that Ontarians were the most loyal to their country; many would say that Ottawa's close and continuous attention to Ontarian interests since 1867 is responsible for this attitude. An equally plausible interpretation of the Carleton survey, of course, is that Ontarians make no real distinction between their province and the country as a whole. This might explain why they have the strongest sense of being Canadians and have little sensitivity to inter-regional tensions.

On the other hand, the reply of Québec and Newfoundland residents alike suggested a greater loyalty to their province than to their country. Sixty per cent of the Québeckers surveyed thought it likely that their province would choose to separate if the Meech Lake accord failed to be accepted. With its collapse on June 23, 1990, there are increasing indications that French-speaking Québeckers see themselves as rejected by "English Canada" as a federal partner.

Being attached to one's province or region need not reduce allegiance to Canada; dual loyalties should be complementary; never should there be conflict. Québeckers and Newfoundlanders unfortunately now appear for various historical, cultural, linguistic and constitutional reasons to have exceptional provincial loyalties not typical of other Canadians. In my experience, Canadians who are the most sensitive to provincial, multicultural and language diversity often hold the strongest sense of being Canadian.

Canada is among the world's longest practitioners of federalism. A unitary form of government would never meet the needs of a country as geographically, linguistically and culturally diversified as ours. Yet, regional differences and priorities require much better public expression in Parliament if the central institution of our national government is to reflect all parts of the country. Regional voices are frequently suffocated by rigid party discipline and the entrenched habit of all three national caucuses to maintain a close eye on what opinion leaders in Toronto-Ottawa-Montréal regard as the national interest on any issue. The constant priority of most MPs in our House of Commons is to defend or attack the government of the day. Therefore, regional concerns usually fail to be expressed because it might fracture the unity each party wants to project during the partisan wars waged daily in the House. Nor can one consider the Senate in its present form as a forum where legitimate regional interests can be voiced. No one in the Senate, except Stanley Waters, today represents anyone except him or herself. In practice, the loyalty of most senators today is to the prime minister and political party through which they gained virtually life-time membership in the best-paid club on earth.

Neither chamber of the Canadian Parliament today encourages the articulate expression of regional concerns that the national legislature of a federation must provide. Accordingly provincial governments years ago assumed the task of defending regional aspirations, not only on areas of provincial constitutional responsibility but in relation to matters such as interest rates, federal procurement policy and tariffs, which are squarely within Ottawa's jurisdiction. In doing so, the provincial governments discharge no constitutional responsibility: they are elected to deal with problems within the provincial jurisdiction, not to be regional voices in the formulation of national policy. This function should be provided in the Parliament of Canada, probably most effectively by a reformed upper chamber.

In the United States a host of factors, including economic diversification in most regions, an enormous mobility of population, and a gradual weakening of the financial and legislative powers of state governments, have "nationalized" the thinking of most Americans. Conversely, regionalism is an enduring, and probably now ascendant, fact of Canadian life. Opinion leaders in Inner Canada who say that Canadians should stop being so attached to their province or local communities misread the nature of Canada. They thereby probably contribute to a significant degree to the reduction of national cohesion across Outer Canada. Our country is far more than Joe Clark's "community of communities," but trivializing provincial attachments doesn't enhance the building of a stronger national unity.

Federal System

Our federal system, to the regret of many Inner Canadians and of some Outer Canadians as well, evolved in the opposite direction from that of our southern neighbour. In 1867, the northern model was intended by its founders to be a blend of the British and American models with a very strong tilt in favour of Ottawa dominating the provinces. Most Fathers of Confederation, including John A. Macdonald, saw a strong central government as necessary for political and economic survival. As the Toronto political scientist, Donald Smiley, has pointed out, "the provinces were to be in precisely the same constitutional relation to the federal government as the individual colonies of British North America had been to the Imperial authorities." The BNA Act rejected the earlier American constitutional model with its emphasis on a comparatively weak national government and stress on the rights of individual states. Without the determination of earlier Québeckers, for example, provincial legislators might not even have gained jurisdiction over education, language and property rights.

The re-shaping of Canadian federalism distinctly away from the preferences of its architects began with the successful campaign for greater provincial rights waged by Oliver Mowat, Liberal Premier of Ontario between 1872 and 1896, and continued with the election in 1896 of the Liberal party led by Wilfred Laurier on a policy of provincial rights. Until his defeat in 1911, Laurier enjoyed a harmony in his relations with provincial governments that has probably never existed before or since. Subsequently, during both World Wars and the Great Depression, Ottawa massively reasserted its dominance. After 1945, it began using its unlimited spending power to encroach at will on areas of provincial jurisdiction. An exception was the case of Québec: for many years, Premier Maurice Duplessis refused to allow provincial universities to accept Ottawa funds for post-secondary education. Canada's federalism in these decades closely paralleled what was happening in the United States, but by the 1960s, in the words of Roger Gibbins, Canada's "national government, unlike its American counterpart, was in rapid retreat across a broad jurisdictional field, as provincial governments began to remake the face of Canadian federalism."

Macdonald's dream of a triumphant Ottawa government began to unravel due to a series of decisions taken by the Judicial Committee of the Privy Council in Britain. Until 1949, the Judicial Committee was Canada's final court of appeal in civil matters. It took the view that the undoubted intention of Canada's founders to form a national Parliament and government dealing with subordinate provinces was irrelevant. The late constitutional expert Frank Scott detected twenty-one additional provincial powers created after 1867 by judicial decision. Ottawa's constitutional right to regulate trade and commerce (which in the U.S. was inflated by federal courts to the point of swamping state legislative authority) was eventually divested of substance. Most federal social legislation passed by Parliament during 1935 in the spirit of the New Deal was also struck down by the Judicial Committee. Since 1949, under the influence of centralizing personalities like Chief Justice Bora Laskin, the Supreme Court of Canada, now having the final constitutional word, moved briskly to strengthen the remaining federal authority. By then, however, the die was cast in favour of strong provincial prerogatives.

A second influence favouring the strengthening of our provincial legislatures and governments resulted from another factor: a great number of extra-constitutional practices have developed outside the reach of our Supreme Court, most notably in the realm of federal-provincial tax spending arrangements. In the fiscal year 1989-90, federal transfer payments to provincial territorial and municipal governments exceeded $34.4 billion, including $7.3 billion in equalization payments or transfers from wealthier to poorer provinces, and more than $19 billion for provincial health care and post-secondary education, $4.8 billion for the Canada Assistance Plan under which provincial and municipal governments assist needy persons for certain welfare and health services, and $10.5 billion in unconditional tax grants. Since most shared-cost programs fall in areas within provincial jurisdiction, Ottawa's ability to have a say over them has been limited. Due to differing provincial priorities, there is a considerable variety in the nature and cost of these programs.

In 1964 the government of Jean Lesage, determined to reinforce provincial authority as part of Québec's "Quiet Revolution," mounted major pressure to exclude Ottawa from spending money in areas within provincial jurisdiction. The first Québec-Canada agreement permitting the province to opt out of such programs with compensation was signed in the mid-1960s.

A different situation arose in Québec in 1976: the Parti Québécois took office with an overwhelming majority, determined to withdraw the province from Confederation. For more than a century, most Québec premiers had sought vigorously to defend their provincial autonomy, particularly in the areas of language and culture, by protecting from Ottawa encroachment any powers assigned by the BNA Act to the provincial jurisdiction. This status quo vanished with the advent of René Levesque as premier. Overnight, the colonial constitutional model of 1867 had fewer supporters amongst Outer Canadians, who felt that the national government functioned primarily by and for Inner Canadians. In the face of a mounting provincial resurgence, Ottawa's legislative and financial power was waning again in something of an uneven retreat. In the mid-1970s, Ottawa was making large fiscal transfers to the provinces without any conditions attached. The best known exception to this federal retreat was the National Energy Program of late 1980 which evoked little enthusiasm among Western Canadians for the restoration of a strong central government in Ottawa.

Another reason for the decreasing support among Outer Canadians for a strongly centralized national government was the insensitivity of our federal institutions to regional interests. Most notably the House of Commons and the Senate have not provided effective regional representation to Outer Canadians. The American federal system developed towards centralization partly because its Senate took to heart the interests of residents of smaller states. With two senators from Alaska (with approximately 534,000 residents) and two from California (with 29.3 million residents), the American Senate is seen as providing political clout to states that lack weight in the House of Representatives. There the large states dominate because its composition is based merely on population. Not so in the Senate: long-serving Senator Quinten Burdick from tiny North Dakota, for example, is chairman of an important legislative committee and is seen as someone who fights effectively for his voters every day of the year. It is also important to note that on issues involving inter-state rights, U.S. senators promote the interests of their voters, not those of their state's governments.

Components of the CF-18 aircraft are reportedly manufactured in 42 of the 50 states. The resulting American perception of regional fair play is understandable. Similarly, Washington's mammoth Super-Collider project was awarded last year to a community in rural Texas. No Canadian anywhere would believe that the Mulroney government would award a project of comparable importance to a location outside the Toronto-Ottawa-Montréal triangle. Every Outer Canadian knows that the Mulroney cabinet awarded the CF-18 maintenance contract to Canadair of Montréal despite a better and lower bid by Winnipeg's Bristol Aerospace. It has also postponed both the polar ice-breaker contract for Vancouver and the promised construction of a natural gas pipeline to Victoria.

Congress

Congressmen, representing single member geographical districts after 1842, became important vehicles for injecting local interests into their national government in both its administrative and legislative branches. The first loyalty of every congressman is to his or her district just as that of senators is to their state. In the words of one political analyst, "The first concern of every congressman seems to be how to get as much as he can out of the nation for his own state." Such an assertion could hardly be made of Canadian Members of Parliament.

In turn, successful American presidents, being elected by voters everywhere, seek to reflect in their person the diversity of their entire nation by shaking off all personal regional colouration. In our own country, there is a serious question today as to whether a resident of other than our three officially favoured cities, Toronto, Montréal and Ottawa, could lead any political party to a majority in a general election.

The constitutional separation of powers between the executive and legislative branches and the weakness of party discipline in congressional voting behaviour greatly enhance effective regional representation in Washington. Presidents and congressmen are elected for fixed terms and none resign if a particular measure is voted down in the Senate or House of Representatives. The congressional system also provides the freedom for effective territorial representation when an issue has clear state implications. Congressmen depart frequently from party lines to represent state interests; elected persons in the American capital don't hesitate to place their state or district interests ahead of their respective party line when voting.

Even the definition of 'a party unity vote' in *The Congressional Quarterly* is astonishing to Canadian Members of Parliament: "when at least 51 per cent of the members of one party vote against more than 51 per cent of the other." Between the years 1975 to 1982, during much of which the Democrats controlled the White House and both Houses of Congress, the *Quarterly* notes that party unity votes occurred in only 44.2 per cent of all recorded Senate votes and in only 39.8 per cent of votes in the House of Representatives. Weak party discipline in Washington enhances the continuing importance of regional influences in the American capital.

My own experience with our House of Commons since 1979 is that MPs from all three parties vote in solid blocs on almost every issue. Government members do so from fear that a lost vote on a measure will be deemed by their prime minister as a loss of confidence. This stems from the early to mid-nineteenth century British concept that a government falls if it loses the support of a majority in the Commons on any vote. It has now been largely abandoned in the UK and other Commonwealth countries.

Canadian MPs have represented, on average, about 87,000 individuals since the 1988 election. In practice, few of them have any real opportunity to put their constituents' interests first in votes in the House of Commons. Real power is concentrated in the hands of the three party leaderships. Canadian democracy itself would benefit substantially if we put our present mind-numbing party discipline where it belongs — in the history books.

Another feature of the congressional system in the U.S. that fosters effective regional input in national policy making is territorial bloc-voting — something quite unknown in Canada's House of Commons. The weakness of party discipline in Congress is one of several factors encouraging the formation of regional voting blocs that cross party lines. Thus legislation detrimental to regional interests can be opposed without fear of the government being defeated, and an early election being called. Representatives from the two political parties of the Mountain states, Sun Belt states, New England states and others vote en bloc or work together in committees to advance common constituency interests.

A good example of how regional representatives can influence the geographic location of federal government procurement, which affects the geographic distribution of the manufacturing sector, is the Southern congressional influence. It played a major role in the post-war concentration of federal military and space expenditures in the South and in the general economic revival and growth of the Sun Belt. If bloc-voting occurred in our House of Commons, possibly through the enactment of a fixed four year term in office, we might see some measures detrimental to Outer Canadians voted down when MPs would cross party lines to put the interests of their regions first.

A related feature of the congressional system in the U.S. is the committee system. Congressional committees and their investigative staffs, together with congressional control over departmental programs and budgets allow Congressmen to fulfil their responsibility of supervising the executive branch with a vigour that is virtually unknown in Canada. Canadian parliamentary committees are, in practice, mostly still dominated by party whips and the committee chairmen mostly government-chosen for their obedience rather than for any ability or special knowledge as independent policy-makers. Approximately 300 American House, Senate and Joint House-Senate committees and sub-committees provide real clout to their members.

It is really at committee meetings rather than on the floor of the House or Senate that American legislators play major political roles. Full regional representation is also provided directly in the composition of committees because on the House side almost 40 per cent of committee seats are reserved for members of specific states. In the discharge of their important oversight role over the executive branch, Congressmen and Senators have numerous tools — some say too many — to promote regional and local causes, including large personal staffs and large numbers of investigative personnel who work directly for committees. American public officials can be summoned to committees on short notice — and in practice must reply to most questions. Their federal counterparts in Canada can be called through subpoena, but are still not compelled to provide information which came to them in their official capacity. In theory, at least, a Canadian Deputy Minister can still refuse to say anything of substance to a Commons or Senate committee.

The American oversight function, which has opened up the national administration to territorial representation, is really only effective because individual congressmen have weight in their own right. Some American analysts, Roger Gibbins notes, have concluded "that federal agencies are, if anything, too sensitive to state desires rather than not sensitive enough. No such charge could be levelled at federal agencies in Canada." Again, one remedy for the Canadian disease in this area might be fixed term parliaments for, say, four years. A reformed and elected Senate is also vital here. Its elected members could attack and defend the government on grounds other than party loyalty if they were not under the thumbs of party whips. If the Canadian cabinet were not responsible to a reformed Senate this would also boost Senate independence.

House of Commons

The House of Commons in Ottawa correctly reflects the nation's majority will on a representation by population basis. Yet few Members of Parliament have provided effective regional voices in it since the dawn of the twentieth century when voting in party blocs became *de rigeur* for all MPs. In our present political culture, if a government or opposition MP's loyalty to his province clashes with the instructions of his party whip, putting constituents' or regional considerations first in his way of voting implies considerable risk to his prospects for party advancement. Regional or state cross-party voting, as exists in the American Congress, is virtually non-existent in our House of Commons. The situation is only a little better in House committees because they are too weak and too much lacking in publicity to have any real impact on policy. That the committees are essentially impotent in policy-making is illustrated by the fact that, since 1969 to the best of my knowledge, only one $10,000 item of proposed Ottawa spending has ever been deleted by any of numerous committees considering the annual budgetary estimates. The sum in issue had reportedly already been spent when the committee rejected it.

In short, Canadian MPs, in Leon Epstein's devastating phrase, today "function in effect as members of an electoral college that is in more or less continuous session between general elections." The respective party leaders require only the brute votes of their MPs; in consequence they are essentially passive observers in the formulation and administration of most national policy. Backbench MPs in Canada are far less able to represent regional interests effectively than are their counterparts in Washington where the congressional system provides the freedom for effective regional representation when an issue has clear regional implications. The heretical but serious question is whether a model closer to the congressional one would not serve Canadians generally better at the end of the twentieth century. Defenders of "British Parliamentary Democracy" have been numerous over the years: suggestions that the model itself might be part of the problems of Outer Canada have rarely even been made.

There are, of course, major flaws in American Congressional government, including unnecessary log-rolling, mammoth delays in committees, and vast costs associated with enhancing interregional harmony. The best solution to problems of representative democracy in Canada might be to adopt attractive features from various systems. In Britain, the matter of Parliament itself has evolved significantly away from some of its earlier twentieth century practices still followed slavishly in Canada. As the Regina political scientist, John Courtney, points out, backbench government members since the mid-1960s have shown an increasing willingness to defy their party whips. Between 1974 and 1978, for example, the government of the day was defeated 123 times on its own legislation, an average of one defeat per government bill. Courtney attributes this trend to a changed sociological mix in the British Parliamentary parties. "The older, largely subservient backbenchers of the past have gradually been replaced by younger, more independent-minded MPs . . . . The goals and political ambitions of these new members in the parliamentary system were soon matched by their frustrations with Parliament, and they have defied their party's leadership in increasing numbers. The change has been welcomed because it introduced a healthy tension into British parliamentary politics and gave new credibility to the role of the parliamentary backbencher."

Senate Reform

Many Outer Canadians regard reform of our upper house as an issue whose time has finally come after 123 years of Confederation. An Angus Reid-Southam poll completed in the spring of 1990 found that Senate reform was a constitutional priority to 53 per cent of British Columbians, 64 per cent of Albertans, 62 per cent of residents of Saskatchewan/ Manitoba, and 46 per cent of Atlantic Canadians. Among Ontarians and Québeckers surveyed in the same poll, however, only 43 per cent of the first and 37 per cent of the second held the same view.

All premiers of the outer eight provinces now appear to support the concept of a Triple E Senate. Since the death of the Meech Lake accord, moreover, the Vander Zalm government, taking the view that its ability to have input on Senate appointments is now gone, has introduced legislation to fill future senate vacancies from British Columbia by elections. There is also pressure on the Getty government to proceed once again to the election of an Alberta candidate to fill the next senate vacancy anticipated in Alberta.

The case for a Triple-E Senate is especially strong because our country has a large concentration of population in two provinces. Following the 1980 federal election which returned Pierre Trudeau as prime minister, Western Canadians knew that none of Ottawa's important institutions — the House of Commons, the Senate, the prime minister and the cabinet — would take their side on any issue. Similarly, since the 1988 election many Atlantic Canadians consider they have been abandoned by the Mulroney government. As to Northerners, they have the feeling of having been neglected by every single government in Ottawa.

The legitimate interests of the eight smaller provinces and territories are rarely afforded much attention by the institutions of our present national government. Arguably, they continue to demonstrate less sensitivity to regional perspectives on issues than is the case for any other democratic federation on earth. This is probably why federal politicians from Inner Canada have successfully blocked substantial change in Ottawa's institutions continuously since 1867.

Virtually all other federal democracies entrench legislative protection for smaller provinces through an upper house. Ours was fatally flawed from the beginning. It is unelected and therefore illegitimate in democratic terms. A second defect was its being unequal in the representation from each province. Any role for the Canadian Senate as an effective legislative voice of Outer Canada thus quickly atrophied. During the 1980s, setting the Ottawa agenda on a host of issues — patriation of the constitution, wage and price controls, the Charter of Rights, the National Energy Program, free trade with the U.S. — became the exclusive preserve of the House of Commons, dominated both numerically and psychologically by MPs from Ontario and Québec. Representation according to population is essential for the Commons, but our long national experience persistently calls for equal representation from each province in an upper house that is urgently in need of reform.

In the American government system, the Senate was established as the primary vehicle for regional representation in the national government. When conflicts occur between Washington and the states, senators defend the interests of their states, playing the role they were elected to perform. In a more recent development, many U.S. Senators have become national political figures, probably at the expense of defending their respective state interests as was traditionally the case. Our political system still provides no mechanism for effective representation from Outer Canada. Canadian senators provide no effective representation from a regional perspective because most attempt to represent the "national view" of the country by transcending provincial and regional interests. More than a century of appointments by Prime Ministers of mostly party war-horses, hacks and fund raisers from both major political parties has cumulatively delivered a mortal blow to our Senate as an institution.

Since Senate reform is above all designed to minimize the obvious centre-periphery cleavage in Canadian politics, it has increasingly become an Outer Canadian cause. It was an important part of the Alberta government's package of constitutional reforms in 1987. Premier Don Getty has so consistently promoted the concept that it is now perceived by the public as a Western issue. Despite numerous studies and an estimated twenty-four different proposals since 1967, Senate reform remains a pipe dream, itself probably the clearest indication of the essential impotence of Outer Canadians among Ottawa policy circles. The Prime Minister's promise of a fresh set of public hearings by a House Committee if the Meech Lake accord had passed was only another indication of how little he understood or cared about the issue.

The Saskatchewan-raised Gordon Robertson, a fellow-in-residence at Ottawa's Institute for Research on Public Policy, has a Western perspective on reform of the upper chamber. "If it was important, as it was in 1968, to recognize that the federal arrangements and balance of 1867 were no longer acceptable to Québec and French Canada, it is equally important now to recognize that the failure of the BNA Act to give proper weight and representation to the West in our national Parliament is no longer acceptable to that region. As I see it, it is not simply a matter of equity and justice, although those are both important. It is also the fact that, until we remedy this defect, our national governments — no matter what their party basis may be from time to time — will have to govern in a climate of western discontent and against the pressures of western governments that speak for that discontent."

It is also important in a post-Meech Canada to deal with Western, Atlantic and Northern causes of discontent with our federal balance and to listen to the grievances of Outer Canadians everywhere. In a supplement to the report of the Macdonald Commission in 1985, Albert Breton of Québec advanced a theory that he calls competitive federalism. In politics, as well as in economics, competition maximizes the well-being of citizens, he argued. The so-called executive federalism with its intergovernmental partnership might not be an adequate prescription for Canadians in meeting the challenges of the future. According to Breton, "responsible government plus federalism is extended democracy simply because there is more competition," and a reformed Senate will work as a natural "monitor" of this federal-provincial competition.

The major role of the reformed Senate would be to give prominence to the regional dimensions of public policies. It would primarily have a "monitoring" function, not only a representative role. If the competition over resources and policies in the national government is to be efficient, it is essential that provincial interests be competing with each other on an equal footing. It is no longer enough that provincial interests be represented appropriately in national debates. "They must be able," argued Breton, "to vie with each other on a basis of 'competitive equality'. Otherwise, the checks and balances that characterize national politics will be biased against the weaker provinces, even if their points of view are represented. A capacity to compete is more than a capacity to talk; it is also, and radically, a capacity to exert a real influence on decisions. That is the real meaning underlying the notion of 'monitored' competition." The Senate can only play this monitoring role if it has legitimacy; therefore, it must be elected. With Breton, I favour such a monitoring function for a Senate constituted of equal numbers of senators for each province elected at fixed intervals and for fixed periods.

Australian Model

The Australian Triple-E Senate provides a good model for Canada today partly because, like Canada, about two-thirds of Australia's population live in two of its six states. We also share a tradition of parliamentary rather than representative democracy. The founding fathers from Australia's four smaller states refused during the 1890s any form of federal union unless it included a second house representing all states equally. Initially in 1901, the Australian Senate had six senators from each state, all elected by state-wide ballots. Since 1906, half of them take their seats on fixed dates every three years. It still holds equal powers with the lower chamber, the House of Representatives, except for some limitations on money bills. Changes in its legislative authority, but not the numbers of senators from each state, can only be made by a referendum which produces an overall majority of votes cast nationally and majorities in any four of the six states.

Between 1901 and 1949, however, the Australian Senate did not effectively advance the interests of the smaller states, overtaken as it was by the national political parties. Typically, these were far more interested in achieving cabinet dominance over the business in both houses than in advancing regional interests. The pressure for obedience grew after 1900 with the rise of the Australian Labour party and its stress on party discipline for its members of parliament. In response, two new parties emerged: the Liberal party in 1946, and its rural ally, the National party in 1948. Eventually the presence in the senate of a large majority of senators from the two party alliances and their respective whips ensured that party loyalty overrode loyalty to one's states in most Senate votes. In consequence of this and other factors, the upper chamber had by the 1940s become a refuge for party hacks and was widely seen as a failure.

In 1948, a Labour government, quite unaware of the radical consequences to follow, introduced proportional voting to elect senators with grouping by parties on the ballots. In essence, the new system, like the old, required voters to rank candidates according to preference. The preferences were then added by a complex arithmetical rule. Successful candidates had to obtain enough votes so that a party's share of the votes cast corresponded with its share of the seats won. For example, the quota for election to the Senate at a half-Senate election is 17 per cent of the votes cast.

As a startling result, the defects inherent in plurality were reduced. (Electoral systems such as Canada's first-past-the-post-wins model could also benefit from it.) Minor party and independent senators suddenly found themselves benefiting from the flow of voters' second or third preferences on the ballots. By 1955, a relatively even split in Senate seats between the two major groupings gave independent and minor party senators the balance of power for the first time. No government has had a majority in the Senate except from 1975 to 1978. It is clearly abnormal to have a majority in both houses. By 1970, the new coalition of political forces allowed the creation of a Senate committee system with real clout.

By the mid-1970s, the Australian Senate had developed enough confidence to attempt to force the lower house into an election. When the Governor General, Sir John Kerr, dismissed the Whitlam Labour government in 1975, the authority of the Senate soared dramatically because it had successfully affirmed its right to refuse the spending of money even to the point of bringing down the cabinet. In 1975 it refused to pass the appropriations unless Whitlam first agreed to call a national election. When he refused, Kerr dissolved both the House and the Senate in a double dissolution. Since 1975, the Senate has been an autonomous body in the sense that because minor parties hold the balance of power the old line parties cannot control its daily agenda.

This means, in practice, that Australia's national Parliament does not practice responsible government in the way Canada and other parliamentary democracies have done since enacting reform bills at different dates during the nineteenth century. It is a hybrid which, to many Australians, is a better system than responsible government in the usual sense. When, to take a recent example, a majority in the House of Representatives prepared to introduce identity cards for Australians, a majority in Senate rejected the measure with no immediate consequences for the government of Robert Hawke.

An increasing number of Australians vote for one of the major parties in the lower house but also for one of a number of minor parties in their Senate. The presence of state-wide electoral contests enhances voter support for independent and minor party candidates, albeit more in some states than others. The Australian Democrats are strong in South Australia and Victoria states. Western Australia has become a fertile ground for senators concerned with single issues, including the environment, and Queensland tends to support the National party. Tasmania has a long tradition of electing independent Senators. In short, the Senate electoral system in place since 1949 has accommodated both regional and partisan diversity well.

Another advantage of proportional voting in terms of regional effectiveness is in the recruitment of candidates. The 1949 model has tended to create two safe Senate seats in each state for the candidates at the top of each major party list at each half-Senate election. Accordingly, vigorous competition for these top spots on the ballot lists has produced increasingly good candidates for party endorsement, further enhancing the Senate as a major player in the governing process. Because the state branches of the major parties, rather than the leaders of national parties, control their candidate selection process, prominent men and women from the various states have entered the national Parliament. Today, there are always talented and forceful representatives of state interests in the Senate — at least from the parties other than Labour — even if the Australian Senate is not a states house in the sense intended by Australia's founders.

The most important role of the Australian Senate today is to balance the executive branch. As in Canada, it appears that party discipline has subordinated most activities in the Australian lower house to the wishes of cabinets. The Australian Senate, however, being powerful in its own right, can effectively check a cabinet when it is not controlled by the party in office. Even more importantly, it ensures close scrutiny of proposed legislation and provides hearings to groups otherwise ignored by the government. All too often, a cabinet tends to establish a club-type relationship with favoured interest groups. Assuming the Senate is not controlled by the political party that forms the government, the cabinet has to sway some senators of a different political complexion or its proposed legislation is doomed to fail. Another area of key Senate activity is the free-wheeling investigations of issues of public interest — often on matters which ministries would prefer to be ignored — in a manner free of government manipulation or control. Australia's national government and democratic spirit have both improved significantly because of this interplay.

The leaderships of both major Australian political groupings resent bitterly the loss of control over the Senate because they each want to monopolize the entire legislative process. Cabinet attempts to undermine the role of the Senate have been numerous. They first attempted to limit its co-equal legislative powers. This was blocked because of the need to have all constitutional amendments approved by a referendum which gain both an overall national majority of votes and majorities in four of the six states. A second campaign sought to remove the fixed terms of senators and to ensure that the elections for both houses occur simultaneously (in order to reduce the likelihood of minor party successes) and to have all elections at the time of a government's choosing. Four constitutional proposals to this end were defeated by Australian voters, most recently during 1988. A third attempt lay in recasting the number of senators from ten to twelve with the hope that calculations of new quotas would work against minor party candidates. In the election of March 1990, the number of minor party and independent senators stayed at ten in a Senate of 76 members.

There is a constant attack on the legitimacy of the Senate in thwarting governments of the day, employing essentially nonsensical rhetoric about

British parliamentary democracy to deny any role for legislators except to pass all government proposals. Senators reply in terms of constitutionalism, checks and balances, the need for a division of powers to offset the absolute control of the lower house by the majority of the day, and the importance of compromise and consensus.

There are numerous lessons here for Senate reform in Canada. From Outer Canada's perspective, the first is the increased responsiveness coming from an institutional check on the present prime ministerial domination of our House of Commons. In the words of Campbell Sherman, a western Australian political scientist, this "invigorates the legislature and greatly increases the effectiveness of parliamentary scrutiny of government administration. It counters the distortions of the policy process that flow from the executive's attempts to reduce the influences of rival views of the national interest, to smother informed debate of its policies in the legislature, and to avoid the necessity of compromise once a measure has partisan endorsement." In other words, effectiveness is a key part of reforming the Canadian upper house. Apologists for the status quo say that an effective Senate would collide with our long-established concept of responsible government. Canada is not tiny Britain in the earlier part of the nineteenth century. An effective Senate works well in Australia and we should adapt it to our conditions in the interest of a more responsive democracy.

I agree with Sherman's view that for the Senate to be effective and politically self-confident it has to result from the direct election of senators. With him, I anticipate that a Canadian Senate based on equal representation from all provinces and elected through a proportional voting system would frequently hold a non-government majority. Two major obstacles for Canadians to overcome are our longstanding political culture, with its increasingly anomalous notion of letting governments govern without restraint, and our fear of an effective upper chamber.

In the aftermath of the Meech Lake failure, it appears particularly important to many Outer Canadians that the Mulroney government not attempt to confirm the present Senate by filling the vacancies with his party faithful. Until Senate reform is dealt with properly, good faith demands that vacancies either be filled by elections or left vacant. Outer Canadians will be watching Brian Mulroney very carefully on this issue, for many believe he and most of his cabinet and caucus like the Senate just as it is, provided it is henceforth dominated by a Conservative majority.

National Interests vs. Regional Concerns

Canada's national government should in both theory and practice represent the national interest as distinct from provincial interests. However, as "national interest" concepts are usually elusive, successive federal governments in pursuing this concept often act in ways in accord with the wishes of one particular region while forsaking all the others.

David Elton and Peter McCormick, professors of political science from the West and prominent advocates of Western issues, offer an Outer Canadian view on "national policies": "There seems to be a strange convention of federal political language that when a program is labelled 'western,' it means the benefits are distributed fairly evenly across the country, and when it is called 'national,' it means the benefits go disproportionately to Central Canada. The pattern is clearly exemplified by the statement of the Prime Minister in the House of Commons, in which he explicitly equated a long-term fighter aircraft maintenance contract (in the 'national' interest) with aid to farmers as a 'western' policy. The comparison overlooks the fact that the aid is for farmers as such, not just those farmers who live in the West, and approximately 20 per cent of the funds made available will go to farmers in Central Canada, while the jobs protected and created by the CF-18 decision will overwhelmingly be found in Central Canada."

Discussions of regionalism in Canada invariably boil down to arguments over which should prevail: regional interests or "the national interest." Nobody argues that national interest should take precedence when it reflects the aspirations of a larger number of citizens. However, by choosing a federal system of government, Canadians rejected the notion that the national majority should always prevail. Federalism means that on some issues, at least occasionally, the will of the population majority will be frustrated. If the biggest battalions of voters were to prevail over smaller ones under any circumstances, we should drop the charade that we have a federal system of government that respects minorities in times of stress. The notion that the national majority will prevail has resulted in much regional discontent and accompanying feelings of regional irrelevancy.

In an increasingly interdependent world, Canada must imaginatively create or alter existing institutions in order that they represent the interests of both Inner and Outer Canadians effectively. Unless we move away from the notion that "the national interest" is merely a code-phrase for the most populous region dominating all corners of the country, frictions between Inner and Outer Canada will probably worsen.

Renewed Federalism

The year 1989 witnessed spectacular developments in Eastern Europe. After forty-five years of totalitarian rule, new governments, inspired by democratic principles and impulses, redrafted their constitutions and introduced sweeping changes affecting almost every aspect of daily life. Why has Canada, a country fortunate to have been governed since its beginnings by democratically-elected governments, taken so long to initiate an effective process of reforms? They would not lead to such revolutionary changes as in Eastern Europe, yet they are of comparable importance to many Canadians, especially to the residents of the outer regions of the country.

RECONCILABLE DIFFERENCES

Outer Canadians need to know that however far from Toronto-Ottawa-Montréal they live, they matter in Ottawa as much as their compatriots in Inner Canada. National policies and institutions must begin to reflect their needs and be targeted to meet their requirements and aspirations as well. They need to know that they will in future be effectively represented during the process of national policy-making by those elected to defend the interests of their communities, provinces or regions. This role can no longer be subordinated to other political considerations. In order for this notion to become a reality, we need as a people to renew our federalism. We need to do so now as badly, or perhaps more so, as when Prime Minister Trudeau promised "renewed federalism" to Québec during the 1980 referendum campaign.

The first initiative should be Senate reform, combined with improved regional representation in many federal government institutions, agencies and wherever policy-making affects certain regions. There is also a need for fair and generous financial assistance and federal government procurement funds that might show a bias this time towards disadvantaged regions of the country. The ongoing nation-wide debates on Senate reform and the repercussions of the failure of the Meech Lake accord have already started the process of renewing Canadian federalism. The impulse is gaining momentum and cannot be stopped. Nor should we wish it to be averted. However, if it is lost now, future generations of Canadians will blame their parents for losing possibly the last opportunity to strengthen our sense of common purpose and unity.

In 1867, the Fathers of Confederation laid down Canada's national objectives as "peace, order and good government." Principles chosen by reform movements or revolutions are somehow often expressed in threes. The American Declaration of Independence set them out as, "life, liberty and the pursuit of happiness." Revolutionary France put the objectives as "liberté, égalité, fraternité." Proponents of our reformed Senate want it to be, "Equal, Elected, Effective." A new national credo for Canada would be difficult to define in three catchy words. Descriptive phrases might help express the principles towards which our federal system should be evolving: effective regional representation and fairness; inter-cultural acceptance and respect; equal economic opportunity for all Canadians.

ELEVEN

OUR FUTURE TOGETHER

The twentieth century, we were promised by Wilfrid Laurier, would belong to Canada. Instead the country is today entangled in a constitutional knot, faces mounting economic problems and is even endangered in its existence as a single country. The demise of the Meech Lake accord, the first-ever separatist Member of Parliament elected for a new Bloc Québécois in the House of Commons, Western premiers musing publicly about their region's fate in the new political climate — these and other issues indicate we are at a pivotal moment in Canada's history.

Our present crisis provides opportunity to move on and follow directions that might lead us to fulfil the dreams and expectations placed in Confederation. Trying to maintain the status quo with a series of crisis-controls and palliative measures will simply no longer do. Only courage, vision and sense of purpose can prevent our country from fragmenting into regional blocs, political and economic structures devoid of the attraction of being a part of one great country.

The late Robert Kennedy used to say: "Some men see things as they are and say 'Why?' I dream things that never were and say 'Why not?' " All of us who have not given up on a united Canada during this difficult period must not hesitate to think things that never were. The vision for the future of Canada I hold is one where the principles of regional equality and fairness will not only be reflected in national institutions, but will serve as eminent precepts for the conduct of decision- and policy-makers. Should the legitimate concerns of the disadvantaged outer parts of our country not be integral parts of the national interest and addressed accordingly? In short, we need to renew our federalism quickly and we all have a role to play in bringing this about. The goal of the exercise here is worthy of everyone's best effort: one united Canada.

What follows is an attempt to propose remedies in the direction of overall reforms. They include constitutional, institutional and economic matters, but are neither exhaustive, comprehensive nor all-encompassing. Consistent with the thrust of this book, they seek to end our present pattern of the centre versus the peripheries which has created two classes of Canadians.

All of the proposed reforms are achievable, but they will probably require a new political leadership convinced that real changes, not cosmetic ones, have to come if we want to keep this country together. My vision of the country relates to the 1990s and beyond.

A New National Policy

We cannot build unity if the things that divide Canadians are not dealt with candidly as part of a genuine renewal process. Examining what Canada is all about must include what the country might become. Repeating worn-out clichés and appealing to a sentimental concept of Canada cannot replace serious attempts to address basic issues at the heart of the many problems facing the country.

Addressing the inequalities resulting from the division of the country into Outer and Inner Canada is vital. The outer regions contribute to the success of the centre, but for more than a century their role in Confederation has been reduced to little more than natural resource hinterlands. Our national Main Street, as the most favoured, populous and prosperous region of the country, must start to share opportunities with them.

The failure of successive federal governments to deal with and reconcile divergent regional needs has produced serious strains and cracks in the fabric of our country. Only once has Canada defined its overriding national goals. In 1879, the "National Policy" set the objectives of populating the country, linking the common market with a national transportation network, and developing our industrial base. The two central provinces, more accurately the southern parts of them, were the beneficiaries of the industrial strategy with the ensuing economic stability and political weight. The Atlantic provinces declined in relative importance and became more and more dependent on federal government handouts. This spawned a bitter sense of regional grievance, one that Western Canadians have shared fully and that is now in my own region, for various reasons, close to an all-time high since the Great Depression.

More than at any other time in our history, we need to formulate a New National Policy. Central to it must be the principle of fairness and equality of opportunities for all, including the residents of the eight outer provinces and of the two territories. All have worked hard to strengthen Inner Canada during the earlier years, often at the expense of their own unrealized potential and aspirations.

Atlantic Canada, Northern Ontario, peripheral Québec, Western Canada and the North — all need to be fully integrated into a national partnership. Their priorities and concerns must be addressed by Ottawa in a manner sensitive to the local needs of each of them.

The alienation, isolation and hopelessness of the inhabitants of Northern Ontario's resource-towns and the Québec single-industry peripheral communities must become a concern for national decision-makers who now dismiss them as part of an unchangeable hinterland experience. Boom-and-bust cycles can be expected to persist in these Northern communities, but innovative approaches to diversify the local economies are available. They include involvement and participation by residents in community-based development programs and the redirection of regional development funds away from centres in our industrial core. Both would bring welcome changes to local economies and improve the quality of life in remote, harsh, yet breathtakingly beautiful environments.

We need to bring Maritimers and Newfoundlanders back into Confederation as equal partners and not as the stereotyped "poor cousins." This will require serious attempts to break the cycle of the region's dependency and reliance on Ottawa grants. There are many views on how best to move the Atlantic provinces to self-reliance, but locally devised programs usually deal best with specific problems. Greater investment in one of the region's largest and real assets, its people, can bring a transition to self-reliance and sustainable economic development. Better joint federal and provincial programs are needed to assist Atlantic Canadians to upgrade their skills, manage new technologies, and provide more support for local research in developing new strategies and technologies. New job creation in non-traditional occupations, particularly in services across Atlantic Canada, is crucial. It would allow people to avoid the costs of migration and to reap the personal benefits of pride and confidence.

The Atlantic Economic Council proposed an Atlantic alliance, believing it would provide the region with a unified voice to help eliminate institutional barriers to growth and to facilitate access to modern communication technologies. It might also increase the demand for Atlantic products both within Canada and abroad and enhance their creation through a better coordinated development policy. Products derived from resources common throughout the region should, in particular, find opportunities for improved access to American and European markets. The entire region must present a unified voice in the planning of national trade policy and in negotiations over marine boundaries and fisheries management.

The expansion of capabilities in such activities as developmental software is also important for the Atlantic region. Its industrial base must be diversified, all opportunities to develop new products and services pursued. Special emphasis must be placed on high and medium technology operations, on activities that are "knowledge-intensive." A range of human skills need to be further developed. Better rail transportation is another part of Atlantic Canadian needs. Residents have long depended on rail passenger transportation, more than most other Canadians. It might not be feasible to restore the regionally-oriented freight rate system of the Intercolonial railway before 1912, which did so much to promote regional manufacturing, but all options should be fully considered in light of the harm done by earlier national governments. Certainly the damage done to the region by the most recent VIA Rail cutbacks should be undone as quickly as possible.

Western Canadians believe their region is vital to the overall nature of Canada. They have sought the democratization of institutions and a pluralistic society in which no cultural background is given preference. Yet, Westerners share the conviction that our potential in human and national resources has been too little explored and developed.

The "New West" is going to be built on, among other things, technological advances in processing natural resources. Ottawa must assist in this process rather than continuing to indicate that it believes Westerners are all wheat farmers. A coherent strategy is needed to achieve western diversification. A first step is obtaining a fair share from Ottawa of regional development spending, federal procurement and export financing. More investment in the region's real asset, its people, is needed to achieve a more skilled and mobile population for new technologies.

The four Western premiers, during their July 1990 conference, discussed general objectives and a common agenda for the region to follow in order to overcome challenges. They agreed to ensure closer co-operation and co-ordination among the Western provinces and a reduction in interprovincial barriers to commerce. The region also needs to define a position on the needs of agriculture and of the food industry in respect to international trade. Improved regional science and technology and research and development efforts can prepare the West for a host of technological changes. An improved information network about new products with greater distribution to the regional business community across the four Western provinces and beyond is badly needed. New export opportunities need to be sought in part because export-driven growth encourages diversification. A good business climate has to be maintained as the success of most initiatives will depend largely on the private sector. Foreign investment has to be attracted to technology sectors and more transfers of proven foreign technologies into the region are necessary.

Western disaffection has to be dealt with, not dismissed casually as a regional phenomenon nurtured by stereotyped Westerners. Westerners need to know that their concerns are ongoing priorities for national leaders. The fact that so many Westerners today feel alienated from the national government shows that the present government, like virtually all before it, is unable to see the West as a fully equal partner. In this context, the Triple-E Senate — the product largely of Western thinking on how to bring the voice of all outer regions more effectively into Ottawa — must not be lost in the aftermath of Meech Lake's collapse. Westerners must continue their campaign to democratize the upper house.

Seven and a half million Westerners seek major changes on both the attitudinal and institutional fronts in Ottawa, but economic and political equality with Ontario and Québec continues to elude our region eight decades after the last two Western provinces joined the union. The more we hear about regional fairness, the more elusive the concept appears to become. National leaders must put their rhetoric into practice in all corners of the federal government. Some national institutions will simply have to be forced to represent all regions fairly; the issue will be an important symbol of national unity for any national government in the 1990s. A host of changes in discriminatory practices inherent to our "executive democracy" under which Westerners have struggled needlessly for decades must be completed rapidly. Then, and only then, will the region be a full partner in Confederation, and the political party in office achieving them become a truly effective instrument of national reconciliation.

The North essentially defines the Canadian personality and sets us apart as a nation. Throughout history we have failed to develop a fair partnership with the residents of at least forty per cent of our national land mass. We ignore the special character of the region and the uniqueness of its peoples and continue to impose on them southern ideas and structures, mostly originating in Western Europe, that were not designed to accommodate northern circumstances. What we really ought to decide is whether we want the North to continue to be a part of Canada. If so, are we prepared to do what is necessary to provide the political and economic conditions in which native and non-native Northerners can govern themselves and be themselves?

Such a policy would also reinforce the Canadian presence across the North. The ongoing issue of Canadian Arctic sovereignty resurfaced with the voyage of the American ice-breaker, "the Polar Sea" — many saw it as a direct challenge to Canadian sovereignty over the waters of the archipelago. Canadians clearly want these northern parts to remain Canadian. The residents are Canadian Inuit; new constitutional arrangements must be achieved to recognize them as equal Canadians. Our unique national character should enable us to accommodate differing cultural, political and economic interests in Canada's North as elsewhere. We have here a rare chance to demonstrate to the world that Canadians really are unique in that they can live successfully with differences.

Until now, Canada's frontiers have lacked a spirit of belonging and a common sense of purpose with the rest of the nation. Disappointment and frustration with the terms of Confederation in distant corners of the country have torn at the very fabric of Canadian nationhood. In order to preserve the country, we must now respect our frontiers in ways which give us all a unifying sense of national purpose, fired by the effort of meeting a common challenge.

The only region widely seen today as a "frontier" is our North, with its richness in human and natural resources. Some Southerners came, lured by its many promises, and left, taking out all that could be turned into profit, bringing disruption and destruction to the centuries-old ways of life there.

We must re-invent this frontier in order to repair the damage that the greed behind the "roads to resources" drive has caused. Canada, as a whole, needs the balance that the ecologically-sensitive North needs — the balance between desired economic development and preservation of an awesome environmental heritage that belongs to all Canadians. Above all, we must bring justice and a dignified way of life to the once self-reliant and proud native peoples, who face poverty and discrimination, powerlessness and assimilation within their own homeland.

In short, the region and its peoples have to be finally brought into Confederation as equal partners, enriching us all. This is the real challenge of the North and Canada.

Related in part to the subordination of the North is the ongoing subjugation of aboriginal Canadians across the country. No other Outer Canadians have been treated worse, or for longer, by successive national governments. Under the Indian Act, enacted in 1876 by the Parliament of Canada and incredibly still in full force today, Ottawa mandated its Indian Affairs Department to control virtually every aspect of Indian life: land use, education, politics, municipal and provincial government matters, economic development. Even some Indian Band Council resolutions must still be approved by the department before going into effect. In brief, the statute purports to encourage Indians, but in practice affords little respect to their culture, religion or traditional way of life. I agree with George Erasmus, President of the Assembly of First Nations, that Ottawa still views aboriginal Canadians as "wards of the government with no real ability to influence their communities."

A positive consequence of the barricades at Oka and Mercier Bridge was the widespread agreement among Canadians that it is time to end the "dialogue of the deaf" between governments and aboriginal peoples. A more serious effort by Ottawa to complete land claims negotiations is essential. Our First Nations also have a good deal to teach other Canadians about self-government, which some of them practised even before Europeans reached North America. I support the key recommendation of the 1983 House of Commons Special Committee on Indian Self-Government that Ottawa must establish a new relationship with the Indian First Nations and that an essential element of the relationship must be Indian self-government.

Economic Development

Despite decades of intervention by governments, regional economic disparities in Canada persist. Gaps in employment opportunities widen and stagnation remains a fact of life in many remote communities throughout Outer Canada. A multitude of Ottawa-designed measures to reduce economic disparities between regions have not brought significant improvements, and the need for a new approach to the problem is evident. The notion of using community programs as tools for economic and business development is thus gaining support in Outer Canada. Residents of small isolated communities in hinterland regions face the choice between a continued dependence on welfare and emigration, or active involvement in local development with assistance. They are taking up the challenge of revitalizing their economies. They are also better aware of their economic problems and opportunities than are officials in distant centres. So many "top-down" policies, devised by distant federal and provincial bureaucrats, have proved unsuccessful. Thriving "bottom-up" initiatives undertaken by isolated communities suggest this might be the welcome break in re-thinking economic development across our country.

The concept of locally generated initiatives as a tool for economic development in depressed communities is still at the experimental stage. Already there is enough evidence that this approach can revitalize the economies of small and isolated communities. Paradoxically, the federal government has a role to play in encouraging decision-making and self-help through local development organizations. No additional spending is required; it is sufficient that the assistance presently earmarked for the region be channelled to local development organizations, and free from bureaucratic domination. This assistance should provide the resources enabling these local organizations to create information networks, to train people and to explore new market opportunities. Smaller and more isolated communities must have priority over urban centres in obtaining govern-ment funding because they face more difficulties in acquiring the money and business information they need.

Local development approaches will not work economic magic; nor can they be panaceas for all economic hardships. Yet they present a viable opportunity for residents of remote parts of the country, if instead of turning to welfare or emigration, they are allowed to shape their own future in the environment in which they grew up and want to live. The involvement of the federal government in assisting such efforts would be seen as a caring response to the needs and concerns of Outer Canadians, and proof that the vision of prosperous Canada extends to all communities. As additional funding is not anticipated for such a strategy — an important consideration in a period of fiscal restraint — policy makers should seriously consider this concept as a tool for improving the economic viability of stagnating communities. The payoffs might be measured in terms of human dignity, an improved quality of life for Outer Canadians and a boosted economic vitality for their depressed communities, as well as a changed perception of the national government as being responsive to local concerns.

Our national policy-makers tend to devise most fiscal, monetary and other economic policies for the entire country on the basis of national averages. Also, some of their policies are specifically targeted to deal with Central Canada's problems. However, sharp discrepancies in regional unemployment rates and the economic performance of provinces suggest that we cease these practices; monetary policies intended to cool the economies in the centre often destroy the economic health of Outer Canada. Ottawa programs and initiatives can no longer be designed on the basis of average national needs as these often have little or limited application for the needs of individual regions and local communities.

More than 75 per cent of the new jobs created since 1983 were in Ontario and Québec. This shows that unemployed Canadians in Outer Canada do not have equal access to job training and employment opportunities. Current accelerating trends in national employment patterns indicate that slow-growth regions and isolated communities will be further disadvantaged.

During the last decade, virtually all of the job creation in the country took place in the service sector. Now, the development opportunities for service-led growth in regions which lack diversified or specialized service centres are not bright. The increasing importance of the service industries, mostly concentrated in relatively few major cities, suggests that regions lacking significant metropolitan centres will face developmental problems.

The national labour market in the 1990s as identified by leading economic analysts will be characterized by increasing employment in service activities, more jobs requiring high knowledge, and further concentration of highly skilled and well paying jobs in large centres. These developments and the way we respond to them will determine both our regional employment opportunities and our overall position in the global economy. Quick and decisive efforts by the national government are needed to bring about adjustments. Effective education and training programs must take these trends into account and serve to develop the human resources of our Outer regions. Investment in people is our best stake in the future.

We must also re-examine our education and training practices. There is mounting evidence that many entering the labour force lack numeracy and language skills, making further training difficult. Also, the training programs of both federal and provincial governments which do not respond to the needs of the labour market must be redesigned: if redundant, inflexible or irrelevant they should be eliminated.

The world is becoming much more competitive and technology is evolving rapidly. To maintain lifestyles we are accustomed to, we must compete with vibrantly developing economies everywhere. Canada's living standards are already falling in relation to those of other industrial nations and our overall competitiveness is slipping due to declining industrial efficiency and limited research and development effort. According to the 1990 World Competitiveness Report, Canada ranks fifth among 23 industrial countries in international competition following Japan, Switzerland, the United States and West Germany. A year earlier, we ranked fourth.

The energy and attention of Canadians has been focused on the Meech

Lake accord tribulations for too long. We need, instead, to deal with the way we prepare Canadians for the challenges of an increasingly techno-logical world. We need a concentrated effort by Ottawa and all of the provinces to respond to the challenge.

A Regional Perspective

The remedies to many of Outer Canada's legitimate grievances are within our national grasp if elected and appointed policy makers in Ottawa can be persuaded to significantly change their attitudes and a host of policies and laws. Regional justice must become a major Ottawa priority, continuously reinforced by an iron political will from every government in Ottawa. For the sake of genuine national unity, any prime minister worthy of the office must be ready to "walk their talk" on the issue.

For most of Canada's 123 years, southern Ontario and metropolitan Québec have offered models of dynamic, diversified, and stable commu-nities in what is now internationally regarded as one of the most successful federal democracies on earth. In terms of Inner Canada by itself, the grand Canadian experiment has succeeded probably beyond any of its founders' dreams. It seems unthinkable to many Outer Canadians that significant numbers of Montréalers now favour effectively breaking their ties with the rest of Canada as the recent by-election in Montréal suggests. Has the virus of secession, evident in so many nations across the world in a *perestroika* age, reached even the core of Québec?

Some in our three favoured cities continue to believe that the real Canada does not exist beyond the viewing distance from Toronto's CN Tower, Montréal's Place Ville Marie, or Ottawa's Peace Tower. If you've real talent, they think, you'll relocate from Outer Canada and become "movers and shakers" where the real action is. Do they really believe that in a world boiling over with secessionists from Lithuania to Tibet that Canada will survive into the 21st century as one country if Ottawa policy makers continue to treat Inner Canadians as their only real constituency?

Within the European Community, as the 1992 unified market fast approaches, large regional disparities exist, but there is at least a growing consensus among Eurocrats and European parliamentarians alike that they must be reduced with all possible speed. From a Canadian perspective, it was facile to argue, as Pierre Trudeau did more than two decades ago, that "the road to prosperity lies in the direction of international integration"; Québeckers, unlike West Europeans, have never known the presumed advantages of full sovereignty. Many Québeckers today clearly believe that their cultural and language differences demand full nationhood with possible economic ties to the rest of Canada to be discussed after separa-tion. This reality gives a special urgency to the regional justice issue now facing our country.

The entire national government deck must be reshuffled so as not to be stacked in favour of Inner Canada. For example, if the chartered banks can be shown to be lending a disproportionate share of their depositors' money to finance realty projects in and around Metro Toronto, a new Minister of Finance should exercise some "moral suasion." Is it better to have yet another mammoth commercial tower in downtown Toronto, or to ensure that small businesses across the country (which already employ more than 40 per cent of us) have better access to bank credit than most now do? This heresy will evoke outrage from the executives of our "Big Six" banks; but if these companies are paying virtually no federal income tax, few individuals are likely to take their howls seriously.

Some judicious carrots and sticks will probably also be necessary to encourage new manufacturing plants and future-oriented businesses to locate across the country. Part of the problem is business culture: too many business people think their facility must be within Inner Canada to be "on the varsity." Ottawa must use the host of levers it holds, including its procurement policies, to achieve a more regionally-balanced manufacturing sector. One obvious means is to encourage newcomers to Canada to settle across Outer Canada. There are limits to this, of course. But current practice seems to perpetuate the bias: one complaint heard about our Hong Kong immigration office is that officials there continue to encourage applicants to choose Toronto or Montréal as their destinations. Wouldn't an Immigration Minister who cares about this issue attempt to ensure that all our missions abroad try more vigorously to persuade immigrants to locate across the entire country?

In the case of tourism, why are so many of the national government's new tourist attractions located in Ottawa-Hull? One initiative in that respect could develop a new formula by which Tourism Canada, when spending abroad on promotion of Canada, would provide a leg-up to peripheral communities whose economy depends on tourism. Instead of borrowing hundreds of millions of dollars to build the National Art Gallery and the Museum of Civilization in the National Capital region, a more nationalized government might have spent a fraction of such sums attempting to spread the National Gallery collection across the country. The Tyrrell Museum of Palaeontology near Drumheller, Alberta, completed in 1987 and run by the provincial government, illustrates the point. Built at a fraction of the cost of Ottawa's Museum of Civilization, it has already attracted more than 600,000 visitors on the basis of its exhibits. Ottawa should be putting its available museum and tourism dollars into similar projects across Canada.

More than ever, our major electronic and print media are concentrated in Toronto and Montréal. In consequence, the news that most Canadians watch or read across the country is filtered through the priorities of Inner Canadian editors. It is essential for national balance and fairness that the attention of the country does not always focus on issues from the perspective of our two largest cities.

The CBC is one of the most vital links between our regions and is essential to enhance our cultural identity. Its mandate should require that it make issues better known to Canadians: region to region, province to province, coast to coast. Regional programming for the most part continues to be done according to Inner Canadian perceptions of regional values and traditions. It should, instead, strive to produce quality productions reflecting authentic regional concerns and culture. The unique identity of communities such as Corner Brook, La Ronge or Iqaluit should also be given the opportunity to be seen and heard nationally. Such coverage is a prerequisite for a better mutual understanding among Canadians in diverse regions and a shared feeling of belonging to one country. This is the real challenge to both public and private media across Canada.

Our national government is a highly centralized organization and a disproportionate number of its key decision-makers have experience only within Inner Canada. For this and other reasons, the capacity of our federal government to represent regional interests and take into account regional circumstances is grossly inadequate. Ottawa officials play key roles in the decision-making process: they are shaping the policies of the government. Major decisions are normally made at the middle and senior levels of departments. Despite their protests to the contrary, cabinet ministers rarely have much influence on the first draft of a policy position paper or on cabinet documents. It is vital to look at the federal bureaucracy from a regional perspective in order to see who are the usually faceless personalities behind policies that affect Canadians in every corner of the country. Better regional representation in the public service could provide more effective participation by Canadians from Outer Canada in national decision-making. Senior public servants must in future be more aware of existing opportunities and limitations in the regions before setting policy; they must be made more responsive to specific needs of the region and more sensitive to regional circumstances.

A few years ago, the Secretary of State for External Affairs, Joe Clark, organized a "cultural immersion" for some six federal deputy ministers in Edmonton. The, seminar conducted by prominent Albertans, was intended to give them a sense of Western Canada, to dispel some old stereotypes and to sensitize them to the needs of the region. It was reportedly a highly successful endeavour and should be expanded and continued on a regular basis. The awareness Ottawa-based officials have of Canada as a whole could also be reinforced by rotating personnel between headquarters in Ottawa and the regions.

A Constitutional Convention

In the post-Meech era, it is difficult to foresee successful constitutional negotiations during the next two or three years. Many Canadians were deeply offended by the "top-down" first ministers' process of last June's eleventh hour negotiations to save the Meech Lake accord. The next stage in updating our constitution must have real democratic legitimacy.

The Federal Republic of Germany's constitutional convention of 1948 might be a model, though it would have to be adapted to Canadian circumstances. One of its appeals for provincial governments is that the West German basic law established a federal system of government which entrenched effective safeguards to protect the rights of the eleven German states. These include a constitutional court, half of whose members are appointed by ministers of the state governments. Rotating and instructed delegates of the state governments constitute the upper house or Bundesrat. The Federal Republic of Germany continues today as a genuinely federal state; the state governments have not been reduced to being mere subordinates of the central government as so often happens in federal systems. The Federal Republic is, today, one of the most successful democracies established since the Second World War. Canadians everywhere can be impressed by the effective guarantees of individual rights and freedoms enshrined in West German basic law. How did it come about?

The West Germans, with a population of 45 million in 1948 and a territory about one-half that of our Yukon, chose sixty-five individuals to draft their new constitution. Canadians and their governments might now agree that sixty-five is a workable number of delegates for a Canadian constitutional convention despite our size and regional differences. Allocating sixty-five positions would be difficult to resolve to everyone's satisfaction, but with good will on all sides it can be achieved. Since Canada, unlike many other democracies, has never had a constituent assembly, it would be healthy to have our citizens elect directly a majority of the delegates.

Thirty-three could be elected on a province-wide basis in elections held on the same day across Canada using voters' lists compiled at the previous federal election. In larger provinces, it might be more practical to elect, say, one delegate from each of a number of districts. Candidates could campaign either as independents or with the endorsement of a political party. No tax monies would be available to subsidize election campaigns, but daily allowances could be paid to delegates for their time at the convention.

Direct election of thirty-three delegates might be rejected by all thirteen governments (including the two territorial ones) for reasons of cost at a time when many taxpayers are wary of any proposal involving more spending of their money. In that case the two levels of government could each appoint thirty-two delegates on the same basis as was done by the legislatures of the West German states to provide representation for all political parties represented in the various assemblies. The remaining thirty-two delegates might be chosen by federal and provincial legislatures according to rules worked out by a federal-provincial conference of first ministers.

The Canadian convention could adopt the basic structures and procedures of the German convention for the best of all possible reasons: they worked. There would be little need for experts to prepare a draft constitution: we already have the BNA Act and many other modern federal constitutions, including the West German basic law, as points of departure and of reference.

A major issue would be whether a new constitution adopted by the constitutional convention would be binding without ratification by Parliament and all ten provincial legislatures. The West German experience indicates that it might be more realistic not to require approval by a majority in any. The premise would be that a majority-approved constitution should not be a creation of Parliament and the legislatures, but rather an enactment of the will of the Canadian people, the real source of both federal and provincial authority. The constitutional convention would represent the Canadian people as a whole.

There could be a condition that unless a majority in each of the thirteen legislatures subsequently ratified the proposed constitution in a free vote, our existing constitution and conventions would continue unaltered in their entirety. This would encourage all delegates to look for compromise-formulas thought to be acceptable to a majority in each of the legislatures. In providing such a veto to a slim majority of politicians in every legislative assembly in the land, the whole process might, however, become a huge waste of time, money, and national goodwill.

I am fully aware that, whatever form the new constitution may take, it will inevitably appear to be less than satisfactory to some of the delegates, to a minority or majority of legislators in each of the federal and provincial legislatures, and to some of the Canadian people. Dissenters might well prefer the status quo to be maintained. Yet national events, in particular the present mood of public opinion in Québec, unmistakably suggest that existing arrangements need to be updated to reflect the realities of today. After what happened in June of 1990, the current political and constitutional practices could result in the eventual dismemberment of our country. Like the West Germans in 1948, we have no choice but to entrench in a new constitution all the features of a truly federal state, a nation in which Canadians, wherever they live, will feel themselves to be full partners.

An important preliminary step to the convening of a constitutional convention should be public hearings held in every province and territory to hear from Canadians. Those on a panel doing the listening could be men and women chosen by members of our national family, including the English- and French-speaking, aboriginals, the West, Atlantic Canada, the North, Québec, Ontario, and the third of our people of origin in neither the United Kingdom nor France. The panel might produce a first draft of what it had heard and circulate it broadly for further public discussion. Once this process is completed, delegates to the constitutional convention could be elected by any method recommended by the panel in time. A national referendum might well be recommended by both the panel and the constitutional convention to ratify any constitutional recommendations.

Senate Reform

Our unloved Canadian Senate was fatally flawed from Confederation onward because senators were both appointed for life and named by the Prime Minister, a double defect completely incompatible with producing effective regional voices in the Canadian Senate. There is now growing public support across Canada for major Senate reform, and possibly enough public awareness that a reformed upper chamber is essential if our national government is to work the way it should.

We Outer Canadians need assurance that our concerns will become continuously part of the national policy agenda, for the first time since 1867. The recent long overdue appointment to the Senate of the first-ever elected Senator, Stan Waters, as well as a rather limp-wristed statement of good intention about Senate reform in the first ministers' political agreement of June, 1990 might be signs on the wall. Perhaps it has finally been realized that a remodelling of the Senate aimed at balancing our federal system cannot be postponed any longer. Still, a meaningful mechanism leading to the overhaul of our upper chamber is not yet in place. With the Meech Lake accord's failure, some even consider Senate reform a dead issue. I believe that the momentum originating in the West to elect senators cannot now be stopped. As we redefine the country's institutions, Senate reform will reappear on the agenda with even more urgency.

Our country faces a set of challenges that would be daunting even at the best of times. The events of the year 1990, a critical one in our history, reinforce a need for a new constitutional deal that would foster harmony and consensus among the various parts and peoples of Canada, the pressing need to reduce a staggering national debt without recourse to a crippling new national consumption tax and the need to build an economy fit to meet the requirements of a highly competitive world-market. A new test is how to harness the negative energy and emotion released by the failure of the Meech Lake accord; how to channel it into a constructive process leading to reforms; how to make sure that these reforms will reflect the real needs and concerns of all parties involved in the Meech Lake process. To meet the demands of our time, we need political leaders who will rise to the occasion. Disillusionment with our current leading politicians probably makes it impossible for us not only to trust them again, but also to believe they can reconcile our differences and bring about healing.

The intellectual vacuum that now permeates Ottawa seems incapable of reconciling the contradictory forces at play. Nor can it deal effectively with regional demands and at the same time rekindle a national spirit of unity. We require national leaders capable of setting a clear agenda for the current political climate and of bringing us together. These must be men and women who have the respect and trust of Canadians generally, and ultimately people whose vision of our country includes regional fairness in all government policies, equal economic opportunity for Canadians everywhere and personal integrity. Above all, we need a higher sense of national purpose and a redefinition of our national objectives, policies and institutions which must better reflect our differences. The concerns of all of us, no matter where we live, must become a part of national policy-making. Only in these terms can we find the nation and the unity the vast majority of Canadians are seeking.

POSTSCRIPT
EXPULSION

One by-product of the GST issue was a demonstration to Canadians of what happens to MPs who dare to side with their constituents instead of the government whip in present day Ottawa.

From virtually the beginning of his period as Finance Minister, Michael Wilson struck me as the embodiment of my late father's view, expressed in the mid-1950s, that the main goal of the national Conservative party was to improve the financial lot of wealthy Torontonians and Montréalers. His changes in personal income taxes following the 1984 election indicated that high-income earners were to be the main beneficiaries while many low and middle-income families faced successive volleys of tax increases. The National Council of Welfare estimates that by 1991 the federal taxes for families with a total income of $25,000 will have risen 60 per cent since 1984.

Reforming Ottawa's corporate income tax meant that the share of federal tax revenues generated by our income tax on companies would fall from 18 per cent in 1980 to an estimated 10 per cent for this fiscal year. Donald Blenkarn, the minister's usually like-thinking chairman of the Finance Committee, and Murray Dorin, the vice-chairman, both said publicly earlier in 1990 that they would like to see the federal corporation tax abolished completely.

When Wilson released his technical paper on the GST in the spring of 1989, I was troubled from a number of standpoints, most notably on the issues of fairness and simplicity. I asked the Library of Parliament and as many other sources as possible for everything they could provide and began to dig into the proposal in depth. Constituents and individuals and groups from many provinces were also sources of much good advice. Like an onion, the more layers I managed to remove the worse it smelled.

For example, many Outer Canadians believe the major motivation for the GST was to release about 75,000 manufacturers, mostly located in southern Ontario and around Montréal, from the burden carried since 1924 of collecting the MST in favour of requiring more than two million small businesses and individuals across the country to collect an even larger amount of revenue from consumers everywhere. When responsible economists estimated that the switch from the MST to the GST represented a tax break of approximately $4 billion on business inputs, mostly for larger companies, my father's earlier view took on an even sharper focus.

Canadians in cities sensed that the new tax would be an additional obstacle for the very large number of small businessmen selling all manner of services and goods to each other. Many instinctively shared the view of the Toronto urbanologist Jane Jacobs on value-added taxes: "no neater little tax contrivance could be imagined for favouring large, relatively self-sufficient enterprises such as multinational corporations with their many subsidiaries and many internal transactions while penalizing symbiotic production. Such a tax," she concluded, "needlessly twists the knife in the very vitals of city economies."

In early October of 1989, I sent a detailed submission to the Commons Finance Committee which reflected my conclusion that the GST would be a major policy error of National Energy Program proportions. A copy was sent to every Conservative MP and senator. It contained a range of serious objections to the proposal. For example, the seven per cent GST levy on transportation services struck me as providing an especially discriminatory blow for Outer Canadians generally, both as consumers and producers. Someone in Nanaimo, St. John's or Yellowknife would be required, for the first time, to pay seven per cent on the cost of shipping a refrigerator — most probably from somewhere in Inner Canada — based on the distance involved. A producer in Outer Canada would have to absorb a similar levy in order to compete in our most populous markets within Inner Canada. The present MST provides a small tax advantage to remote manufacturers of finished products — so the MST provides one of the few competitive advantages Outer Canadians enjoy.

Except for a brief period in Denmark, my submission stressed, countries with a value-added consumption tax invariably raise the rate significantly after its introduction. Handing Ottawa a fresh means of raising vast quantities of new tax monies would inevitably reduce the current public pressure to bring the national finances and debt under control. As nations with value-added taxes all appear to have higher levels of government spending than those which don't, the introduction of the GST would, in my view, only ratchet up overall spending by Ottawa to new and higher levels.

The submission stressed the view of the Atlantic Provinces' Economic Council that the ability of a manufacturer or retailer to pass on the GST to consumers in Atlantic Canada would be greater than in regions of greater population concentration where market competition is more vigorous. The GST is simply a means of collecting, from residents of nine of our ten provinces, a second and differently calculated retail sales tax which would prove a nightmare for most of those required by law to collect it. I've since learned that if the Senate passes the tax as is, Canada will be the only nation on earth with a two-tier sales tax, most probably calculated differently, in nine provinces. A recent study by the Institute for Policy Analysis estimates that a harmonized federal-provincial goods and services tax would cost more than 200,000 jobs in the first years of implementation.

I agreed with a study which was done by the Cambridge Research Institute that where a value-added tax is designed to raise additional revenues — as this one undoubtedly was, despite Michael Wilson's repeated claims that it would be revenue neutral — price increases are greater than where such taxes do not raise more taxes than what they replace. A Conservative MP from Britain had admitted to me that Margaret Thatcher's virtual doubling of the value-added tax to 15 per cent during 1979 was one major reason why the U.K. inflation rate rose from 8 per cent in 1979 to 20 per cent in 1980.

The cost of the GST in reduced revenues and employment and additional administrative costs to businesses which are price sensitive would be high. Wilson's technical paper suggested that a series of taxes and rebates on eleven transactions occurring between the iron ore and washing machine dealer stage would produce only $54 in GST revenue for Ottawa. But at what administrative cost and loss of sales to all those required to be Ottawa's collectors along the way? A spokesman for the Boy Scout movement in Western Canada had told me they expected their revenues at the earlier nine per cent rate would drop by eighteen per cent under the tax: nine per cent in revenues and nine per cent to collect it. What would be the full costs of this measure for our large voluntary sector nationally?

The experience of the European Community nations with value-added taxes is not encouraging. In some, business felt it was simply pre-financing government because it had to file tax returns monthly, while rebates came quarterly. Evasion of the tax in Europe appeared to be considerable, especially in the service sector, either through barter arrangements without invoices or through selling services free of the tax and then either not recording the sale or invoicing for less than the full amount charged. European consumers minimize their tax payments by making as many purchases as possible abroad. In Canada, a similar measure would both encourage our nationals to buy more taxable items in the United States and discourage all visitors to Canada from buying within Canada.

In a cover letter sent with my submission to all Conservative MPs, I attempted to dissuade them from the party whip's argument that voting against the GST bill would constitute a gross parliamentary heresy. I referred them to a study on confidence votes done by Eugene Forsey and Graham Eglington. It noted that between 1867 and 1872 there were dozens upon dozens of Commons decisions in which Conservative MPs voted against measures of the first John A. Macdonald administration without impairing the ability of his cabinet to govern effectively. In 1914, R.B. Bennett of Calgary both spoke out strongly against and voted against a proposed railway agreement of his own Prime Minister, Robert Borden, with no consequences for the dissident MP and future Conservative party national leader.

More advanced parliamentary systems permit MPs to vote against their respective political parties. In Britain, taxation bills have not been regarded as confidence votes since 1834. In our own country, the defeat of the Trudeau government in 1983 on a clause of an Income Tax Amendment was not deemed a confidence vote.

In mid-October, I received a reply from Donald Blenkarn which I felt was neither persuasive nor substantive in any respect. He wrote, for example, "Once you have covered your needs for food and shelter and clothing, then what you spend starts to have more and more of a volunteer nature to it." Only a Tory MP-lawyer-businessman-hobby farmer could make such a statement. How, I asked in a six page rejoinder, would he answer low and middle income Canadians? Moreover, how would greater savings be encouraged by a tax which would reduce the standard of living for most Canadian families? Both of us sent copies of our letters to the Conservative national caucus.

Additional letters went back and forth on the subject among Blenkarn, myself and other Conservative caucus members. None received from other caucus members contained much common sense or logic. From private conversations with Conservative MPs during the period, I concluded that few of them could make a persuasive case for the proposal. Most had simply accepted it on blind faith from the Finance Minister and were searching for ways to defend it to hostile constituents.

I sent many objections on behalf of concerned organizations and individuals to Michael Wilson. None of his replies dealt realistically with their concerns, usually because most of the responses were based on suppositions that were absurd in the real world of commerce. His officials were equally unconvincing. On one occasion, I attempted to obtain a study from them on the regional consequences of the GST. It never arrived.

I went through a period of conscience-searching while wondering if I should sit as an independent MP because of my deepening opposition to the GST and other policies of the government. After speaking with a number of friends and supporters, I resolved to soldier on within the caucus. My hope, albeit an increasingly faint one as time went by, was to dissuade colleagues, some of ten years' standing, that the GST was socially and economically wrong and politically suicidal.

This personal goal worked reasonably well for a number of weeks until it became clear that a majority of the Alberta Conservative caucus wanted Alex Kindy, the MP for Calgary Northeast, and myself to leave each Tuesday night when discussion of their strategy to sell the GST to Alberta voters began. This struck Kindy and me as reasonable since by this point neither side was going to move on the basic issue. Both sides agreed that we would leave at this point near the end of each caucus meeting. It breaches no canon of caucus secrecy to say that since the 1984 election, the national Conservative caucus functions primarily as a forum in which provincial caucuses tell the prime minister and other colleagues what's on their members' minds.

Several weeks later, I arrived for the regular Tuesday night Alberta caucus meeting to find the prime minister was also attending. No sooner had we all taken our seats than someone proposed that I leave because the GST would be discussed. Assuming that Mulroney knew my position on the tax from copies of letters sent to him and from various media accounts of speeches I'd made against it, I bit my tongue and said virtually nothing before leaving. Thereafter, I did not return to either the Alberta or national caucus before the April 10 final vote in the Commons on third reading, because it was pointless. The positions of both the national and Alberta Conservative caucuses and myself on the GST were irreconcilable. Some weeks after the prime minister's visit, Dr. Kindy and I both received a one-sentence letter from the chairman of the Alberta Conservative caucus, Bobbie Sparrow, telling us that we'd been suspended from the caucus. In fairness, she telephoned first to say the letter was coming, but there was little discussion of the substance.

Shortly before the final vote, I signed individual letters to all government MPs recapitulating why I would oppose the bill. I pointed out that numerous constituents (approximately 7,500) and others had, in one form or another, indicated their opposition to the measure; all but one member of the Edmonton Southeast Conservative Association executive had voted for a motion recommending that I vote against the measure. I reminded them that the Canadian Bankers Association and the Business Council on National Issues were prominent among the few groups supporting the measure across Canada. The letter ended by saying that I'd stand with my constituents, personal convictions and Canadians generally and vote "nay."

The government response was almost immediate after Kindy and I voted against third reading of the GST bill. To the media outside the House, I indicated that, for a decade, I'd voted only once against my party except on some Meech Lake amendments and intended to attend the national caucus the next morning to defend my right to do so on principle. It was not to be. Remarks made by the government whip, Jim Hawkes, to the media later that evening indicated Kindy and I had already been expelled from the government caucus. How, we both wondered, could this unprecedented occurrence in the Conservative national caucus have happened without any species of hearing? Why had Hawkes not even bothered to telephone either of us when he prided himself on being able to reach every government MP within minutes at any time?

Kindy and I learned later that the other members of the Alberta Conservative caucus had held an emergency meeting soon after the vote and voted to expel both of us. Hawkes then evidently approached House Speaker John Fraser and told him that the two of us were to be removed from the government side of the Commons. Fraser, for whom I have the highest respect and affection, simply had no choice under our present outdated parliamentary practices but to comply despite the absence of any species of due process. I'm certain that as Speaker he had no inkling at all as to how the two heretics had been banished.

Late the same night, Alex and I discussed the situation on the telephone and agreed that attempting to attend the next morning's national caucus, a political lynching in the making, would be foolish. He took an early flight for Calgary to face his voters; I decided to catch a noon flight to Edmonton but beforehand to do my best during the morning to ensure that the Prime Minister's "press line" on the matter, whatever it was, was not the only one available for the Ottawa media. By the time Mulroney came out of the national caucus in the late morning to announce that it had decided to expel Kindy and myself, copies of the new seating plan had already been distributed to journalists by the Speaker's office . Later, when I asked one of them why no one quizzed the Prime Minister on this obvious contradiction in his story, he shrugged and replied, "Why bother?" It was, however, gratifying to learn that several MPs present in the national caucus had objected strongly to the lack of any hearing before expelling two colleagues. The national caucus chairman, Bob Layton, appointed by the Prime Minister, wrote a very short letter of dismissal the same day, "we are sorry that you have chosen to withdraw your support for and confidence in the government. Your decision requires me to advise that you will no longer be recognized as a Member of our National caucus."

Arriving in Edmonton in the late afternoon, I went directly to a press conference and announced that in the unusual circumstances, I would sit as an independent Progressive Conservative for the time being. William Stewart, president of the Edmonton Southeast Conservative Association, who confronted the journalists with me, was strongly supportive of my position. Virtually all other members of the 25-member riding executive had been encouraging as well. It was, however, a painful situation in every respect. An Edmonton reporter said the Prime Minister had denounced me as someone who had never spoken up for Alberta on the GST. "That comment would melt the Blarney Stone," I quipped. From comments Mulroney had made personally to me, I knew that he was perfectly aware of my position on the tax before the vote.

After campaigning for the party for twenty-five years in nine of the ten provinces, including thirteen constituencies in Québec during the heat of the 1984 election campaign, I did not consider myself a fair-weather party supporter as was claimed by the party leader. Instead, I felt like many in Eastern Europe who had for years supported a very different political party but now found themselves no longer able to accept it or to believe its leadership. It strongly appeared from hundreds of letters, telephone calls and comments I later received from individuals all over the country that Canadians generally disapproved of the nature of the Prime Minister's strong personal attack against someone who disagreed in principle with a government proposal.

Only the Senate can still stop the GST. I think it is better to be right with our unreformed Senate on the issue than to be wrong with a popularly elected House of Commons whose government members had voted together, dismissing Edmund Burke's wise advice that an MP must never surrender his judgement to anyone.

Government MPs and like-minded editorial writers argue that the Senate is unelected. However, the argument seems rather hollow considering that members of the majority who voted for the bill didn't reflect the views of their constituents while "dissenters" were expelled from the government ranks. The incident might, therefore, help to convince Canadians that our current parliamentary practices must be changed. In a House of Commons where one party has a majority, the prime minister dictates his instructions to the MPs of his party, completely dominating them for the period between elections.

We reformers are not advocating total independence on the part of MPs, only that the parliamentary rules clearly specify under what narrow conditions a defeat of a measure in the House will also cause a government to fall. The present situation, under which virtually any lost vote can be declared by a prime minister to have been a confidence vote, should be unacceptable to any Canadian democrat at the end of the twentieth century. Our present practice, largely abandoned among parliamentary democracies, persists only because it makes life easier for prime ministers. It attracts much public ridicule of government MPs and elected office holders at both our national and provincial levels.

Westminster, as the mother of parliaments, itself offers a way out of the present situation. There, for several decades government private members have voted regularly against their party leadership. In one period during the mid-1970s, the government averaged one defeat in the House per government bill without falling. Older and mostly docile backbenchers in Britain are being replaced by more independent, smarter and younger MPs concerned about their occupational credibility. In our own much larger and more diverse country, it strikes me that allowing MPs greater freedom to represent our constituents would also help all political parties to better discharge their national role as vehicles of reconciliation.

SELECTED REFERENCES

Chapter 1 — MAIN STREET

Yeates, Maurice. *Main Street: Windsor to Quebec City*, Toronto: Macmillan of Canada, 1975.

_____, *Land in Canada's Urban Heartland*. Ottawa: Lands Directorate, Environment Canada, Land Use in Canada series, No. 27, 1985.

_____, The Industrial Heartland: Its Changing Role and Internal Structure, in *Heartland and Hinterland, A Geography of Canada*, L.D. McCann ed., 1987, Scarborough: Prentice-Hall Canada Inc., 1987.

Warkentin, John. *Canada: A Geographical Interpretation*, Toronto: Methuen, 1968.

Careless, J.M.S. *Frontier and Metropolis: Regions, Cities, and Identities in Canada Before 1914*. Toronto: University of Toronto Press, 1989.

McLeod Arnopoulos, Sheila and Clift, Dominique. *The English Fact in Quebec* (2nd edition). Kingston and Montreal: McGill-Queen's University Press, 1980.

Rudin, Ronald, *The Forgotten Quebecers: A history of English-speaking Quebec 1759-1980*, Quebec: Intitut québécois de recherche sur la culture, 1985.

McRae, Kenneth D., *The Federal Capital*, Studies of the Royal Commission on Bilingualism and Biculturalism, Ottawa, 1969.

Hamelin, Jean and Beaudoin, Louise, "Les cabinets provinciaux 1867-1967", dans Richard Desrosiers, *Le Personnel Politique Québécois*. Montréal: Les Éditions du Boréal Express, 1972.

Gailloux, Michel. "Les disparités régionales: plus ça change, plus c'est pareil", La Revue Commerce, octobre 1981.

Thibodeau, Jean-Claude et Polèse, Mario. *Les effets d'entraînement de Montréal sur les autres regions du Québec*. Montréal: Institut National de la Recherche Scientifique, fevrier 1976.

SELECTED REFERENCES

❧

Bourassa, Guy et Léveillée, Jacques, dir., *Le système politique de Montréal.* Montréal: L'Association canadienne-française pour l'avancement des sciences, Les Cahiers No. 43, 1986.

National Capital Commission, 1988-89 Annual Report.

Statistics Canada, *Manufacturing Industries of Canada: Sub-provincial areas.* Cat. 31-209, 1985.

_____, *Manufacturing Industries of Canada: National and Provincial Areas.* Cat. 31-203, 1986.

_____, *Labour Force by Industry Sex and Province.* Cat. 71-001 monthly, December 1989.

_____, *Personal Income and Personal Disposable Income Aggregates for Counties or Census Divisions and for Sub-provincial Regions.* 1987, Cat. 13-216.

_____, *1986 Census of Canada, Family Income.* Cat. 98-128, July 1989.

_____, *Summary of Canadian International Trade.* Cat. 65-001, December 1989.

_____, *Air Passenger Origin and Destination.* Domestic Report, Cat. 51-204, 1988.

_____, *Preliminary 1989 Estimates: GDP at Market Prices.*

Israelson, David. "Housing crunch kills the dreams", seventh of 10-part series: Choking on Success, *Globe and Mail*, May 20, 1989.

The Municipality of Metropolitan Toronto, Annual Report 1987, and 1988.

Eddie, David. "Welcome to Toronto", *Saturday Night*, January/February 1990.

Fullerton, Douglas. "Whither the National Capital: Ottawa's Symbolic Role More Important than Ever". *Canadian Geographic*, December 1987/January 1988.

The Financial Post. Summer, 1989.

Chapter 2 — DOWN HOME

Hamilton, William B., "Regional Identity: A Maritime Quest", Centre for Canadian Studies, Mount Allison University, Sackville, N.B., 1985.

Bruce, Harry, *Down Home*, Toronto: Key Porter Books Ltd., 1988.

Rawlyk, George (ed.), *The Atlantic Provinces and The Problems of Confederation*, Report to the Task Force on Canadian Unity, St. John's: Breakwater, 1973.

Wynn, Graeme, "The Maritimes: The Geography of Fragmentation and Underdevelopment", in L.D. McCann, ed. *Heartland and Hinterland: A Geography of Canada*, Scarborough: Prentice Hall Canada, 1982.

Staveley, Michael, "Newfoundland: Economy and Society at the Margin", in L.D. McCann, (ed.), *Heartland and Hinterland*, ibid.

SELECTED REFERENCES

Acheson, T.W., "The National Policy and the Industrialization of the Maritimes", 1880-1914, *Acadiensis*, 1 (Spring 1972).

Thornton, Patricia A., "The Problem of Out-Migration from Atlantic Canada, 1871 and 1921: A New Look", *Acadiensis*, 15 (Autumn 1985).

Forbes, Ernest R., "Misguided Symmetry: the Destruction of Regional Transportation Policy for the Maritimes" in David Jay Bercuson (ed.), *Canada and the Burden of Unity*, Toronto: Macmillan of Canada, 1977.

_____, "Consolidating Disparity: The Maritimes and the Industrialization of Canada During the Second World War", *Acadiensis*, Vol. XV, No. 2, Spring 1986.

McCann, L.D., "Metropolitanism and Branch Businesses in the Maritimes, 1881-1931", *Acadiensis*, 13 (Autumn 1983).

Reid, John G., *Six Crucial Decades*, Halifax, Nimbus Publishing Ltd. 1987.

_____, "Towards the Elusive Synthesis: The Atlantic Provinces in Recent General Treatments of Canadian History", *Acadiensis*, Vol. 16, No. 2, Spring 1987.

Alexander, David, "Economic Growth in Atlantic Region, 1880-1940", in *Eastern and Western Perspectives*, Papers from the Joint Atlantic Canada/Western Canadian Studies Conference, ed. David Bercuson and Phillip Buckner, Toronto, University of Toronto Press, 1981.

Economic Council of Canada, *Newfoundland, From Dependency to Self-Reliance*, 1980.

Copithorne, Lawrence, Economic Council of Canada, *Newfoundland Revisited*, Discussion paper No. 296, 1986.

Atlantic Provinces Economic Council, *Atlantic Canada Today*, Halifax: Formac Publishing Ltd., 1987.

_____, *Atlantic Report*, Vol. XXIV, No. 2, June 1989.

Submission to the Department of Finance, Pre-budget consultations, March 15, 1989.

_____, *Newsletter*, Vol. 33, No. 3 and 4, March, April, May 1989.

_____, "New England and Atlantic Canada: A Comparative Study", September 1985.

_____, "The Atlantic Vision - 1990", 1979.

Harris, Michael, "Atlantic Blues", *Canadian Business*, October 1989.

Ward, Stephen, "40 Years After", *St. John's Evening Telegram*, April 1, 1989.

Smallwood, Joseph R., "Our First Day in Canada", ibid.

Nichol, Don, "State of the Union", *Globe and Mail*, March 31, 1989.

Sullivan, J.M., "As chose our fathers: 40 years of Confederation", *Atlantic Insight*, April 1989.

SELECTED REFERENCES

Chapter 3 — LIFE ON THE SHIELD

Gagnon, Alain G., *Développement Régional*, État et Groupes Populaires, Le Cas de L'Est du Québec.

Dugas, Clermont, *Les Régions Périphériques, Défi au développement du Québec*, Sillery, Québec: Presses de L'Université du Québec, 1983.

_____, "Hinterland Politics: The Case of Northwest Ontario, *Canadian Journal of Political Science*, Vol. X:4, December, 1977.

Wallace, Iain, "The Canadian Shield: The Development of a Resource Frontier", in *Heartland and Hinterland, A Geography of Canada*, op. cit.

Miller, Tom, "Cabin Fever: The Province of Ontario and Its Norths", in *The Government and Politics of Ontario*, 2nd edition, Donald C. MacDonald (ed.) Toronto: Van Nostrand Reinhold Ltd., 1980.

Scott, Don, "Northern Alienation", in *Government and Politics of Ontario*, Donald C. MacDonald (ed.), Toronto: The Macmillan Company of Canada Ltd., 1975.

Bray, Matt and Epp, Ernie (eds.), *Magnificent Land, An Illustrated History of Northern Ontario*, Toronto: Ontario Ministry of Northern Affairs, 1984.

Morissonneau, Christian, "The Quebec North in the 19th Century: Myth and Symbol", *Forces*, No. 20, 1972.

Sarrazin, Jean, "The Québec North", *Forces*, No. 48, 1979.

Le Nord du Québec, profil régional, Publications gouvernementales du ministère des Communication en Collaboration avec le Service des Communications de l'office de planification et de développement du Québec, Gouvernement du Québec, 1983.

St-Pierre, Marc, "La fin d'un grand rêve collectif, Québec abandonne les villes nordiques", *Le Soleil*, October 6, 1984.

MacRae, Penny, "Schefferville, la reine du fer, est devenue une ville fantôme que n'habitent plus les Amérindiens", *La Presse*, December 15, 1983.

Eggertson, Laura, "Staking a Claim in Elliot Lake", *Ottawa Citizen*, March 31, 1990.

Le Québec Statistique, édition 1985-1986, Bureau de la Statistique du Québec.

Le Ministère de la main-d'oeuvre et de la sécurité du revenu, *La main - d'oeuvre et l'emploi au Québec et dans ses régions*, Bilan 1988 et perspectives 1989-1990, Québec: Les Publications du Québec, 1989.

Chapter 4 — OUT WEST

Hollifield, Kathryn and Scarfe, Brian L., *Western Canada in the World Economy*, (draft) Western Centre for Economic Research and the C.D. Howe Institute, March 1988.

Chambers, Edward J. and Percy, Michael B., *Western Canada in the International Economy*, (draft), Western Centre for Economic Research, February 1990.

Mansell, Robert L., and Schlenker, Ronald C., *An Analysis of the Regional Distribution of Federal Fiscal Balances: Updated Data*, unpublished study, Department of Economics, University of Calgary, May 1990.

Mansell, Robert L., *Alberta's Economic Performance in the 1980s: The Impacts of Energy Policies and Prices*, unpublished paper, Department of Economics, University of Calgary, July 31, 1989.

Kilgour, David, *Uneasy Patriots: Western Canadians in Confederation*, Edmonton: Lone Pine Publishing, 1988.

"What The West Wants", Western Premiers Conference (excerpts), *New Federation*, February/March 1990.

Canada West Foundation, "Defining Diversification", *Western Perspectives*, Calgary: August 1989.

_____, "Time for Action, Reducing Interprovincial Barriers to Trade", *Western Perspectives*, May 1989.

Koch, George, "A New Chance for the West", *Alberta Report*, July 9, 1990.

Morton, Peter, "Farm Incomes to Plummet", *Financial Post*, April 4, 1990.

_____, "The New West Flexes its Muscles", *Globe and Mail*, July 26, 1990.

Braid, Don, "West Slowly Winning Media Attention", *Calgary Herald*, January 22, 1989.

Hayter, Roger, "Export Performance and Export Potentials: Western Canada's Exports of Manufactured End Products", *The Canadian Geographer*, Vol. 30, No. 1, Spring 1986.

Chapter 5 — UP NORTH

Canadian Arctic Resources Committee, *National and Regional Interests in the North*, Third National Workshop on People, Resources and the Environment North of 60°; Ottawa: 1984.

_____, *Changing Times, Challenging Agendas: Economic and Political Issues in Canada's North*, National Symposium on the North, Vol. 1, Ottawa: CARC, 1988.

_____, *A Question of Rights: Northern Wildlife Management and the Anti-Harvest Movement*, National Symposium on the North, Vol. 2, Ottawa: CARC, 1989.

_____, *Northern Perspectives*, issues:.

- "Future Imperfect, A controversial report on the the prospects for Inuit society strikes a nerve in the NWT", #1, Vol. 17, 1989.

- "Canada in the Circumpolar World", #2, Vol. 15, 1987.

- "The Wolf at the Door/The Anti-harvest Campaign Strikes at the Heart of Aboriginal Economies", #2, Vol. 14, 1986.

SELECTED REFERENCES

- "Nunavut", #2, Vol. 10, 1982.

- "Northern Ellesmere", #4, Vol. 10, 1982.

- "Yukon Wilderness... but for how long?", #4, Vol. 8, 1980.

- "Native Northerners: Are They Obstacles to Progress?", #1, Vol. 6, 1978.

Fenge, Terry and Rees, William E., (eds.), *Hinterland or Homeland, Land-use Planning in Northern Canada*, Ottawa: CARC, 1987.

Merritt, John, Fenge, Terry, et al, (eds.), *Nunavut: Political Choices and Manifest Destiny*, Ottawa: Canadian Arctic Resources Committee, 1989.

Usher, Peter J., "The North: One Land, Two Ways of Life", in *Heartland and Hinterland, A Geography of Canada*, L.D. McCann (ed.) second ed., Scarborough: Prentice-Hall Canada Inc., 1987.

Hamelin, Louis-Edmond, *Canadian Nordicity: It's Your North Too*, trans. William Barr, Montreal: Harvest House, 1978.

Zaslow, Morris, The Opening of the Canadian North 1870-1914, Toronto: McLelland and Stewart, 1971.

Granatstein, J.L., A Fit of Absence of Mind: Canada's National Interest in the North to 1968, in *The Arctic in Question*, E.J. Dosman, Toronto: Oxford University Press, 1976.

Whittington, Michael S., *Native Economic Development Corporations: Political and Economic Change in Canada's North*, Canadian Arctic Resources Committee Policy Paper 4, July 1986.

_____, co-ordinator, *The North*, The Royal Commission on the Economic Union and Development Prospects for Canada, Vol. 72, Toronto: University of Toronto Press, 1985.

Frankling, Freddie T., (ed.), *Northern Hydrocarbon Development in the Nineties: A Global Perspective*, Proceedings of a Conference, Carleton University, Ottawa: Geotechnical Science Laboratories, 1989.

Richardson, Boyce, (ed.), *Drumbeat: Anger and Renewal in Indian Country*, Toronto: Summerhill Press, The Assembly of First Nations, 1989.

Robertson, Gordon, *Northern Provinces: A Mistaken Goal*, Montreal: The Institute for Research on Public Policy, 1985.

Yukon Tourism Industry, *Highlights Report 1987-1988.*

The Tourism Industry Association of the Northwest Territories, *Economic Impact of the Northwest Territories Tourism Industry*, June 1988.

Indian Affairs and Northern Development, *Looking North: Canada's Arctic Commitment*, Ottawa, 1989.

Maslove, Allan, and Hawkes, David, "The Northern Population", *Canadian Social Trends*, Statistics Canada, Winter, 1989.

Butler, Elaine, "An Ecotourist in Bathurst Inlet", *Borealis*, 1(4), 1990.

Chapter 6 — CANADIANS SPEAK OUT

Camu, Pierre, "Prologue: Aspects of Social Differentiation in Canada", in G.M. Robinson (ed.), *A Social Geography of Canada*, Edinburgh: North British Publishing, 1988 .

Elkins, David, "The Sense of Place" in David Elkins and Richard Simeon, *Small Worlds: Provinces and Parties in Canadian Political Life*, Toronto: Methuen, 1980.

Economist, "Banners Yet Waving", August 12, 1989.

Windsor Star, "Once-boring Canada Viewed as Fascinating", October 13, 1989.

Economist, "Yes, You are the Superpower", February 24, 1990.

Montgomery, Charlotte, "Search for Flag was 'Search for Country'", *Globe and Mail*, February 15, 1990.

Stewart, Edison, "More of Us Concerned About Unity", *Toronto Star*, May 14, 1990.

Bai, David H., "Multiculturalism in the 1980s and Beyond", (draft), Edmonton: University of Alberta, May 1986.

Winsor, Hugh, "Tired of Constitutional Talk, Canadians Say", (The Globe and Mail-CBC News Poll), *Globe and Mail*, July 9, 1990.

Chapter 7 — DEALER'S CHOICE

Department of Regional and Industrial Expansion, Annual Report 1987-1988.

Department of Regional Industrial Expansion and the Department of Industry, Science and Technology, Annual Report 1988-1989.

Ottawa's Senior Executive Guide, 1988 and 1989.

Financial Post, Summer 1989.

Small Business, February 1989.

Transport 2000, Submission to the House of Commons Standing Committee on Transport, October 1989.

Senate of Canada, Proceedings of the Special Committee of the Senate on Bill C-21, No. 25, Report of the Committee.

Savoie, Donald J., *The Politics of Public Spending in Canada*, Toronto: University of Toronto Press, 1990.

_____, "In and Out of Ottawa", Jackson, Robert, Jackson, Doreen, and Baxter-Moore, Nicolas, *Contemporary Canadian Politics*, Scarborough, Ontario: Prentice-Hall Canada, 1987.

Supply and Services, Supply Program Contracting - geographic locations in Canada by vendor supply point, Fiscal Years 1988-1989, 1987-1988, 1986-1987.

DND Estimated Expenditures by Electoral District FY 88/89, The Directorate of Costing Services, National Defence, 1990.

SELECTED REFERENCES

DND Expenditures and Contracts Awarded by Canadian Regions FY 87/88, National Defence.

Tupper, Allan, *Public Money in the Private Sector: Industrial Assistance Policy and Canadian Federalism*, The Institute of Intergovernmental Relations, Queen's University, 1982.

Treddenick, J.M., *Regional Impacts of Defence Spending*, Kingston: Centre for Studies in Defence Resources Management, Department of Political and Economic Science, Royal Military College, No. 4, June 1984.

Walker, David F., "Canadian Regional Development Policy", in Hecht, Alfred (ed.), *Regional Developments in the Peripheries of Canada and Europe*, Winnipeg: Department of Geography, University of Manitoba, 1983.

Employment and Immigration Canada, *Immigration to Canada: A Statistical Overview*, 1989.

Canada Employment and Immigration Advisory Council, *Regional Unemployment in Canada: A Nation Out of Balance*, Interim Report, November 1989.

Gower, David, "Regional Unemployment", in Statistics Canada, *Canadian Social Trends*, Spring 1990.

Economic Council of Canada, *Good Jobs, Bad Jobs, Employment in the Service Economy*, 1990.

Public Service Commission, Annual Report 1989.

Data on regional employment and procurement of individual federal departments and crown corporations have been obtained from the author's correspondence with the respective departments and agencies.

Wilson, Jane, "R and D: Canadian Commitment Lags Behind World Levels", *Ottawa Citizen*, September 30, 1989.

Statistics Canada, Federal Government Employment in Metropolitan Areas, September 1987.

_____, The Labour Force, cat. 71001, September, 1989, April 21, 1990, May 19, 1990.

_____, *The Regional Distribution of R and D in Canada, 1979 to 1987*, cat. 88-001.

_____, *Personal Income Per Capita by Province and Canada*, 1987, cat. 13-216.

_____, *Preliminary 1989 Estimates, GDP at Market Prices*, May 3, 1990.

_____, *Manufacturing Industries of Canada: National and Provincial Areas*, 1986, cat. 31-203, 71-001, monthly: December 1989.

Cohen, Andrew, "High Rates Help Ontario, Hurt Rest", *Financial Post*, October 30, 1989.

Snyder, Jack, "Orlando Near Top in Growth", *Orlando Sentinel*, March 3, 1990.

Beale, Elizabeth, "UI Reform Impact Unevenly Spread", *Financial Post*, April 21, 1989.

Chapter 8 — PRESSURE POINTS

Siegel, Arthur, *Politics and the Media in Canada*, Toronto: McGraw-Hill Ryerson Ltd., 1983.

Vipond, Mary, *The Mass Media in Canada*, Toronto: James Lorimer and Company, Publishers, 1989.

Audley, Paul, *Canada's Cultural Industries: Broadcasting, Publishing, Records and Film*, Ottawa: Canadian Institute for Economic Policy, 1983.

National Media Archive, *On Balance*, Vancouver: Fraser Institute, June, 1989, February, March and July/August, 1990.

Collins, Richard, "Broadcasting and National Culture in Canada", *British Journal of Canadian Studies*, No. 4, 1989.

Statistics Canada, *Federal Government Expenditures on Culture by Province and Region, 1987-1988*.

Standing Committee on Communications and Culture, *Minutes of Proceedings and Evidence*, House of Commons, Canada, issue Nos. 43-48, 55, 1987.

CBC Fact Book, 1988.

Canada Council, *Exploration Applications, Grants and Amounts by Region, January 1988 -January 1989 Competitions.*

_____, *32nd Annual Report*, 1989.

_____, *Provincial and Metropolitan Accounts*, 1986.

Cooper, Barry with Lydia Miljan and Maria Vigilante, *Bias on the CBC - A Study of Network AM Radio*, original version of the Report presented to the Canadian Communications Association, Winnipeg, June 1986.

Task Force on Broadcasting Policy, Report, Supply and Services, Canada, September, 1986.

CRTC, Report of the Committee of Inquiry into the National Broadcasting Service, March 14, 1977.

Robertson, Gordon, *A House Divided, Meech Lake, Senate Reform and the Canadian Union*, Halifax: The Institute for Research on Public Policy, 1989.

Behiels, Michael D. (ed.), *The Meech Lake Primer: Conflicting Views of the 1987 Constitutional Accord*, Ottawa: University of Ottawa Press, 1989.

Gibbins, Roger, *Meech Lake and Canada: Perspectives from the West*, Edmonton: Academic Printing and Publishing, 1988.

Wells, Clyde K., *The Meech Lake Accord*, an address to the Canadian Club at Montreal, January 19, 1990.

Geraets, Théodore F., *Meech Lake Revisited, Equality? Distinctness? Separatism?*, unpublished paper, February 1990.

SELECTED REFERENCES

Special Committee to Study the Proposed Companion Resolution to the Meech Lake Accord, Minutes of Proceedings and Evidence, House of Commons, Canada, issue No. 1-4, April, 1990.

Report of the Special Committee to Study the Proposed Resolution to the Meech Lake Accord, May, 1990.

Forsey, Eugene, *Notes on the Meech Lake Accord*, unpublished paper, 1987.

Betrame, Julian, "Meech Poll", *Ottawa Citizen*, April 7, 1990.

"Mr. McKenna's Compromise", *Halifax Chronicle Herald*, March 23, 1989.

"Meech Lake Last Words", *Policy Options*, June 1990.

Department of Finance, Canada, Account of the Cost of Selective Tax Measures, August 1985.

_____, Tax Reform 1987, Sales Tax Reform, ("White Paper"), Ottawa, 1987.

_____, 1989 Budget: Goods and Services Tax, Ottawa, 1989.

_____, Goods and Services Tax: Technical Document, Ottawa, August, 1989.

_____, Goods and Services Tax, as tabled in the House of Commons, December 19, 1989.

Hamilton, Bob, Chan-Yan Kuo, *The Goods and Services Tax: A General Equilibrium Analysis*, Department of Finance, Working Paper 89-3.

Standing Committee on Finance, Report on the Technical Papers on the Goods and Services Tax, November 1983.

Atlantic Provinces Economic Council, Submission to the Department of Finance, March 15, 1989.

St. Albert Chamber of Commerce General Resolution on the Proposed GST, January 1990.

New Brunswick Federation of Home and School Associations, Inc., The Proposed GST and Education, January 1990.

Alberta Association of Municipal Districts and Counties, Position Paper - National Goods and Services Tax, February 1990.

Health Unit Association of Alberta, "Alberta Health Units and the GST", January 17, 1990.

Government of Alberta, "Protecting Alberta's Future... Why we Oppose the Federal Goods and Services Tax", November 1989.

Alexander, L.L., Submission to the Standing Committee on Finance, Goods and Services Tax, September 1989.

Coalition of Canadian Transport Associations and Carriers, "Options for Sales Tax Reform, A Review of the Impact of Stage II Proposals on the Transportation Industry", Canada, August 1987.

Western Canadian Wheat Growers, letter on the impact of the proposed GST on the farm sector, August 21, 1989.

Canadian Federation of Independent Business, "It's An Anti-GST Avalanche", *News and Views*, mandate 147 (12/89).

Smith, Dan T., et al, for Cambridge Research Institute, *What You Should Know About the Value-Added Tax*, Homewood, Illinois: Dow Jones-Irwin, 1973.

Due, John F., "New Zealand Goods and Services (Value-Added) Tax - A Model for Other Countries", *Canadian Tax Journal*, Vol. 36, No. 1, January-February 1988.

Surrey, Stanley, S., "Value-Added Tax: The Case Against", *Harvard Business Review*, November-December 1970.

Tait, Alan, "Is the Introduction of a Value-Added Tax Inflationary?", *Finance and Development*, Vol. 18, No. 2, June 1981.

Tax Reform for Fairness, Simplicity and Economic Growth, The Treasury Department , United States, Report to the President, Vol. 3, Value-Added Tax, November 1984.

The Value-Added Tax in the European Economic Community, Comptroller General of the United States, Report to Congress, December 1980.

Brookes, Warren T., "A Value-Added Tax Would Harm the Economy", *Nation's Business*, July 1989.

Canadian Consumer, "A Tax on Spending, Why the New Federal Goods and Services Tax will be Bad News for All Consumers", Vol. 19, No. 6, 1989.

Problemes Economiques, La TVA dans le monde et le problème de sa généralisation, n° 2.091, 21 septembre 1988.

Callaghan, Catherine, "Verdict on the GST", *Small Business*, March 1990.

Farrell, Jim, "Alta. Tops Anti-GST Poll", *Edmonton Journal*, January 12, 1990.

Toronto Star, "Senate Should Block GST, 68% Tell Poll", May 24, 1990.

Chapter 9 — KICKSTARTING DEVELOPMENT

de Vos, Dirk, *Sector Policies of Other Countries*, (Draft) February 1989.

Savoie, Donald J., *Regional Economic Development: Canada's Search for Solutions*, Toronto: University of Toronto Press, 1986.

Savoie, Donald J. (ed.), *The Canadian Economy: A Regional Perspective*, Toronto, Methuen, 1986.

McAllister, Ian, "Regional Development: How the EC and Canada Tackle the Issues - With Lessons for Each", *Europe*, Vol. 6, No. 4, Winter 1986\87.

Cannon, James B., "Directions in Canadian Regional Policy", *Canadian Geographer*, No. 3, 1989.

Economist, "Regional Mismatch", July 29, 1989.

Cameron, David M., *Regional Economic Disparities: The Challenge to Federalism and Public Policy*, Canadian Public Policy, Autumn 1981.

SELECTED REFERENCES

Regional Economic Disparities - Causes and Remedies, Report of the Royal Commission on the Economic Union and Development Prospects for Canada, Ottawa, Supply and Services, 1985, Vol. II.

Wadley, David, *Restructuring the Regions,* Paris: Organisation for Economic Co-operation and Development, 1986.

Bradfield, Michael, *Regional Economics: Analysis and Policies in Canada,* Toronto: McGraw-Hill Ryerson Ltd., 1988.

Coffey, William J. and McRae, James J., *Service Industries in Regional Development,* Halifax: The Institute for Research on Public Policy, 1989.

Economic Council of Canada, *From the Bottom Up: The Community Economic Development Approach,* A Statement, 1990.

_____, *The Perspective 2000 Conference,* A Synopsis, 1990.

Chapter 10 — RECONCILABLE DIFFERENCES

Gibbins, Roger, *Conflict and Unity: An Introduction to Canadian Political Life,* Toronto: Methuen, 1985.

_____, *Regionalism - Territorial Politics in Canada and the United States,* Toronto: Butterworths, 1982.

Robertson, Gordon, "The Global Challenge and Canadian Federalism", *Canadian Public Administration,* Vol. 32, No. 1, Spring 1989.

Breton, Albert, Supplementary Statement, Report, Royal Commission on the Economic Union of Development Prospects for Canada, Vol. 3.

McCormick, Peter and Elton, David, The Western Economy and Canadian Unity, *Western Perspectives,* Calgary, Canada West Foundation, March 1987.

Sharman, Campbell, "The Australian Triple-E Senate: Lessons for Canadian Senate Reform?", *Western Perspectives,* Canada West Foundation, Calgary, May 1989.

McMillan, John, Evans, Gareth, and Storey, Haddon, *Australia's Constitution: Time for Change?,* Sydney: The Law Foundation of New South Wales, 1983.

Reid, G.S. (ed.), *The Role of Upper Houses Today,* Proceedings of the Fourth Annual Workshop of the Australian Study of Parliament Group, 1983.

Evans, Harry, "Proposals for Constitutional Change in Australia", *The Parliamentarian,* July 1982.

_____, *Constitutionalism and Party Government in Australia,* Australian Study of Parliament Group, Occasional Paper No. 1, August 1988.

"Adjusting Senate Reform to the Meech Lake Companion Amendment", *Western Perspectives,* Calgary: Canada West Foundation, April 1990

INDEX

INDEX

INDEX

Hibernia, 42, 47
hinterland, 17-19, 25, 51-52, 54-57, 65-66, 89, 91, 103, 121, 125, 135, 145, 152, 181, 216-217, 221
Hodge, Gerald, 158
Hotson, John, 137
House of Representatives, 171, 201-202, 208-209
Howe, C.D., 36-38, 60
hunting, 58-59, 62, 94, 96-98
Hurtig, Mel, 178-179

- I -

immigration, 61, 75, 130, 145, 147, 169, 172-173, 187, 224
Indian Affairs and Northern Development, 110, 220
Indians, 58, 63, 91, 94-95, 97, 99-100, 112-113, 179, 220
Innu, 97-98
Intercolonial Railway, 34-35
interest rates, 27, 54, 74, 84, 87, 122, 135-136, 161, 179, 190
International Development Research Centre, 149
Inuit, 62, 89, 91-97, 99-101, 105, 108-111, 219
Inuvialuit, 99

- J -

Jacob, Jane, 232
Jalava, Mauri, 122
job creation, 105, 217, 222

- K -

Kenora, 51, 53, 57-59
Kindy, Alex, 234-236
Klondike, 89, 94, 100, 109

- L -

Labour Canada, 149
Labrador, 39-41, 44, 52, 54-56, 62, 97-98, 101-102, 123, 165
Lacroix, Jean-Michel, 117
language relations, 127-128, 131
Laurier, Wilfrid, 29, 71-74, 82, 93, 199, 215
Lee, Derek, 125
Leefe, John, 125
Lewis, Brian, 122-123

- M -

Macdonald, John A., 20, 34-35, 70-72, 74, 121, 136, 199-200, 233
magazines, 167, 179
mail rates, 157
Makuto, Moffatt S., 125
Manitoba, 26, 28, 32, 57, 59, 71-75, 79, 84, 101, 123, 147, 152, 154-155, 158-159, 168, 173, 177, 186, 197, 205
Mansell, Robert, 78, 86-87
manufacturing, 19-26, 34-37, 42, 46, 48-49, 54, 84, 103, 136, 141-143, 158, 203, 218, 224
high-tech, 46, 60, 84, 151, 153
Maritimes, 31-38, 44, 121, 125, 137, 157, 164, 188
Martin, Ray, 119
Mazankowski, Don, 155
McAndrew, Jack, 164
McCreath, Peter, 125
McDonough, Alexa, 165
McKenna, Frank, 170
Meech Lake, 33, 39, 42, 70, 75-76, 111-112, 115-116, 122, 127-131, 146, 159, 163, 168-177, 181, 198, 205, 207, 211, 213, 215, 218, 225, 228, 235
melting pot, 131
Members of Parliament (MPs), 32-33, 69, 71, 75, 79, 116, 124, 159, 178, 198, 202-206, 231, 233-237
Métis, 58, 82, 91, 92, 99, 110, 112
metropolis, 17, 19, 24, 26, 27-28, 52-53, 103
metropolitan area, 19, 21-22, 138, 166
Miller, Tom, 57
minerals, 52, 54, 101, 102
mining, 26, 52, 54-55, 65, 73, 102-104, 138, 154, 170, 175, 216
Montréal, 18-25, 27, 35, 38, 46, 53, 61-62, 64-66, 69, 76, 78, 80, 90, 100, 118-119, 121, 124, 127, 136, 141-142, 145-146, 149-154, 158-159, 162, 164-167, 169, 174, 179, 186, 198, 201-202, 213, 223-224, 231-232
Morton, William, 20, 74
mosaic, 52, 81, 95, 118, 129, 130-131
Mowat, Oliver, 199
Mulroney, Brian, 25, 42, 48, 62-63, 69-70, 75-76, 80-81, 85, 86-87, 98, 102, 131, 139, 142, 154, 157, 159, 169, 174-175, 177, 181, 188, 201, 206, 211, 235-236
multiculturalism, 58, 83, 117, 130
munitions, 150
Museum of Civilization, 29-30, 224

- N -

National Capital Commission, 29
National Capital Region, 29, 149, 154
National Energy Program, 70, 76, 136, 201, 206, 232
National Gallery, 29, 168, 224
national identity, 39, 117, 119, 120, 123, 131
national interest, 98, 123-124, 198, 211-212, 215
National Media Archive, 163
National Policy, 20-21, 34-35, 71, 74, 121, 136, 216
national unity, 39, 79, 115-116, 118, 123-124, 126-127, 135, 153, 161-163, 166, 179, 189, 199, 219, 223
native, 56, 58, 62, 66, 89-91, 93-102, 104-108, 110-111, 113, 118, 122, 125, 137, 165, 179, 212, 219-220

253

INDEX

THE AUTHOR

David Kilgour was born in Winnipeg and educated at the universities of Manitoba, Toronto and Paris. He has been a prosecuting attorney in Vancouver, a defence counsel in Winnipeg and a constitutional adviser to the Alberta government. Earlier, he worked as a labourer-teacher for Frontier College in northern Ontario, a bank clerk in Québec City and a trail rides guide in Banff National Park. Since 1979, he has represented southeast Edmonton in the House of Commons. During 1990, he was one of two persons (with Vaclav Havel) to receive the MASARYK AWARD from the Czechoslovak Association of Canada. He is the author of the prize-winning book *Uneasy Patriots — Western Canadians in Confederation.* He and his wife, Laura, have four children and live in Edmonton and Aylmer, Québec.